Command-Line Rust
A Project-Based Primer for Writing Rust CLIs

Ken Youens-Clark

Beijing · Boston · Farnham · Sebastopol · Tokyo

Command-Line Rust

by Ken Youens-Clark

Copyright © 2022 Charles Kenneth Youens-Clark. All rights reserved.

Published by O'Reilly Media, Inc., 1005 Gravenstein Highway North, Sebastopol, CA 95472.

O'Reilly books may be purchased for educational, business, or sales promotional use. Online editions are also available for most titles (*https://oreilly.com*). For more information, contact our corporate/institutional sales department: 800-998-9938 or *corporate@oreilly.com*.

Acquisitions Editor: Suzanne McQuade
Development Editors: Rita Fernando and Corbin Collins
Production Editors: Caitlin Ghegan, Kristen Brown, and Gregory Hyman
Copyeditor: Kim Sandoval

Proofreader: Rachel Head
Indexer: Ellen Troutman-Zaig
Interior Designer: David Futato
Cover Designer: Karen Montgomery
Illustrator: Kate Dullea

January 2022:   First Edition

Revision History for the First Edition
2022-01-13:   First Release
2023-02-03:   Second Release
2024-03-29:   Third Release

See *https://oreilly.com/catalog/errata.csp?isbn=9781098109431* for release details.

978-1-098-10943-1

[LSI]

Table of Contents

Preface

I already know the ending \ It's the part that makes your face implode
—They Might Be Giants, "Experimental Film" (2004)

To become proficient at a language, you must write many programs in that language. I remember back when this new language called "JavaScript" came out in 1995. I decided to learn it, so I bought a big, thick reference book and read it cover to cover. The book was well written and thoroughly explained the language in great detail, from strings to lists and objects. But when I finished the book, I still couldn't write JavaScript to save my life. Without applying this knowledge by writing programs, I learned very little. I've since improved at learning how to learn a language, which is perhaps the most valuable skill you can develop as a programmer. For me, that means rewriting programs I already know, like tic-tac-toe.

Rust is the new kid on the block now, and perhaps you've picked up this book to see what it's all about. This book is not a reference on the language. Those already exist, and they're quite good. Instead, I've written a book that challenges you to write many small programs that probably will be familiar to you. Rust is reputed to have a fairly steep learning curve, but I believe this approach will help you quickly become productive with the language.

Specifically, you're going to write Rust versions of core Unix command-line tools such as head and cal. This will teach you more about the tools and why they are so wildly useful while also providing the context to use Rust concepts like strings, vectors, and filehandles. If you are not familiar with Unix or command-line programming, then you will learn about concepts like program exit values, command-line arguments, output redirection, pipes to connect one program's output (STDOUT or *standard out*) to the input of another program (STDIN or *standard in*), and how to use STDERR (*standard error*) to segregate error messages from other output. The programs you write will reveal patterns that you'll be able to use when you create your own Rust programs—patterns like validating parameters, reading and writing files, parsing text, and using regular expressions. Many of these tools and concepts don't even exist on

Windows, so users of that platform will create decent versions of several core Unix programs.

What Is Rust (and Why Is Everybody Talkin' About It)?

Rust (*https://www.rust-lang.org*) is "a language empowering everyone to build reliable and efficient software." Rust was created by Graydon Hoare and many others around 2006, while Hoare was working at Mozilla Research. It gained enough interest and users that by 2010 Mozilla had sponsored the development effort. In the 2023 Stack Overflow Developer Survey (*https://survey.stackoverflow.co/2023/*), over 90,000 developers ranked Rust as the "most loved" language for the eighth year running.

Figure P-1. Here is a logo I made from an old Rush logo. As a kid playing the drums in the 1980s, I listened to a lot of Rush. Anyway, Rust is cool, and this logo proves it.

The language is syntactically similar to C, so you'll find things like `for` loops, semicolon-terminated statements, and curly braces denoting block structures. Crucially, Rust can guarantee memory safety through the use of a *borrow checker* that tracks which part of a program has safe access to different parts of memory. This safety does not come at the expense of performance, though. Rust programs compile to native binaries and often match or beat the speed of programs written in C or C++. For this reason, Rust is often described as a systems programming language that has been designed for performance and safety.

Rust is a *statically typed* language like C/C++ or Java. This means that a variable can never change its type, such as from a number to a string, for example. You don't always have to declare a variable's type in Rust because the compiler can often figure it out from the context. This is in contrast to *dynamically typed* languages like Perl, JavaScript, or Python, where a variable can change its type at any point in the program, like from a string to a filehandle.

Rust is *not* an object-oriented (OO) language like C++ or Java, as there are no classes or inheritance in Rust. Instead, Rust uses a `struct` (structure) to represent complex data types and *traits* to describe how types can behave. These structures can have methods, can mutate the internal state of the data, and might even be called *objects* in the documentation, but they are not objects in the formal sense of the word.

Rust has borrowed many exciting concepts from other languages and programming paradigms, including purely functional languages such as Haskell. For instance, variables in Rust are *immutable* by default, meaning they can't be changed from their initial value; you have to specifically inform the compiler that they are mutable. Functions are also *first-class* values, which means they can be passed as arguments to other so-called *higher-order functions*. Most exciting to my mind is Rust's use of *enumerated* and *sum* types, also called *algebraic data types* (ADTs), which allow you to represent, for instance, that a function can return a `Result` that can be either an `Ok` containing some value or an `Err` containing some other kind of value. Any code that deals with these values must handle all possibilities, so you're never at risk of forgetting to handle an error that could unexpectedly crash your program.

Who Should Read This Book

You should read this book if you want to learn the basics of the Rust language by writing practical command-line programs that address common programming tasks. I imagine most readers will already know some basics about programming from at least one other language. For instance, you probably know about creating variables, using loops to repeat an action, creating functions, and so forth. I imagine that Rust might be a difficult first language as it uses types extensively and requires understanding some fine details about computer memory. I also assume you have at least some idea of how to use the command line and know some basic Unix commands, like how to create, remove, and change into directories. This book will focus on the practical side of things, showing you what you need to know to get things done. I'll leave the nitty-gritty to more comprehensive books such as *Programming Rust*, 2nd ed., by Jim Blandy, Jason Orendorff, and Leonora F. S. Tindall (O'Reilly); *The Rust Programming Language* by Steve Klabnik and Carol Nichols (No Starch Press), and *Rust In Action* (*https://oreil.ly/Izwlo*) by Tim McNamara (Manning). I highly recommend that you read one or more of those along with this book to dig deeper into the language itself.

You should also read this book if you'd like to see how to write and run tests to check Rust programs. I'm an advocate for using tests not only to verify that programs work properly but also as an aid to breaking a problem into small, understandable, testable parts. I will demonstrate how to use tests that I have provided for you as well as how to use *test-driven development* (TDD), where you write tests first and then write code that passes those tests. I hope that this book will show that the strictness of the Rust compiler combined with testing leads to better programs that are easier to maintain and modify.

Why You Should Learn Rust

There are plenty of reasons to learn Rust. First, I find that Rust's type checking prevents me from making many basic errors. My background is in more dynamically typed languages like Perl, Python, and JavaScript where there is little to no checking of types. The more I used statically typed languages like Rust, the more I realized that dynamically typed languages force much more work onto me, requiring me to verify my programs and write many more tests. I gradually came to feel that the Rust compiler, while very strict, was my dance partner and not my enemy. Granted, it's a dance partner who will tell you every time you step on their toes or miss a cue, but that eventually makes you a better dancer, which is the goal after all. Generally speaking, when I get a Rust program to compile, it usually works as I intended.

Second, it's easy to share a Rust program with someone who doesn't know Rust or is not a developer at all. If I write a Python program for a workmate, I must give them the Python source code to run and ensure they have the right version of Python and all the required modules to execute my code. In contrast, Rust programs are compiled directly into a machine-executable file. I can write and debug a program on my machine, build an executable for the architecture it needs to run on, and give my colleague a copy of the program. Assuming they have the correct architecture, they will not need to install Rust and can run the program directly.

Third, I often build containers using Docker or Singularity to encapsulate workflows. I find that the containers for Rust programs are often orders of magnitude smaller than those for Python programs. For instance, a Docker container with the Python runtime may require several hundred MB. In contrast, I can build a bare-bones Linux virtual machine with a Rust binary that may only be tens of MB in size. Unless I really need some particular features of Python, such as machine learning or natural language processing modules, I prefer to write in Rust and have smaller, leaner containers.

Finally, I find that I'm extremely productive with Rust because of the rich ecosystem of available modules. I have found many useful Rust crates—which is what libraries are called in Rust—on *crates.io*, and the documentation at *Docs.rs* is thorough and easy to navigate.

The Coding Challenges

In this book, you will learn how to write and test Rust code by creating complete programs. Each chapter will show you how to start a program from scratch, add features, work through error messages, and test your logic. I don't want you to passively read this book on the bus to work and put it away. You will learn the most by writing your own solutions, but I believe that even typing the source code I present will prove beneficial.

The problems I've selected for this book hail from the Unix command-line coreutils (*https://oreil.ly/fYV82*), because I expect these will already be quite familiar to many readers. For instance, I assume you've used head and tail to look at the first or last few lines of a file, but have you ever written your own versions of these programs? Other Rustaceans (*https://www.rustaceans.org*) (people who use Rust) have had the same idea, so there are plenty of other Rust implementations (*https://oreil.ly/RmiBN*) of these programs you can find on the internet. Beyond that, these are fairly small programs that each lend themselves to teaching a few skills. I've sequenced the projects so that they build upon one another, so it's probably best if you work through the chapters in order.

One reason I've chosen many of these programs is that they provide a sort of ground truth. While there are many flavors of Unix and many implementations of these programs, they usually all work the same and produce the same results. I use macOS for my development, which means I'm running mostly the BSD (Berkeley Standard Distribution) or GNU (*https://www.gnu.org*) (GNU's Not Unix) variants of these programs. Generally speaking, the BSD versions predate the GNU versions and have fewer options. For each challenge program, I use a shell script to redirect the output from the original program into an output file. The goal is then to have the Rust programs create the same output for the same inputs. I've been careful to include files encoded on Windows as well as simple ASCII text mixed with Unicode characters to force my programs to deal with various ideas of line endings and characters in the same way as the original programs.

For most of the challenges, I'll implement only a subset of the original programs as they can get pretty complicated. I also have chosen to make a few small changes in the output from some of the programs so that they are easier to teach. Consider this to be like learning to play an instrument by playing along with a recording. You don't have to play every note from the original version. The important thing is to learn common patterns like handling arguments and reading inputs so you can move on to writing your material. As a bonus challenge, try writing these programs in other languages so you can see how the solutions differ from Rust.

Getting Rust and the Code

To start, you'll need to install Rust. One of my favorite parts about Rust is the ease of using the rustup tool for installing, upgrading, and managing Rust. It works equally well on Windows and Unix-type operating systems (OSs) like Linux and macOS. You will need to follow the installation instructions (*https://oreil.ly/camNw*) for your OS. If you have already installed rustup, you might want to run **rustup update** to get the latest version of the language and tools, as Rust updates about every six weeks. Execute **rustup doc** to read copious volumes of documentation. You can check your version of the rustc compiler with the following command:

```
$ rustc --version
rustc 1.76.0 (07dca489a 2024-02-04)
```

All the tests, data, and solutions for the programs can be found in the book's GitHub repository (*https://oreil.ly/pfhMC*). You can use the Git source code management tool (*https://git-scm.com*) (which you may need to install) to copy this to your machine. The following command will create a new directory on your computer called *command-line-rust* with the contents of the book's repository:

```
$ git clone https://github.com/kyclark/command-line-rust.git
```

You should *not* write your code in the directory you cloned in the preceding step. You should create a separate directory elsewhere for your projects. I suggest that you create your own Git repository to hold the programs you'll write. For example, if you use GitHub and call it *rust-solutions*, then you can use the following command to clone your repository. Be sure to replace *YOUR_GITHUB_ID* with your actual GitHub ID:

```
$ git clone https://github.com/YOUR_GITHUB_ID/rust-solutions.git
```

One of the first tools you will encounter in Rust is Cargo (*https://oreil.ly/OhYek*), which is its build tool, package manager, and test runner. Each chapter will instruct you to create a new project using Cargo, and I recommend that you do this inside your solutions directory. You will copy each chapter's *tests* directory from the book's repository into your project directory to test your code. If you're curious what testing code looks like with Cargo and Rust, you can run the tests for Chapter 1. Change into the book's *01_hello* directory and run the tests with **cargo test**:

```
$ cd command-line-rust/01_hello
$ cargo test
```

If all goes well, you should see some passing tests (in no particular order):

```
running 3 tests
test false_not_ok ... ok
test true_ok ... ok
test runs ... ok
```

 I tested all the programs on macOS, Linux, Windows 10/PowerShell, and Ubuntu Linux/Windows Subsystem for Linux (WSL). While I love how well Rust works on both Windows and Unix operating systems, two programs (findr and lsr) work slightly differently on Windows due to some fundamental differences in the operating system from Unix-type systems. I recommend that Windows/PowerShell users consider also installing WSL and working through the programs in that environment.

All the code in this book has been formatted using `rustfmt`, which is a handy tool for making your code look pretty and readable. You can use **cargo fmt** to run it on all the source code in a project, or you can integrate it into your code editor to run on demand. For instance, I prefer to use the text editor `vim`, which I have configured to automatically run `rustfmt` every time I save my work. I find this makes it much easier to read my code and find mistakes.

I recommend you use Clippy (*https://oreil.ly/XyzTS*), a linter for Rust code. *Linting* is automatically checking code for common mistakes, and it seems most languages offer one or more linters. Both `rustfmt` and `clippy` should be installed by default, but you can use **rustup component add clippy** if you need to install it. Then you can run **cargo clippy** to have it check the source code and make recommendations. No output from Clippy means that it has no suggestions.

March 2024 Update

This book was originally published in 2022. The Rust language and crates evolved quickly in the following two years, and I am grateful to O'Reilly for allowing me to update my code examples to reflect these changes. I have simplified the programs to make them easier to teach and improved the test output by using the `pretty_assertions` crate. The biggest change by far is in the `clap` (command-line argument parser) crate used in every program starting from Chapter 2. The `clap` crate was at version 2.33 when I wrote the book and had just one method (builder) to parse arguments. The version jumped to 4 soon after publication and introduced a second method (derive). I rewrote all my programs to use these new patterns, being sure to isolate the parsing so that the reader is free to substitute any code they would prefer. The code examples in this version of the book can be found using `git check` out of the branches *clap_v4* and *clap_v4_derive* for the builder and derive patterns, respectively.

Now you're ready to write some Rust!

Conventions Used in This Book

The following typographical conventions are used in this book:

Italic
    Indicates new terms, URLs, email addresses, filenames, and file extensions.

`Constant width`
    Used for program listings, as well as within paragraphs to refer to program elements such as variable or function names, databases, data types, environment variables, statements, and keywords.

Constant width bold

In blocks of code, unless stated otherwise, this style calls special attention to elements being described in the surrounding discussion. In discursive text, it highlights commands that can be used by the reader as they follow along.

Constant width italic

Shows text that should be replaced with user-supplied values or by values determined by context.

 This element signifies a tip or suggestion.

 This element signifies a general note.

 This element indicates a warning or caution.

Using Code Examples

Supplemental material (code examples, exercises, etc.) is available for download at *https://oreil.ly/commandlinerust_code*.

If you have a technical question or a problem using the code examples, please send email to *bookquestions@oreilly.com*.

This book is here to help you get your job done. In general, if example code is offered with this book, you may use it in your programs and documentation. You do not need to contact us for permission unless you're reproducing a significant portion of the code. For example, writing a program that uses several chunks of code from this book does not require permission. Selling or distributing examples from O'Reilly books does require permission. Answering a question by citing this book and quoting example code does not require permission. Incorporating a significant amount of example code from this book into your product's documentation does require permission.

We appreciate, but generally do not require, attribution. An attribution usually includes the title, author, publisher, and ISBN. For example: "*Command-Line Rust* by Ken Youens-Clark (O'Reilly). Copyright 2022 Charles Kenneth Youens-Clark, 978-1-098-10943-1."

If you feel your use of code examples falls outside fair use or the permission given above, feel free to contact us at *permissions@oreilly.com*.

O'Reilly Online Learning

 For more than 40 years, *O'Reilly Media* has provided technology and business training, knowledge, and insight to help companies succeed.

Our unique network of experts and innovators share their knowledge and expertise through books, articles, and our online learning platform. O'Reilly's online learning platform gives you on-demand access to live training courses, in-depth learning paths, interactive coding environments, and a vast collection of text and video from O'Reilly and 200+ other publishers. For more information, visit *https://oreilly.com*.

How to Contact Us

Please address comments and questions concerning this book to the publisher:

O'Reilly Media, Inc.
1005 Gravenstein Highway North
Sebastopol, CA 95472
800-889-8969 (in the United States or Canada)
707-827-7019 (international or local)
707-829-0104 (fax)
support@oreilly.com
https://www.oreilly.com/about/contact.html

We have a web page for this book, where we list errata, examples, and any additional information. You can access this page at *https://oreil.ly/commandLineRust*.

Email *bookquestions@oreilly.com* to comment or ask technical questions about this book.

For news and information about our books and courses, visit *https://oreilly.com*.

Find us on LinkedIn: *https://linkedin.com/company/oreilly-media*

Watch us on YouTube: *https://www.youtube.com/oreillymedia*

Acknowledgments

My first debt of gratitude is to the Rust community for creating such an incredible language and body of resources for learning. When I started writing Rust, I quickly learned that I could try to write a naive program and just let the compiler tell me what to fix. I would blindly add or subtract & and * and clone and borrow until my program compiled, and then I'd figure out how to make it better. When I got stuck, I invariably found help at *https://users.rust-lang.org*. Everyone I've encountered in Rust, from Twitter to Reddit, has been kind and helpful.

I would like to thank the BSD and GNU communities for the programs and documentation upon which each chapter's project is based. I appreciate the generous licenses that allow me to include portions of the help documentation from their programs:

- *https://www.freebsd.org/copyright/freebsd-license*
- *https://creativecommons.org/licenses/by-nd/4.0*

I further wish to thank my development editors, Corbin Collins and Rita Fernando, and my production editors, Caitlin Ghegan, Greg Hyman, and Kristen Brown. I am deeply indebted to the technical reviewers Carol Nichols, Brad Fulton, Erik Nordin, and Jeremy Gailor, who kept me on the straight and narrow path, as well as others who gave of their time to make comments, including Joshua Lynch, Andrew Olson, Jasper Zanjani, and William Evans. I also owe thanks to my bosses over the last few years, Dr. Bonnie Hurwitz at the University of Arizona and Amanda Borens at the Critical Path Institute, who have tolerated the time and effort I've spent learning new languages such as Rust in my professional job.

In my personal life, I could not have written this book without the love and support of my wife, Lori Kindler, and our three extremely interesting children. Finally, I would also like to thank my friend Brian Castle, who tried so hard in high school to redirect my musical tastes from hard and progressive rock to alternative bands like Depeche Mode, The Smiths, and They Might Be Giants, only the last of which really took.

CHAPTER 1

Truth or Consequences

And the truth is, we don't know anything
    — They Might Be Giants, "Ana Ng" (1988)

In this chapter, I'll show you how to organize, run, and test a Rust program. I'll be using a Unix platform (macOS) to explain some basic ideas about command-line programs. Only some of these ideas apply to the Windows operating system, but the Rust programs themselves will work the same no matter which platform you use.

You will learn how to do the following:

- Compile Rust code into an executable
- Use Cargo to start a new project
- Use the $PATH environment variable
- Include external Rust crates from *crates.io*
- Interpret the exit status of a program
- Use common system commands and options
- Write Rust versions of the `true` and `false` programs
- Organize, write, and run tests

Getting Started with "Hello, world!"

It seems the universally agreed-upon way to start learning a programming language is printing "Hello, world!" to the screen. Change to a temporary directory with `cd /tmp` to write this first program. We're just messing around, so we don't need a real directory yet. Then fire up a text editor and type the following code into a file called *hello.rs*:

```
fn main() {  ❶
    println!("Hello, world!");  ❷
}  ❸
```

❶ Functions are defined using fn. The name of this function is main.

❷ println! (*print line*) is a macro and will print text to STDOUT (pronounced *standard out*). The semicolon indicates the end of the statement.

❸ The body of the function is enclosed in curly braces.

Rust will automatically start in the main function. Function arguments appear inside the parentheses that follow the name of the function. Because there are no arguments listed in main(), the function takes no arguments. The last thing I'll point out here is that println! (*https://oreil.ly/GGmNx*) looks like a function but is actually a *macro* (*https://oreil.ly/RFXMp*), which is essentially code that writes code. All the other macros I use in this book—such as assert! (*https://oreil.ly/SQHyp*) and vec! (*https:// oreil.ly/KACU4*)—also end with an exclamation point.

To run this program, you must first use the Rust compiler, rustc, to *compile* the code into a form that your computer can execute:

```
$ rustc hello.rs
```

On Windows, you will use this command:

```
> rustc.exe .\hello.rs
```

If all goes well, there will be no output from the preceding command, but you should now have a new file called *hello* on macOS and Linux or *hello.exe* on Windows. This is a binary-encoded file that can be directly executed by your operating system, so it's common to call this an *executable* or a *binary*. On macOS, you can use the file command to see what kind of file this is:

```
$ file hello
hello: Mach-O 64-bit executable x86_64
```

You should be able to execute the program to see a charming and heartfelt message:

```
$ ./hello  ❶
Hello, world!
```

❶ The dot (.) indicates the current directory.

I will shortly discuss the $PATH environment variable that lists the directories to search for programs to run. The current working directory is never included in this variable to prevent malicious code from being surreptitiously executed. For instance, a bad actor could create a program named ls that executes rm -rf / in an attempt to delete your entire filesystem. If you happened to execute that as the root user, it would ruin your whole day.

On Windows, you can execute it like so:

```
> .\hello.exe
Hello, world!
```

Congratulations if that was your first Rust program. Next, I'll show you how to better organize your code.

Organizing a Rust Project Directory

In your Rust projects, you will likely write many files of source code and will also use other people's code from places like *crates.io*. It's best to create a directory for each project, with a *src* subdirectory for the Rust source code files. On a Unix system, you'll first need to remove the *hello* binary with the command **rm hello** because that is the name of the directory you will create. Then you can use the following command to make the directory structure:

```
$ mkdir -p hello/src ❶
```

❶ The mkdir command will make a directory. The -p option says to create parent directories before creating child directories. PowerShell does not require this option.

Move the *hello.rs* source file into *hello/src* using the mv command:

```
$ mv hello.rs hello/src
```

Use the cd command to change into that directory and compile your program again:

```
$ cd hello
$ rustc src/hello.rs
```

You should now have a hello executable in the directory. I will use the tree command (which you might need to install) to show you the contents of my directory:

```
$ tree
.
├── hello
└── src
    └── hello.rs
```

This is the basic structure for a simple Rust project.

Creating and Running a Project with Cargo

An easier way to start a new Rust project is to use the Cargo tool. You can delete your temporary *hello* directory:

```
$ cd ..  ❶
$ rm -rf hello  ❷
```

❶ Change into the parent directory, which is indicated with two dots (..).

❷ The -r *recursive* option will remove the contents of a directory, and the -f *force* option will skip any errors.

If you would like to save the following program, change into the solutions directory for your projects. Then start your project anew using Cargo like so:

```
$ cargo new hello
      Created binary (application) `hello` package
```

This should create a new *hello* directory that you can change into. I'll use tree again to show you the contents:

```
$ cd hello
$ tree
.
├── Cargo.toml  ❶
└── src  ❷
    └── main.rs  ❸
```

❶ *Cargo.toml* is a configuration file for the project. The extension *.toml* stands for Tom's Obvious, Minimal Language.

❷ The *src* directory is for Rust source code files.

❸ *main.rs* is the default starting point for Rust programs.

You can use the following cat command (for *concatenate*) to see the contents of the one source file that Cargo created (in Chapter 3, you will write a Rust version of cat):

```
$ cat src/main.rs
fn main() {
    println!("Hello, world!");
}
```

Rather than using rustc to compile the program, this time use **cargo run** to compile the source code and run it in one command:

```
$ cargo run
   Compiling hello v0.1.0 (/private/tmp/hello)  ❶
    Finished dev [unoptimized + debuginfo] target(s) in 1.26s
```

```
    Running `target/debug/hello`
Hello, world! ❷
```

❶ The first three lines are information about what Cargo is doing.

❷ This is the output from the program.

If you would like for Cargo to not print status messages about compiling and running the code, you can use the -q, or --quiet, option:

```
$ cargo run --quiet
Hello, world!
```

Cargo Commands

How did I know about the -q|--quiet option? Run **cargo** with no arguments and note that it will print some lengthy documentation. Good command-line tools will tell you how to use them, like how the cookie in *Alice in Wonderland* says "Eat me." Notice that *Usage* is one of the first words in the documentation. It's common to call this helpful message the *usage* statement. The programs in this book will also print their usage. You can request help for any of Cargo's commands using **cargo help** *command*.

After running the program using Cargo, use the ls command to list the contents of the current working directory. (You will write a Rust version of ls in Chapter 14.) There should be a new directory called *target*. By default, Cargo will build a *debug* target (*https://oreil.ly/1Fs8Q*), so you will see the directory *target/debug* that contains the build artifacts:

```
$ ls
Cargo.lock  Cargo.toml  src/        target/
```

You can use the tree command from earlier or the find command (you will write a Rust version of find in Chapter 7) to look at all the files that Cargo and Rust created. The executable file that ran should exist as *target/debug/hello*. You can execute this directly:

```
$ ./target/debug/hello
Hello, world!
```

To summarize, Cargo found the source code in *src/main.rs*, used the main function there to build the binary *target/debug/hello*, and then ran it. Why was the binary file called *hello*, though, and not *main*? To answer that, look at *Cargo.toml*:

```
$ cat Cargo.toml
[package]
name = "hello" ❶
```

```
version = "0.1.0"  ❷
edition = "2021"  ❸

# See more keys and their definitions at  ❹
# https://doc.rust-lang.org/cargo/reference/manifest.html

[dependencies]  ❺
```

❶   This was the name of the project I created with Cargo, so it will also be the name
     of the executable.

❷   This is the version of the program.

❸   This is the edition (*https://oreil.ly/4fgvX*) of Rust that should be used to compile
     the program. Editions are how the Rust community introduces changes that are
     not backward compatible. I will use the 2021 edition for all the programs in this
     book.

❹   This is a comment line that I will include only this one time. You can remove this
     line from your file, if you like.

❺   This is where you will list any external crates your project uses. This project has
     none at this point, so this section is blank.

 Rust libraries are called *crates*, and they are expected to use *seman-tic version numbers* in the form `major.minor.patch`, so that `1.2.4` is major version 1, minor version 2, patch version 4. A change in the major version indicates a breaking change in the crate's public application programming interface (API).

Writing and Running Integration Tests

"More than the act of testing, the act of designing tests is one of the best bug preventers known. The thinking that must be done to create a useful test can discover and eliminate bugs before they are coded—indeed, test-design thinking can discover and eliminate bugs at every stage in the creation of software, from conception to specification, to design, coding, and the rest."

—Boris Beizer, *Software Testing Techniques* (Van Nostrand Reinhold)

Even though "Hello, world!" is quite simple, there are still things that could bear testing. There are two broad categories of tests I will show in this book. *Inside-out* or *unit testing* is when you write tests for the functions inside your program. I'll introduce unit testing in Chapter 5. *Outside-in* or *integration testing* is when you write tests that run your programs as the user might, and that's what we'll do for this program. The convention in Rust projects is to create a *tests* directory parallel to the *src* directory for testing code, and you can use the command `mkdir tests` for this.

The goal is to test the `hello` program by running it on the command line as the user will do. Create the file *tests/cli.rs* for *command-line interface* (CLI) with the following code. Note that this function is meant to show the simplest possible test in Rust, but it doesn't do anything useful yet:

```
#[test] ❶
fn works() {
    assert!(true); ❷
}
```

❶ The `#[test]` attribute tells Rust to run this function when testing.

❷ The `assert!` macro (*https://oreil.ly/SQHyp*) asserts that a Boolean expression is `true`.

Your project should now look like this:

```
$ tree -L 2
.
├── Cargo.lock ❶
├── Cargo.toml
├── src ❷
│   └── main.rs
├── target ❸
│   ├── CACHEDIR.TAG
│   ├── debug
│   └── tmp
└── tests ❹
    └── cli.rs
```

❶ The *Cargo.lock* file (*https://oreil.ly/81q3a*) records the exact versions of the dependencies used to build your program. You should not edit this file.

❷ The *src* directory is for the Rust source code files to build the program.

❸ The *target* directory holds the build artifacts.

❹ The *tests* directory holds the Rust source code for testing the program.

All the tests in this book will use `assert!` to verify that some expectation is `true`, or `assert_eq!` (*https://oreil.ly/P6Bfw*) to verify that something is an expected value. Since this test evaluates the literal value `true`, it will always succeed. To see this test in action, execute `cargo test`. You should see these lines among the output:

```
running 1 test
test works ... ok
```

To observe a failing test, change `true` to `false` in the *tests/cli.rs* file:

```
#[test]
fn works() {
    assert!(false);
}
```

Among the output, you should see the following failed test:

```
running 1 test
test works ... FAILED
```

 You can have as many `assert!` and `assert_eq!` calls in a test function as you like. At the first failure of one of them, the whole test fails.

Now, let's create a more useful test that executes a command and checks the result. The `ls` command works on both Unix and Windows PowerShell, so we'll start with that. Replace the contents of *tests/cli.rs* with the following code:

```
use std::process::Command; ❶

#[test]
fn runs() {
    let mut cmd = Command::new("ls"); ❷
    let res = cmd.output(); ❸
    assert!(res.is_ok()); ❹
}
```

❶ Import `std::process::Command` (*https://oreil.ly/ErqAX*). The `std` tells us this is in the *standard* library and is Rust code that is so universally useful it is included with the language.

❷ Create a new `Command` to run `ls`. The `let` keyword (*https://oreil.ly/cYjVT*) will bind a value to a variable. The `mut` keyword (*https://oreil.ly/SH6Qr*) will make this variable *mutable* so that it can change.

❸ Run the command and capture the output, which will be a `Result` (*https://oreil.ly/EYxds*).

❹ Verify that the result is an `Ok` variant, indicating the action succeeded.

By default, Rust variables are immutable, meaning their values cannot be changed.

Run **cargo test** and verify that you see a passing test among all the output:

```
running 1 test
test runs ... ok
```

Update *tests/cli.rs* with the following code so that the `runs` function executes `hello` instead of `ls`:

```
use std::process::Command;

#[test]
fn runs() {
    let mut cmd = Command::new("hello");
    let res = cmd.output();
    assert!(res.is_ok());
}
```

Run the test again and note that it fails because the `hello` program can't be found:

```
running 1 test
test runs ... FAILED
```

Recall that the binary exists in *target/debug/hello*. If you try to execute `hello` on the command line, you will see that the program can't be found:

```
$ hello
-bash: hello: command not found
```

When you execute any command, your operating system will look in a predefined set of directories for something by that name.[1] On Unix-type systems, you can inspect the PATH environment variable of your shell to see this list of directories, which are delimited by colons. (On Windows, this is $env:Path.) I can use tr (*translate characters*) to replace the colons (:) with newlines (\n) to show you my PATH:

```
$ echo $PATH | tr : '\n' ❶
/opt/homebrew/bin
/Users/kyclark/.cargo/bin
/Users/kyclark/.local/bin
/usr/local/bin
/usr/bin
```

---

1 Shell aliases and functions can also be executed like commands, but I'm only talking about finding programs to run at this point.

```
/bin
/usr/sbin
/sbin
```

❶ $PATH tells `bash` to interpolate the variable. Use a pipe (|) to feed this to `tr`.

Even if I change into the *target/debug* directory, `hello` still can't be found due to the aforementioned security restrictions that exclude the current working directory from my PATH:

```
$ cd target/debug/
$ hello
-bash: hello: command not found
```

I must explicitly reference the current working directory for the program to run:

```
$ ./hello
Hello, world!
```

Next, I need to find a way to execute binaries that exist only in the current crate.

Adding Project Dependencies

Currently, the `hello` program exists only in the *target/debug* directory. If I copy it to any of the directories in my PATH (note that I include the *$HOME/.local/bin* directory for private programs), I can execute it and run the test successfully. But I don't want to copy my program to test it; rather, I want to test the program that lives in the current crate. I can use the crate `assert_cmd` (*https://oreil.ly/Lw-gr*) to find the program in my crate directory. I will also add the crate `pretty_assertions` (*https://oreil.ly/VqD62*) to use a version of the `assert_eq!` macro that shows differences between two strings better than the default version.

I first need to add these as development dependencies (*https://oreil.ly/pezix*) to *Cargo.toml*. This tells Cargo that I need these crates only for testing and benchmarking:

```
[package]
name = "hello"
version = "0.1.0"
edition = "2021"

[dependencies]

[dev-dependencies]
assert_cmd = "2.0.13"
pretty_assertions = "1.4.0"
```

I can then use `assert_cmd` to create a `Command` that looks in the Cargo binary directories. The following test does not verify that the program produces the correct output, only that it appears to succeed. Update your *tests/cli.rs* with the following code so that the `runs` function will use `assert_cmd::Command` instead of `std::process::Command`:

```
use assert_cmd::Command; ❶

#[test]
fn runs() {
    let mut cmd = Command::cargo_bin("hello").unwrap(); ❷
    cmd.assert().success(); ❸
}
```

❶ Import `assert_cmd::Command`.

❷ Create a `Command` to run `hello` in the current crate. This returns a `Result`, and the code calls `Result::unwrap` (*https://oreil.ly/SV6w1*) because the binary should be found. If it isn't, then `unwrap` will cause a panic and the test will fail, which is a good thing.

❸ Use `Assert::success` (*https://oreil.ly/b2aIV*) to ensure the command succeeded.

 I'll have more to say about the `Result` type in later chapters. For now, just know that this is a way to model something that could succeed or fail for which there are two possible variants, `Ok` and `Err`, respectively.

Run **cargo test** again and verify that you now see a passing test:

```
running 1 test
test runs ... ok
```

Understanding Program Exit Values

What does it mean for a program to run successfully? Command-line programs should report a final exit status to the operating system to indicate success or failure. The Portable Operating System Interface (POSIX) standards dictate that the standard exit code is 0 to indicate success (think *zero* errors) and any number from 1 to 255 otherwise. I can show you this using the `bash` shell and the `true` command. Here is the manual page from **man true** for the version that exists on macOS:

```
TRUE(1)                    BSD General Commands Manual                    TRUE(1)

NAME
     true -- Return true value.

SYNOPSIS
     true
```

```
DESCRIPTION
     The true utility always returns with exit code zero.

SEE ALSO
     csh(1), sh(1), false(1)

STANDARDS
     The true utility conforms to IEEE Std 1003.2-1992 (''POSIX.2'').

BSD                          June 27, 1991                          BSD
```

As the documentation notes, this program does nothing except return the exit code zero. If I run **true**, it produces no output, but I can inspect the bash variable $? to see the exit status of the most recent command:

```
$ true
$ echo $?
0
```

The false command is a corollary in that it always exits with a nonzero exit code:

```
$ false
$ echo $?
1
```

All the programs you will write in this book will be expected to return zero when they terminate normally and a nonzero value when there is an error. You can write versions of true and false to see this. Start by creating a *src/bin* directory using **mkdir src/bin**, then create *src/bin/true.rs* with the following contents:

```
fn main() {
    std::process::exit(0); ❶
}
```

❶ Use the std::process::exit function (*https://oreil.ly/hrM3X*) to exit the program with the value zero.

Your *src* directory should now have the following structure:

```
$ tree src/
src/
├── bin
│   └── true.rs
└── main.rs
```

Run the program and manually check the exit value:

```
$ cargo run --quiet --bin true ❶
$ echo $?
0
```

❶ The --bin option is the name of the binary target to run.

Add the following test to *tests/cli.rs* to ensure it works correctly. It does not matter if you add this before or after the existing `runs` function:

```
#[test]
fn true_ok() {
    let mut cmd = Command::cargo_bin("true").unwrap();
    cmd.assert().success();
}
```

If you run **cargo test**, you should see the results of the two tests:

```
running 2 tests
test true_ok ... ok
test runs ... ok
```

 The tests are not necessarily run in the same order they are declared in the code. This is because Rust is a safe language for writing *concurrent* code, which means code can be run across multiple threads. The testing takes advantage of this concurrency to run many tests in parallel, so the test results may appear in a different order each time you run them. This is a feature, not a bug. If you would like to run the tests in order, you can run them on a single thread via **cargo test -- --test-threads=1**.

Rust programs will exit with the value zero by default. Recall that *src/main.rs* doesn't explicitly call `std::process::exit`. This means that the `true` program can do nothing at all. Want to be sure? Change *src/bin/true.rs* to the following:

```
fn main() {}
```

Run the test suite and verify it still passes. Next, let's write a version of the `false` program with the following source code in *src/bin/false.rs*:

```
fn main() {
    std::process::exit(1); ❶
}
```

❶ Exit with any value between 1 and 255 to indicate an error.

Manually verify that the exit value of the program is not zero:

```
$ cargo run --quiet --bin false
$ echo $?
1
```

Then add this test to *tests/cli.rs* to verify that the program reports a failure when run:

```
#[test]
fn false_not_ok() {
    let mut cmd = Command::cargo_bin("false").unwrap();
```

```
        cmd.assert().failure(); ❶
    }
```

❶ Use the `Assert::failure` function (*https://oreil.ly/WLwK8*) to ensure the com-
    mand failed.

Run **cargo test** to verify that the programs all work as expected:

```
running 3 tests
test runs ... ok
test true_ok ... ok
test false_not_ok ... ok
```

Another way to write the `false` program uses `std::process::abort` (*https://oreil.ly/
HPsKS*). Change *src/bin/false.rs* to the following:

```
fn main() {
    std::process::abort();
}
```

Again, run the test suite to ensure that the program still works as expected.

Testing the Program Output

While it's nice to know that my `hello` program exits correctly, I'd like to ensure it
actually prints the correct output to `STDOUT`, which is the standard place for output to
appear and is usually the console. Update your `runs` function in *tests/cli.rs* to the
following:

```
use assert_cmd::Command;
use pretty_assertions::assert_eq; ❶

#[test]
fn runs() {
    let mut cmd = Command::cargo_bin("hello").unwrap();
    let output = cmd.output().expect("fail"); ❷
    assert!(output.status.success()); ❸
    let stdout = String::from_utf8(output.stdout).expect("invalid UTF-8"); ❹
    assert_eq!(stdout, "Hello, world!\n"); ❺
}
```

❶ Import the `pretty_assertions::assert_eq` macro for comparing values instead
    of the standard Rust version.

❷ Call `Command::output` (*https://oreil.ly/29jfF*) to execute the `hello` command. Use
    `Result::expect` (*https://oreil.ly/InBqs*) to get the output of the command or die
    with the message "fail."

❸ Verify that the command succeeded.

❹ Convert the output of the program to UTF-8, which I'll discuss more in Chapter 4.

❺ Compare the output from the program to an expected value. Note that this will use the `pretty_assertions` version of the `assert_eq` macro.

Run the tests and verify that `hello` does, indeed, work correctly. Next, change *src /main.rs* to add some more exclamation points:

```
fn main() {
    println!("Hello, world!!!");
}
```

Run the tests again to observe a failing test:

```
running 3 tests
test true_ok ... ok
test false_not_ok ... ok
test runs ... FAILED

failures:

---- runs stdout ----
thread runs panicked at tests/cli.rs:10:5:
assertion failed: `(left == right)`

Diff < left / right > :
<Hello, world!!!
>Hello, world!
```

The preceding test result is trying very hard to show you how the *expected* output (the "right") differs from the *actual* output (the "left"). The terminal output even includes red and green text and highlighted text that cannot be reproduced here. While this is a trivial program, I hope you can see the value in automatically checking all aspects of the programs we write.

Exit Values Make Programs Composable

Correctly reporting the exit status is a characteristic of well-behaved command-line programs. The exit value is important because a failed process used in conjunction with another process should cause the combination to fail. For instance, I can use the logical *and* operator `&&` in `bash` to chain the two commands `true` and `ls`. Only if the first process reports success will the second process run:

```
$ true && ls
Cargo.lock  Cargo.toml  src/       target/    tests/
```

If instead I execute **false && ls**, the result is that the first process fails and `ls` never runs. Additionally, the exit status of the whole command is nonzero:

```
$ false && ls
$ echo $?
1
```

Ensuring that command-line programs correctly report errors makes them composable with other programs. It's extremely common in Unix environments to combine many small commands to make ad hoc programs on the command line. If a program encounters an error but fails to report it to the operating system, then the results could be incorrect. It's far better for a program to abort so that the underlying problems can be fixed.

Summary

This chapter introduced you to some key ideas about organizing a Rust project and some basic ideas about command-line programs. To recap:

- The Rust compiler rustc compiles Rust source code into a machine-executable file on Windows, macOS, and Linux.

- The Cargo tool will create a new Rust project as well as compile, run, and test the code.

- By default, **cargo new** creates a new Rust program that prints "Hello, world!"

- Command-line tools like ls, cd, mkdir, and rm often accept command-line arguments like file or directory names as well as options like -f or -p.

- POSIX-compatible programs should exit with a value of 0 to indicate success and any value between 1 and 255 to indicate an error.

- You learned to add crate dependencies to *Cargo.toml* and use the crates in your code.

- You created a *tests* directory to organize testing code, and you used #[test] to mark functions that should be executed as tests.

- You learned how to test a program's exit status as well as how to check the text printed to STDOUT.

- You learned how to write, run, and test alternate binaries in a Cargo project by creating source code files in the *src/bin* directory.

- You wrote your implementations of the true and false programs along with tests to verify that they succeed and fail as expected. You saw that by default a Rust program will exit with the value zero and that the std::process::exit function can be used to explicitly exit with a given code. Additionally, the std::process::abort function can be used to exit with a nonzero error code.

In the next chapter, I'll show you how to write a program that uses command-line arguments to alter the output.

CHAPTER 2

Test for Echo

By the time you get this note / We'll no longer be alive /
We'll have all gone up in smoke / There'll be no way to reply
  — They Might Be Giants, "By the Time You Get This" (2018)

In Chapter 1, you wrote three programs—`hello`, `true`, and `false`—that take no arguments and always produce the same output. In this chapter, I'll show you how to use arguments from the command line to change the behavior of the program at runtime. The challenge program you'll write is a clone of `echo`, which will print its arguments on the command line, optionally terminated with a newline.

In this chapter, you'll learn how to do the following:

- Process command-line arguments with the `clap` crate
- Use Rust types like strings, vectors, slices, and the unit type
- Use expressions like `match`, `if`, and `return`
- Use `Option` variants to represent `Some` value or `None`
- Handle errors using the `Result` variants of `Ok` and `Err`
- Understand the difference between stack and heap memory
- Test for text that is printed to `STDOUT` and `STDERR`
- Use `Iterator::collect` to turn an iterator into a vector
- Create a struct

How echo Works

In each chapter, you will be writing a Rust version of an existing command-line tool, so I will begin each chapter by describing how the tool works so that you understand what you'll be creating. The features I describe are also the substance of the test suite I provide. For this challenge, you will create a Rust version of the echo program, which is blissfully simple. To start, echo will print its arguments to STDOUT:

```
$ echo Hello
Hello
```

I'm using the bash shell, which assumes that any number of spaces delimit the arguments, so arguments that have spaces must be enclosed in quotes. In the following command, I'm providing four words as a single argument:

```
$ echo "Rust has assumed control"
Rust has assumed control
```

Without the quotes, I'm providing four separate arguments. Note that I can use a varying number of spaces when I provide the arguments, but echo prints them using a single space between each argument:

```
$ echo Rust  has assumed    control
Rust has assumed control
```

If I want the spaces to be preserved, I must enclose them in quotes:

```
$ echo "Rust  has assumed    control"
Rust  has assumed    control
```

It's extremely common—but not mandatory—for command-line programs to respond to the flags -h or --help to print a helpful usage statement. If I try that with echo, it will simply print the flag:

```
$ echo --help
--help
```

Instead, I can read the manual page for echo by executing **man echo**. You'll see that I'm using the BSD version of the program from 2003:

```
ECHO(1)                    BSD General Commands Manual                    ECHO(1)

NAME
     echo -- write arguments to the standard output

SYNOPSIS
     echo [-n] [string ...]

DESCRIPTION
     The echo utility writes any specified operands, separated by single blank
     (' ') characters and followed by a newline ('\n') character, to the stan-
     dard output.
```

The following option is available:

-n   Do not print the trailing newline character. This may also be
       achieved by appending '\c' to the end of the string, as is done by
       iBCS2 compatible systems. Note that this option as well as the
       effect of '\c' are implementation-defined in IEEE Std 1003.1-2001
       (''POSIX.1'') as amended by Cor. 1-2002. Applications aiming for
       maximum portability are strongly encouraged to use printf(1) to
       suppress the newline character.

       Some shells may provide a builtin echo command which is similar or iden-
       tical to this utility. Most notably, the builtin echo in sh(1) does not
       accept the -n option. Consult the builtin(1) manual page.

EXIT STATUS
     The echo utility exits 0 on success, and >0 if an error occurs.

SEE ALSO
     builtin(1), csh(1), printf(1), sh(1)

STANDARDS
     The echo utility conforms to IEEE Std 1003.1-2001 (''POSIX.1'') as
     amended by Cor. 1-2002.

BSD   April 12, 2003   BSD

By default, the text that echo prints on the command line is terminated by a newline character. As shown in the preceding manual page, the program has a single -n option to omit the final newline. Depending on the version of echo you have, this may not appear to affect the output. For instance, the BSD version I'm using shows this:

```
$ echo -n Hello
Hello
$ ❶
```

❶   The BSD echo shows my command prompt, $, on the next line.

The GNU version on Linux shows this:

```
$ echo -n Hello
Hello$ ❶
```

❶   The GNU echo shows my command prompt immediately after Hello.

Regardless of which version of echo you have, you can use the bash redirect operator > to send STDOUT to a file:

```
$ echo Hello > hello
$ echo -n Hello > hello-n
```

The diff tool will display the *differences* between two files. This output shows that the second file (*hello-n*) does not have a newline at the end:

```
$ diff hello hello-n
1c1
< Hello
---
> Hello
\ No newline at end of file
```

Getting Started

This challenge program will be called echor, for echo plus r for Rust. (I can't decide if I pronounce this like *eh-core* or *eh-koh-ar*.) Change into the directory for your solutions and start a new project using Cargo:

```
$ cargo new echor
     Created binary (application) `echor` package
```

Change into the new directory to see a familiar structure:

```
$ cd echor
$ tree
.
├── Cargo.toml
└── src
    └── main.rs
```

Use Cargo to run the program:

```
$ cargo run
Hello, world! ❶
```

❶ The default program always prints "Hello, world!"

You've already seen this source code in Chapter 1, but I'd like to point out a couple more things about the code in *src/main.rs*:

```
fn main() {
    println!("Hello, world!");
}
```

As you saw in Chapter 1, Rust will start the program by executing the main function in *src/main.rs*. All functions return a value, and the return type may be indicated with an arrow and the type, such as -> u32 to say the function returns an unsigned 32-bit integer. The lack of any return type for main implies that the function returns what Rust calls the *unit* type. Also, note that the println! macro (*https://oreil.ly/Edncj*) will automatically append a newline to the output, which is a feature you'll need to control when the user requests no terminating newline.

The unit type (*https://oreil.ly/BVKGJ*) is like an empty value and is signified with a set of empty parentheses: (). The documentation says this "is used when there is no other meaningful value that could be returned." It's not quite like a null pointer or undefined value in other languages, a concept first introduced by Tony Hoare (no relation to Rust creator Graydon Hoare), who called the null reference his "billion-dollar mistake." Since Rust does not (normally) allow you to dereference a null pointer, it must logically be worth at least a billion dollars.

Accessing the Command-Line Arguments

The first order of business is getting the command-line arguments to print. In Rust, you can use `std::env::args` (*https://oreil.ly/4lJGE*) for this. In Chapter 1, you used the `std::process` crate to handle external processes. Here, you'll use `std::env` to interact with the *environment*, which is where the program will find the arguments. If you look at the documentation for the function, you'll see it returns something of the type `Args`:

```
pub fn args() -> Args
```

If you go to the link for the `Args` documentation (*https://oreil.ly/Wtkqr*), you'll find it is a *struct*, which is a kind of data structure in Rust. If you look along the lefthand side of the page, you'll see things like trait implementations, other related structs, functions, and more. We'll explore these ideas later, but for now, just poke around the docs and try to absorb what you see.

Edit *src/main.rs* to print the arguments. You can call the function by using the full path followed by an empty set of parentheses:

```
fn main() {
    println!(std::env::args()); // This will not work
}
```

Execute the program using **cargo run**, and you should see the following error:

```
error: format argument must be a string literal
  --> src/main.rs:2:14
   |
 2 |     println!(std::env::args()); // This will not work
   |              ^^^^^^^^^^^^^^^^
   |
help: you might be missing a string literal to format with
   |
 2 |     println!("{}", std::env::args()); // This will not work
   |              +++++

error: could not compile `echor` due to previous error
```

Here is your first spat with the compiler. It's saying that you cannot directly print the value that is returned from that function, but it's also suggesting how to fix the problem. It wants you to first provide a literal string that has a set of curly braces ({}) that will serve as a placeholder for the printed value, so change the code accordingly:

```
fn main() {
    println!("{}", std::env::args()); // This will not work either
}
```

Run the program again and see that you're not out of the woods because there is another compiler error. Note that I omit the "compiling" and other lines to focus on the important output:

```
$ cargo run
error[E0277]: `Args` doesn't implement `std::fmt::Display`
 --> src/main.rs:2:20
  |
2 |     println!("{}", std::env::args()); // This will not work
  |                    ^^^^^^^^^^^^^^^^ `Args` cannot be formatted with
  |                                     the default formatter
  |
  = help: the trait `std::fmt::Display` is not implemented for `Args`
  = note: in format strings you may be able to use `{:?}` (or {:#?} for
    pretty-print) instead
  = note: this error originates in the macro `$crate::format_args_nl`
    (in Nightly builds, run with -Z macro-backtrace for more info)
```

There's a lot of information in that compiler message. First off, there's something about the trait std::fmt::Display (*https://oreil.ly/gaxyv*) not being implemented for Args. A *trait* in Rust is a way to define the behavior of an object in an abstract way. If an object implements the Display trait, then it can be formatted for user-facing output. Look again at the "Trait Implementations" section of the Args documentation and notice that, indeed, Display is not mentioned there.

The compiler suggests you should use {:?} instead of {} for the placeholder. This is an instruction to print a Debug version of the structure (*https://oreil.ly/zPdzZ*), which will format the output in a debugging context. Refer again to the Args documentation to see that Debug is listed under "Trait Implementations." Change the code to the following:

```
fn main() {
    println!("{:?}", std::env::args()); // Success at last!
}
```

Now the program compiles and prints something vaguely useful:

```
$ cargo run
Args { inner: ["target/debug/echor"] }
```

If you are unfamiliar with command-line arguments, it's common for the first value to be the path of the program itself. It's not an argument per se, but it is useful information. Let's see what happens when I pass some arguments:

```
$ cargo run Hello world
Args { inner: ["target/debug/echor", "Hello", "world"] }
```

Huzzah! It would appear that I'm able to get the arguments to my program. I passed two arguments, Hello and world, and they showed up as additional values after the binary name. I know I'll need to pass the -n flag, so I'll try that next:

```
$ cargo run Hello world -n
Args { inner: ["target/debug/echor", "Hello", "world", "-n"] }
```

It's also common to place the flag before the values, so let me try that:

```
$ cargo run -n Hello world
error: Found argument '-n' which wasn't expected, or isn't valid in this context

USAGE:
    cargo run [OPTIONS] [--] [args]...

For more information try --help
```

That doesn't work because Cargo thinks the -n argument is for itself, not the program I'm running. To fix this, I need to separate Cargo's options using two dashes:

```
$ cargo run -- -n Hello world
Args { inner: ["target/debug/echor", "-n", "Hello", "world"] }
```

In the parlance of command-line program parameters, the -n is an *optional* argument because you can leave it out. Typically, program options start with one or two dashes. It's common to have *short* names with one dash and a single character, like -h for the *help* flag, and *long* names with two dashes and a word, like --help. You will commonly see these concatenated like -h|--help to indicate one or the other. The options -n and -h are often called *flags* because they don't take a value. Flags have one meaning when present and the opposite when absent. In this case, -n says to omit the trailing newline; otherwise, print as normal.

All the other arguments to echo are *positional* because their position relative to the name of the program (the first element in the arguments) determines their meaning. Consider the command chmod to *change* the *mode* of a file or directory. It takes two positional arguments, a mode like 755 first and a file or directory name second. In the case of echo, all the positional arguments are interpreted as the text to print, and they should be printed in the same order they are given. This is not a bad start, but the arguments to the programs in this book are going to become much more complex. We will need a more robust method for parsing the program's arguments.

Adding clap as a Dependency

Although there are various methods and crates for parsing command-line arguments, I will exclusively use the clap (*command-line argument parser*) crate (*https://oreil.ly/DHIR3*). To get started, I need to tell Cargo that I want to download this crate and use it in my project. I can do this by adding it as a dependency to *Cargo.toml*, specifying the version:

```
[package]
name = "echor"
version = "0.1.0"
edition = "2021"

[dependencies]
clap = "4.5.0"
```

 The version "4.5.0" means I want to use exactly this version. I could use just "4" to indicate that I'm fine using the latest version in the major version "4.x" line. There are many other ways to indicate the version, and I recommend you read about how to specify dependencies (*https://oreil.ly/mvf9F*).

The next time I try to build the program, Cargo will download the clap source code (if needed) and all of its dependencies. For instance, I can run **cargo build** to just build the new binary and not run it. You may be curious about where these packages go. Cargo places the downloaded source code into *.cargo* in your home directory, and the build artifacts go into the *target/debug/deps* directory of the project. This brings up an interesting part of building Rust projects: each program you build can use different versions of crates, and each program is built in a separate directory. If you have ever suffered through using shared modules, as is common with Perl and Python, you'll appreciate that you don't have to worry about conflicts where one program requires some old obscure version and another requires the latest bleeding-edge version in GitHub. Python, of course, offers *virtual environments* to combat this problem, and other languages have similar solutions. Still, I find Rust's approach to be quite comforting.

A consequence of Rust placing the dependencies into *target* is that this directory is now quite large. You can use the *disk usage* command **du -shc .** to find that the project now weighs in at about 35 MB, and almost all of that lives in *target/debug/deps*. If you run **cargo help**, you will see that the clean command will remove the *target* directory. You might do this to reclaim disk space if you aren't going to work on the project for a while, at the expense of having to recompile in the future.

Parsing Command-Line Arguments Using clap

To learn how to use `clap` to parse the arguments, you need to read the documentation, and I like to use *Docs.rs* (*https://oreil.ly/CdbFz*) for this. This crate offers two patterns for creating a parser called *derive* and *builder*, and the GitHub branches *main* and *clap_v4_builder* show how to write all the programs using both patterns, respectively. After consulting the `clap` docs, I wrote the following version of *src/main.rs* that creates a new `clap::Command` struct (*https://oreil.ly/F7z87*) to parse the command-line arguments using the builder pattern:

```
use clap::Command; ❶

fn main() {
    let _matches = Command::new("echor") ❷
        .version("0.1.0") ❸
        .author("Ken Youens-Clark <kyclark@gmail.com>") ❹
        .about("Rust version of `echo`") ❺
        .get_matches(); ❻
}
```

❶ Import the `clap::Command` struct.

❷ Create a new `Command` with the name `echor`.

❸ Use semantic version information.

❹ Include your name and email address so people know where to send the money.

❺ This is a short description of the program.

❻ Tell the `Command` to parse the arguments.

> In the preceding code, the leading underscore in the variable name `_matches` is functional. It tells the Rust compiler that I do not intend to use this variable. Without the underscore, the compiler would warn about an unused variable.

With this code in place, I can run the `echor` program with the `-h` or `--help` flags to get a usage document. Note that I didn't have to define this flag or write the implementation for printing the usage, as `clap` does this for me:

```
$ cargo run -- -h
Rust version of `echo`

Usage: echor
```

```
Options:
  -h, --help     Print help
  -V, --version  Print version
```

In addition to the help flags, I see that clap also automatically handles the flags -V and --version to print the program's version:

```
$ cargo run -- --version
echor 0.1.0
```

Next, I need to define the parameters using the clap::Arg (*https://oreil.ly/350vY*) struct and clap::ArgAction (*https://oreil.ly/B1W4s*) enum, which is an *enumeration* of possible values. To do this, I add the following code:

```
use clap::{Arg, ArgAction, Command}; ❶

fn main() {
    let matches = Command::new("echor")
        .version("0.1.0")
        .author("Ken Youens-Clark <kyclark@gmail.com>")
        .about("Rust version of `echo`")
        .arg(
            Arg::new("text") ❷
                .value_name("TEXT")
                .help("Input text")
                .required(true)
                .num_args(1..),
        )
        .arg(
            Arg::new("omit_newline") ❸
                .short('n') ❹
                .action(ArgAction::SetTrue) ❺
                .help("Do not print newline"),
        )
        .get_matches();

    println!("{:#?}", matches); ❻
}
```

❶ Import Arg, ArgAction, and Command from the clap crate.

❷ Create a new Arg with the name text. This is a required positional argument that must appear at least once and can be repeated.

❸ Create a new Arg with the name omit_newline. This is a flag that has only the short name -n.

❹ Note that the single-character short value is enclosed in single quotes to denote the char type (*https://oreil.ly/6EPcF*).

❺ Set the argument to `true` when the flag is present or `false` when absent.

❻ Pretty-print the arguments.

> Earlier I used `{:?}` to format the debug view of the arguments. Here I'm using `{:#?}` to include newlines and indentations to help me read the output. This is called *pretty-printing* because, well, it's prettier.

If you request the usage again, you will see the new parameters:

```
$ cargo run -- --help
Rust version of `echo`

Usage: echor [OPTIONS] <TEXT>...

Arguments:
  <TEXT>...  Input text ❶

Options:
  -n             Do not print newline ❷
  -h, --help     Print help
  -V, --version  Print version
```

❶ The required input text is one or more positional arguments.

❷ The -n flag to omit the newline is optional.

Run the program with some arguments and inspect the structure of the arguments. I will elide some of the output here for brevity:

```
$ cargo run -- -n Hello world
ArgMatches {
    valid_args: [
        "text",
        "omit_newline",
        "help",
        "version",
    ],
    ...
}
```

If you run the program with no arguments, you will get an error indicating that you failed to provide the required arguments:

```
$ cargo run
error: the following required arguments were not provided:
  <TEXT>...

Usage: echor <TEXT>...
```

```
For more information, try '--help'.
```

This was an error, and so you can inspect the exit value to verify that it's not zero:

```
$ echo $?
2
```

If you try to provide any argument that isn't defined, it will trigger an error and a nonzero exit value:

```
$ cargo run -- -x
error: unexpected argument '-x' found

  tip: to pass '-x' as a value, use '-- -x'

Usage: echor [OPTIONS] <TEXT>...

For more information, try '--help'.
```

 You might wonder how this magical stuff is happening. Why is the program stopping and reporting these errors? If you read the documentation for Command::get_matches (*https://oreil.ly/kLBnZ*), you'll see that the method will exit the program on failure, print any error messages, and report an appropriate exit value.

There's a subtle thing happening with the error messages. When you use `println!`, the output appears on STDOUT, but the usage and error messages are all appearing on STDERR, which you first saw in Chapter 1. To see this in the `bash` shell, you can run echor and redirect channel 1 (STDOUT) to a file called *out* and channel 2 (STDERR) to a file called *err*:

```
$ cargo run 1>out 2>err
```

You should see no output because it was all redirected to the *out* and *err* files. The *out* file should be empty because there was nothing printed to STDOUT, but the *err* file should contain the output from Cargo and the error messages from the program:

```
$ cat err
    Finished dev [unoptimized + debuginfo] target(s) in 0.08s
     Running `target/debug/echor`
error: the following required arguments were not provided:
  <TEXT>...

Usage: echor <TEXT>...

For more information, try '--help'.
```

So you see that another hallmark of well-behaved command-line programs is to print regular output to STDOUT and error messages to STDERR. Some errors are severe enough that you should halt the program, but sometimes they should just be noted in the course of running. For instance, in Chapter 3 you will write a program that processes input files, some of which will intentionally not exist or will be unreadable. I will show you how to print warnings to STDERR about these files and skip to the next argument without halting.

Creating the Program Output

Now that I'm able to parse the program's arguments, the next step is to use these values to generate the same output as echo. To start, I want to extract the text argument, which can be one or more strings. I can place multiple values into a vector using Vec (*https://oreil.ly/kmRm-*), and the strings are represented with String (*https://oreil.ly/7HxgU*). In the following code, I first call ArgMatches::get_many (*https://oreil.ly/hsoE5*) to retrieve multiple values for an argument. This call may or may not succeed, so the return value is represented using an Option (*https://oreil.ly/aEft3*), which has the variants None for no value and Some for an existing value. I know that clap will require the user to supply at least one value, so it is safe to call Option::unwrap (*https://oreil.ly/bBiXR*) to extract the values from the Some variant. The result is an Iterator (*https://oreil.ly/YN4DW*) of string values that need to be cloned. Finally, I use Iterator::collect (*https://oreil.ly/9ocju*) to put the strings into the type Vec (*https://oreil.ly/pZU3A*), which is a contiguous growable array type:

```
let text: Vec<String> = ❶
    matches.get_many("text").unwrap().cloned().collect();
```

❶ The type annotation follows the colon and is required because Iterator::collect can return many different types.

 If you call Option::unwrap on a None, it will cause a panic (*https://oreil.ly/DrERd*) that will crash your program. You should only call unwrap if you are positive the value is the Some variant.

Copy vs. Clone/Stack vs. Heap

I want to take a moment to explain why I cloned the strings. If you look at the documentation for `ArgMatches::get_many` (*https://oreil.ly/3_P-S*), you'll see similar code that uses `copied` because the values are integers rather than strings. In both instances, Rust is duplicating the data, but the *type* of the data determines whether it is copied or cloned—operations that are tied to the kind of memory that Rust uses.

Before programming in Rust, I'd only ever considered one amorphous idea of computer memory. Having studiously avoided languages that required me to allocate and free memory, I was only vaguely aware of the efforts that dynamic languages make to hide these complexities from me. In Rust, I've learned that not all memory is accessed in the same way. First there is the *stack*, where items of known sizes are accessed in *last-in, first-out* (LIFO) order. The classic analogy is to a stack of cafeteria trays where new items go on top and are taken back off the top. Because the items on the stack have a fixed size, Rust can set aside a particular chunk of memory and find it quickly. Data types like integers that live on the stack can be easily replicated via an action called *copy*.

The other type of memory is the *heap*, where the sizes of the values may change over time. The strings of input to our program fit this description because they may be of any length and there may be any number of them. The documentation for the `Vec` (vector) type (*https://oreil.ly/u5T4g*) describes this structure as a "contiguous growable array type." *Growable* is the key word here, as the number and sizes of the elements in a vector can change during the lifetime of the program. Rust makes an initial estimation of the amount of memory it needs for the vector. If the vector grows beyond the original allocation, Rust will find another chunk of memory to hold the data. To find the memory where the data lives, Rust stores the memory address on the stack. This is called a *pointer* because it points to the actual data, and so is also said to be a *reference* to the data. Items that live on the heap may be very large, so copying the data requires you to acknowledge this difference via the action called *clone*. The Rust compiler will always ensure that you are correctly copying or cloning data as needed for a given data type.

The `omit_newline` argument is a bit easier, as it's either present or not. The `Arg Matches::get_flag` (*https://oreil.ly/xwY9J*) will return a value of the type `bool` (*https://oreil.ly/4Zh0A*), or Boolean, which is either `true` or `false`. I omit the type annotation as the compiler infers the type:

```
let omit_newline = matches.get_flag("omit_newline");
```

Finally, I want to print the values. Because `text` is a vector of strings, I can use `Vec::join` (*https://oreil.ly/i8IBx*) to join all the strings on a single space into a new string to print. Inside the echor program, `clap` will be creating the vector. To

demonstrate how `Vec::join` works, I'll show you how to create a vector using the
`vec!` macro (*https://oreil.ly/SAlnL*):

```
let text = vec!["Hello", "world"];
```

 The values in Rust vectors must all be of the same type. Dynamic
languages often allow lists to mix types like strings and numbers,
but Rust will complain about "mismatched types." Here I want a list
of literal strings, which must be enclosed in double quotes. The `str`
type (*https://oreil.ly/DREEk*) in Rust represents a valid UTF-8
string. I'll have more to say about UTF in Chapter 4.

`Vec::join` will insert the given string between all the elements of the vector to create
a new string. I can use `println!` to print the new string to STDOUT followed by a
newline:

```
println!("{}", text.join(" "));
```

It's common practice in Rust documentation to present facts using `assert!` (*https://
oreil.ly/SQHyp*) to say that something is `true` or `assert_eq!` (*https://oreil.ly/P6Bfw*) to
demonstrate that one thing is equivalent to another. In the following code, I can
assert that the result of `text.join(" ")` is equal to the string `"Hello world"`:

```
assert_eq!(text.join(" "), "Hello world");
```

When the `-n` flag is present, the output should omit the newline. I will instead use the
`print!` macro (*https://oreil.ly/nMLGY*), which does not add a newline, and I will
choose to add either a newline or the empty string depending on the value of
`omit_newline`. You might expect me to write something like this:

```
fn main() {
    let matches = ...; // Same as before
    let text: Vec<String> =
        matches.get_many("text").unwrap().cloned().collect();
    let omit_newline = matches.get_flag("omit_newline");

    let ending = "\n"; ❶
    if omit_newline {
        ending = ""; // This will not work ❷
    }
    print!("{}{ending}", text.join(" ")); ❸
}
```

❶ Assume a default value of the newline.

❷ Change the value to the empty string if the newline should be omitted.

❸ Use `print!`, which will not add a newline to the output.

But if I try to run this code, Rust complains that I cannot reassign the value of ending:

```
$ cargo run -- Hello world
error[E0384]: cannot assign twice to immutable variable `ending`
  --> src/main.rs:30:9
   |
28 |     let ending = "\n";
   |         ------
   |         |
   |         first assignment to `ending`
   |         help: consider making this binding mutable: `mut ending`
29 |     if omit_newline {
30 |         ending = ""; // This will not work
   |         ^^^^^^^^^^^ cannot assign twice to immutable variable

For more information about this error, try `rustc --explain E0384`.
error: could not compile `echor` (bin "echor") due to previous error
```

As you saw in Chapter 1, Rust variables are immutable by default. The compiler suggests adding mut to make the ending variable mutable to fix this error:

```
fn main() {
    let matches = ...; // Same as before
    let text: Vec<String> =
        matches.get_many("text").unwrap().cloned().collect();
    let omit_newline = matches.get_flag("omit_newline");

    let mut ending = "\n"; ❶
    if omit_newline {
        ending = "";
    }
    print!("{}{ending}", text.join(" "));
}
```

❶ Add mut to make this a mutable value.

There's a much better way to write this. In Rust, if is an expression, not a statement as it is in languages like C and Java.[1] An *expression* returns a value, but a statement does not. Here's a more Rustic way to write this:

```
let ending = if omit_newline { "" } else { "\n" };
```

An if without an else will return the unit type. The same is true for a function without a return type, so the main function in this program returns the unit type.

---

1 Python has both an if statement and an if expression.

Since I use ending in only one place, I don't need to assign it to a variable. Here is the final way I would write the main function:

```
fn main() {
    let matches = ...; // Same as before
    let text: Vec<String> =
        matches.get_many("text").unwrap().cloned().collect();
    let omit_newline = matches.get_flag("omit_newline");
    print!("{}{}", text.join(" "), if omit_newline { "" } else { "\n" });
}
```

With these changes, the program appears to work correctly; however, I'm not willing to stake my reputation on this. I need to, as the Russian saying goes, "Доверяй, но проверяй."[2] This requires that I write some tests to run my program with various inputs and verify that it produces the same output as the original echo program.

Writing Integration Tests

We will use the assert_cmd and pretty_assertions crates for testing echor. We'll also use the predicates crate (*https://oreil.ly/OMtFW*), as it will make writing some of the tests easier and anyhow (*https://oreil.ly/ZcUzF*) for handling errors. Update *Cargo.toml* with the following:

```
[package]
name = "echor"
version = "0.1.0"
edition = "2021"

[dependencies]
clap = "4.5.0"

[dev-dependencies]
anyhow = "1.0.79"
assert_cmd = "2.0.13"
predicates = "3.0.4"
pretty_assertions = "1.4.0"
```

I often write tests that ensure my programs fail when run incorrectly. For instance, this program ought to fail and print help documentation when provided no arguments. Create the *tests* directory, and then start your *tests/cli.rs* with the following:

```
use assert_cmd::Command;
use predicates::prelude::*; ❶

#[test]
fn dies_no_args() {
```

---

2 "Trust, but verify." This rhymes in Russian and so sounds cooler than when Reagan used it in the 1980s during nuclear disarmament talks with the USSR.

```
    let mut cmd = Command::cargo_bin("echor").unwrap();
    cmd.assert() ❷
        .failure()
        .stderr(predicate::str::contains("Usage"));
}
```

❶ The predicates crate helps to check the program's output.

❷ Run the program with no arguments and assert that it fails and prints a usage
    statement to STDERR.

 I often put the word *dies* somewhere in the test name to make it
clear that the program is expected to fail under the given conditions. If I run **cargo test dies**, then Cargo will run all the tests
with names containing the string *dies*.

Run **cargo test** to ensure that your program passes. Next, let's also add a test to
ensure the program exits successfully when provided an argument:

```
#[test]
fn runs() {
    let mut cmd = Command::cargo_bin("echor").unwrap();
    cmd.arg("hello").assert().success(); ❶
}
```

❶ Run echor with the argument hello and verify it exits successfully.

I can now run **cargo test** to verify that I have a program that runs, validates user
input, and prints usage.

```
running 2 tests
test runs ... ok
test dies_no_args ... ok
```

Creating the Test Output Files

Next, I would like to ensure that the program creates the same output as echo. To
start, I need to capture the output from the original echo for various inputs so that I
can compare these to the output from my program. In the *02_echor* directory of the
GitHub repository (*https://oreil.ly/pfhMC*) for the book, you'll find a bash script
called *mk-outs.sh* that I used to generate the output from echo for various arguments.
You can see that, even with such a simple tool, there's still a decent amount of *cyclo-
matic complexity*, which refers to the various ways all the parameters can be combined. I need to check one or more text arguments both with and without the newline
option:

```
$ cat mk-outs.sh
#!/usr/bin/env bash  ❶

OUTDIR="tests/expected"  ❷
[[ ! -d "$OUTDIR" ]] && mkdir -p "$OUTDIR"  ❸

echo     "Hello there"   > $OUTDIR/hello1.txt  ❹
echo     "Hello" "there" > $OUTDIR/hello2.txt  ❺
echo -n "Hello  there"   > $OUTDIR/hello1.n.txt  ❻
echo -n "Hello" "there" > $OUTDIR/hello2.n.txt  ❼
```

❶ A special comment (aka a *shebang*) that tells the operating system to use the environment to execute bash for the following code.

❷ Define a variable for the output directory.

❸ Test if the output directory does not exist and create it if needed.

❹ One argument with two words.

❺ Two arguments separated by more than one space.

❻ One argument with two spaces and no newline.

❼ Two arguments with no newline.

If you are working on a Unix platform, you can copy this program to your project directory and run it like so:

```
$ bash mk-outs.sh
```

It's also possible to execute the program directly, but you may need to execute **chmod +x mk-outs.sh** if you get a *permission denied* error:

```
$ ./mk-outs.sh
```

If this worked, you should now have a *tests/expected* directory with the following contents:

```
$ tree tests
tests
├── cli.rs
└── expected
    ├── hello1.n.txt
    ├── hello1.txt
    ├── hello2.n.txt
    └── hello2.txt

1 directory, 5 files
```

If you are working on a Windows platform, then I recommend you copy the directory and files into your project.

Comparing Program Output

Now that we have some test files, it's time to compare the output from echor to the output from the original echo. The first output file was generated with the input *Hello there* as a single string, and the output was captured into the file *tests/expected /hello1.txt*. In the following test, I will run echor with the same argument and compare the output to the contents of that file. I must add use std::fs to *tests/cli.rs* to bring in the standard *filesystem* module. I replace the runs function with the following:

```
#[test]
fn hello1() {
    let outfile = "tests/expected/hello1.txt"; ❶
    let expected = fs::read_to_string(outfile).unwrap(); ❷
    let mut cmd = Command::cargo_bin("echor").unwrap(); ❸
    cmd.arg("Hello there").assert().success().stdout(expected); ❹
}
```

❶ This is the output from echo generated by *mk-outs.sh*.

❷ Use fs::read_to_string (*https://oreil.ly/dZGzk*) to read the contents of the file. This returns a Result that might contain a string if all goes well. Use the Result::unwrap method with the assumption that this will work.

❸ Create a Command to run echor in the current crate.

❹ Run the program with the given argument and assert it finishes successfully and that STDOUT is the expected value.

 Using fs::read_to_string is a convenient way to read a file into memory, but it's also an easy way to crash your program—and possibly your computer—if you happen to read a file that exceeds your available memory. You should only use this function with small files. As Ted Nelson says, "The good news about computers is that they do what you tell them to do. The bad news is that they do what you tell them to do."

If I run **cargo test** now, I should see output from two tests (in no particular order):

```
running 2 tests
test hello1 ... ok
test dies_no_args ... ok
```

Using the Result Type

I've been using the `Result::unwrap` method in a way that assumes each fallible call will succeed. For example, in the `hello1` function, I assumed that the output file exists and can be opened and read into a string. During my limited testing, this may be the case, but it's dangerous to make such assumptions. I should be more cautious, so I'm going to start checking these possible failures, and I find `anyhow::Result` (*https://oreil.ly/NOGKW*) is easier to use than the default `Result` type.

Up to this point, my test functions have returned the unit type. Now they will return `anyhow::Result`, changing my test code in some subtle ways. Previously I used `Result::unwrap` to unpack `Ok` values and panic in the event of an `Err`, causing the test to fail. In the following code, I replace `unwrap` with the `?` operator to either unpack an `Ok` value or propagate the `Err` value to the return type. That is, this will cause the function to return the `Err` variant of `Result` to the caller, which will in turn cause the test to fail. If all the code in a test function runs successfully, I return `Ok` containing the unit type to indicate the test passes. Note that while Rust does have the `return` keyword (*https://oreil.ly/rtZW1*) to return a value from a function, the idiom is to omit the semicolon from the final expression to implicitly return that result. Update your *tests/cli.rs* to the following:

```
use anyhow::Result; ❶
use assert_cmd::Command;
use predicates::prelude::*;
use std::fs;

#[test]
fn dies_no_args() -> Result<()> { ❷
    let mut cmd = Command::cargo_bin("echor")?; ❸
    cmd.assert()
        .failure()
        .stderr(predicate::str::contains("Usage"));
    Ok(()) ❹
}

#[test]
fn hello1() -> Result<()> {
    let expected = fs::read_to_string("tests/expected/hello1.txt")?;
    let mut cmd = Command::cargo_bin("echor")?;
    cmd.arg("Hello there").assert().success().stdout(expected);
    Ok(())
}
```

❶ Use `anyhow::Result` over the default `Result` type.

❷ The `Ok` variant will contain the unit type, and the `Err` variant will contain an `Error` (*https://oreil.ly/-W7sE*).

❸ Use ? instead of `Result::unwrap` to unpack an `Ok` value or propagate an `Err`.

❹ Omit the final semicolon to return this value.

The next test passes two arguments, `"Hello"` and `"there"`, and expects the program to print "Hello there":

```
#[test]
fn hello2() -> Result<()> {
    let expected = fs::read_to_string("tests/expected/hello2.txt")?;
    let mut cmd = Command::cargo_bin("echor")?;
    cmd.args(vec!["Hello", "there"]) ❶
        .assert()
        .success()
        .stdout(expected);
    Ok(())
}
```

❶ Use the `Command::args` method (*https://oreil.ly/G5FYd*) to pass a vector of arguments rather than a single string value.

I have a total of four files to check, so it behooves me to write a helper function. I'll call it `run` and will pass it the argument strings along with the expected output file. Rather than use `vec!` to create a vector for the arguments, I'm going to use a `std::slice` (*https://oreil.ly/NHidS*). Slices are a bit like vectors in that they represent a list of values, but they cannot be resized after creation. Be sure to add use `pretty_assertions::assert_eq` for the following code to get nice string comparisons:

```
fn run(args: &[&str], expected_file: &str) -> Result<()> { ❶
    let expected = fs::read_to_string(expected_file)?; ❷
    let output = Command::cargo_bin("echor")? ❸
        .args(args)
        .output()
        .expect("fail");

    let stdout = String::from_utf8(output.stdout).expect("invalid UTF-8"); ❹
    assert_eq!(stdout, expected); ❺
    Ok(()) ❻
}
```

❶ The `args` will be a slice of `&str` values, and the `expected_file` will be a `&str`. The return value is a `Result`.

❷ Try to read the contents of the `expected_file` into a string.

❸ Attempt to run echor in the current crate with the given arguments and unpack the output.

❹   Attempt to convert the program's STDOUT to a string.

❺   Ensure that the output is the same as the expected value.

❻   If all the previous code worked, return Ok containing the unit type.

 You will find that Rust has many types of "string" variables. The type str is appropriate here for literal strings in the source code. The & shows that I intend only to borrow the string for a little while. I'll have more to say about strings, borrowing, and ownership later.

Following is the final contents of *tests/cli.rs* showing how I use the helper function to run all four tests:

```
use anyhow::Result;
use assert_cmd::Command;
use predicates::prelude::*;
use pretty_assertions::assert_eq;
use std::fs;

#[test]
fn dies_no_args() -> Result<()> {
    Command::cargo_bin("echor")?
        .assert()
        .failure()
        .stderr(predicate::str::contains("Usage"));
    Ok(())
}

fn run(args: &[&str], expected_file: &str) -> Result<()> {
    let expected = fs::read_to_string(expected_file)?;
    let output = Command::cargo_bin("echor")?
        .args(args)
        .output()
        .expect("fail");

    let stdout = String::from_utf8(output.stdout).expect("invalid UTF-8");
    assert_eq!(stdout, expected);
    Ok(())
}

#[test]
fn hello1() -> Result<()> {
    run(&["Hello there"], "tests/expected/hello1.txt") ❶
}

#[test]
fn hello2() -> Result<()> {
```

```
        run(&["Hello", "there"], "tests/expected/hello2.txt")  ❷
    }

    #[test]
    fn hello1_no_newline() -> Result<()> {
        run(&["Hello  there", "-n"], "tests/expected/hello1.n.txt")  ❸
    }

    #[test]
    fn hello2_no_newline() -> Result<()> {
        run(&["-n", "Hello", "there"], "tests/expected/hello2.n.txt")  ❹
    }
```

❶ Run the program with a single string value as input. Note the lack of a terminating semicolon, as this function will return whatever the run function returns.

❷ Run the program with two strings as input.

❸ Run the program with a single string value as input and the -n flag to omit the newline. Note that there are two spaces between the words.

❹ Run the program with two strings as input and the -n flag appearing first.

As you can see, I can write as many functions as I like in *tests/cli.rs*. Only those marked with #[test] are run when testing. If you run **cargo test** now, you should see five passing tests:

```
running 5 tests
test dies_no_args ... ok
test hello1 ... ok
test hello1_no_newline ... ok
test hello2_no_newline ... ok
test hello2 ... ok
```

Using clap Derive

Now I will show you how to write the same clap code using the derive pattern and the preceding test suite to ensure that the program still works as expected. First, you will need to update *Cargo.toml* to include this crate feature:

```
[dependencies]
clap = { version = "4.5.0", features = ["derive"] }
```

You can also use Cargo to add the dependency for you:

```
$ cargo add clap --features derive
```

Key to the derive pattern is the definition of a struct (*https://oreil.ly/n4Dsk*) to represent the command-line arguments. A struct is similar to a class definition in object-oriented languages and allows you to mix various Rust types into a single data structure. As in the preceding code, I will use Vec<String> to represent the string values and bool for whether or not to include the final newline. Additionally, the struct will have comments (*https://oreil.ly/WN4t7*), which can start with two or three slashes. Three slashes denote documentation, aka *doc comments*. In the previous chapter, you saw #[test] was used to annotate a test function. My Args struct will use similar annotations to tell clap how to create the user interface.

Move your *src/main.rs* to some other filename and start fresh with the following:

```
use clap::Parser; ❶

#[derive(Debug, Parser)] ❷
#[command(author, version, about)] ❸
/// Rust version of `echo` ❹
struct Args { ❺
    /// Input text
    #[arg(required(true))] ❻
    text: Vec<String>, ❼

    /// Do not print newline
    #[arg(short('n'))] ❽
    omit_newline: bool, ❾
}
```

❶ Import the clap::Parser (*https://oreil.ly/IrHOL*) trait.

❷ The derive (*https://oreil.ly/0zHLo*) attribute expands the capabilities of the struct. Here, I'm using the standard Debug to allow for debug printing of the struct and the imported clap::Parser.

❸ command (*https://oreil.ly/SkUg1*) will turn the struct into a clap::Command object. The values for *author* and *version* can be derived from *Cargo.toml*.

❹ This doc comment becomes the program's *about* description.

❺ Define a struct called Args.

❻ Each member of the struct becomes a clap::Arg (*https://oreil.ly/AQZFy*). This #[arg] annotation additionally specifies that text is a required (*https://oreil.ly/a0UyH*).

❼ Create an argument named *text*. The type annotation Vec<String> indicates that this argument can hold multiple string values.

❽ Define a short flag -n for the following argument.

❾ The omit_newline is a Boolean value that will default to false.

Change the main function to the following:

```
fn main() {
    let args = Args::parse(); ❶
    dbg!(args); ❷
}
```

❶ Parse the command-line arguments into a Args struct.

❷ Use the dbg! (*debug*) macro (*https://oreil.ly/a7BdC*) to pretty-print the arguments.

The derive code is more terse but creates the same interface. Run with -h|--help to view the usage documentation and with no arguments to ensure the input text is still required. Finally, run with the correct arguments to view the Args struct:

```
$ cargo run -- -n Hello world
[src/main.rs:18] args = Args { 
    text: [ ❶
        "Hello",
        "world",
    ],
    omit_newline: true, ❷
}
```

❶ The field args.text provides access to a Vec<String>.

❷ The field args.omit_newline is a bool value.

 Run **cargo test** to see the passing and failing tests. Stop reading and see if you can use the Args struct to write a passing version of the program.

Following is how I wrote the main function to use the Args struct:

```
fn main() {
    let args = Args::parse();
    print!(
        "{}{}",
        args.text.join(" "),
        if args.omit_newline { "" } else { "\n" }
    );
}
```

This is a perfect example of refactoring your program. First, you must get something that works correctly, which you can verify using tests. Then you rely on the strictness of the Rust compiler and your tests to change your program.

Summary

Now you have written 20-30 lines of Rust code (depending on whether you use builder or derive) in *src/main.rs* for the echor program and five tests in *tests/cli.rs* to verify that your program meets some measure of specification. Consider what you've achieved:

- You learned that basic program output is printed to STDOUT and errors should be printed to STDERR.
- You've written a program that takes the options -h or --help to produce help, -V or --version to show the program's version, and -n to omit a newline along with one or more positional command-line arguments.
- You wrote a program that will print usage documentation when run with the wrong arguments or with the -h|--help flag.
- You learned how to print all the positional command-line arguments joined on spaces.
- You learned to use the print! macro to omit the trailing newline if the -n flag is present.
- You can run integration tests to confirm that your program replicates the output from echo for at least four test cases covering one or two inputs both with and without the trailing newline.
- You learned to use several Rust types, including the unit type, strings, vectors, slices, Option, and Result.
- You learned how to read the entire contents of a file into a string.
- You learned how to execute an external command from within a Rust program, check the exit status, and verify the contents of both STDOUT and STDERR.
- You used two clap patterns for parsing command-line arguments, builder and derive, the latter of which required creating and annotating a struct.

All this, and you've done it while writing in a language that won't let you make common mistakes that lead to buggy programs or security vulnerabilities. Feel free to give yourself a high five or enjoy a slightly evil *mwuhaha* chuckle as you consider how Rust will help you conquer the world. Now that I've shown you how to organize and write tests and data, I'll use the tests earlier in the next program to start using *test-driven development*, where I write tests first and then write code to satisfy the tests.

CHAPTER 3

On the Catwalk

When you are alone / You are the cat, you are the phone / You are an animal
— They Might Be Giants, "Don't Let's Start" (1986)

In this chapter, the challenge is to write a clone of cat, which is so named because it can con*cat*enate many files into one file. That is, given files *a*, *b*, and *c*, you could execute cat a b c > all to stream all the lines from these three files and redirect them into a file called *all*. The program will accept a couple of different options to prefix each line with the line number.

You'll learn how to do the following:

- Use testing-first development
- Test for the existence of a file
- Create a random string for a filename that does not exist
- Read regular files or STDIN (pronounced *standard in*)
- Use eprintln! to print to STDERR and format! to format a string
- Write a test that provides input on STDIN
- Define mutually exclusive arguments
- Use the enumerate method of an iterator

How cat Works

I'll start by showing how cat works so that you know what is expected of the challenge. The BSD version of cat does not print the usage for the -h|--help flags, so I must use **man cat** to read the manual page. For such a limited program, it has a surprising number of options, but the challenge program will implement only a subset of these:

```
CAT(1)                     BSD General Commands Manual                    CAT(1)

NAME
     cat -- concatenate and print files

SYNOPSIS
     cat [-benstuv] [file ...]

DESCRIPTION
     The cat utility reads files sequentially, writing them to the standard
     output.  The file operands are processed in command-line order.  If file
     is a single dash ('-') or absent, cat reads from the standard input.  If
     file is a UNIX domain socket, cat connects to it and then reads it until
     EOF.  This complements the UNIX domain binding capability available in
     inetd(8).

     The options are as follows:

     -b      Number the non-blank output lines, starting at 1.

     -e      Display non-printing characters (see the -v option), and display
             a dollar sign ('$') at the end of each line.

     -n      Number the output lines, starting at 1.

     -s      Squeeze multiple adjacent empty lines, causing the output to be
             single spaced.

     -t      Display non-printing characters (see the -v option), and display
             tab characters as '^I'.

     -u      Disable output buffering.

     -v      Display non-printing characters so they are visible.  Control
             characters print as '^X' for control-X; the delete character
             (octal 0177) prints as '^?'.  Non-ASCII characters (with the high
             bit set) are printed as 'M-' (for meta) followed by the character
             for the low 7 bits.

EXIT STATUS
     The cat utility exits 0 on success, and >0 if an error occurs.
```

Throughout the book I will also show the GNU versions of programs so that you can consider how the programs can vary and to provide inspiration for how you might expand beyond the solutions I present. Note that the GNU version does respond to --help, as will the solution you will write:

```
$ cat --help
Usage: cat [OPTION]... [FILE]...
```

```
Concatenate FILE(s), or standard input, to standard output.

  -A, --show-all          equivalent to -vET
  -b, --number-nonblank   number nonempty output lines, overrides -n
  -e                      equivalent to -vE
  -E, --show-ends         display $ at end of each line
  -n, --number            number all output lines
  -s, --squeeze-blank     suppress repeated empty output lines
  -t                      equivalent to -vT
  -T, --show-tabs         display TAB characters as ^I
  -u                      (ignored)
  -v, --show-nonprinting  use ^ and M- notation, except for LFD and TAB
      --help     display this help and exit
      --version  output version information and exit

With no FILE, or when FILE is -, read standard input.

Examples:
  cat f - g  Output f's contents, then standard input, then g's contents.
  cat        Copy standard input to standard output.

GNU coreutils online help: <http://www.gnu.org/software/coreutils/>
For complete documentation, run: info coreutils 'cat invocation'
```

 The BSD version predates the GNU version, so the latter implements all the same short flags to be compatible. As is typical of GNU programs, it also offers long flag aliases like - -number for -n and - -number-nonblank for -b. I will show you how to offer both options, like the GNU version.

For the challenge program, you will implement only the options -b|--number -nonblank and -n|--number. I will also show you how to read regular files and STDIN when given a filename argument of a dash (-). To demonstrate cat, I'll use some files that I have included in the *03_catr* directory of the repository. Change into that directory:

```
$ cd 03_catr
```

The *tests/inputs* directory contains four files for testing:

- *empty.txt*: an empty file
- *fox.txt*: a single line of text
- *spiders.txt*: a haiku by Kobayashi Issa with three lines of text
- *the-bustle.txt*: a lovely poem by Emily Dickinson that has two four-line stanzas of text separated by one blank line

Empty files are common, if useless. The following command produces no output, so we'll expect our program to do the same:

```
$ cat tests/inputs/empty.txt
```

Next, I'll run `cat` on a file with one line of text:

```
$ cat tests/inputs/fox.txt
The quick brown fox jumps over the lazy dog.
```

 I have already used `cat` several times in this book to print the contents of a single file, as in the preceding command. This is another common usage of the program outside of its original intent of concatenating files.

The `-n|--number` and `-b|--number-nonblank` flags will both number the lines. The line number is right-justified in a field six characters wide followed by a tab character and then the line of text. To distinguish the tab character, I can use the `-t` option to display nonprinting characters so that the tab shows as ^I, but note that the challenge program is not expected to do this. In the following command, I use the Unix pipe (|) to connect STDOUT from the first command to STDIN in the second command:

```
$ cat -n tests/inputs/fox.txt | cat -t
     1^IThe quick brown fox jumps over the lazy dog.
```

The *spiders.txt* file has three lines of text that should be numbered with the `-n` option:

```
$ cat -n tests/inputs/spiders.txt
     1  Don't worry, spiders,
     2  I keep house
     3  casually.
```

The difference between `-n` (on the left) and `-b` (on the right) is apparent only with *the-bustle.txt*, as the latter will number only nonblank lines:

```
$ cat -n tests/inputs/the-bustle.txt    $ cat -b tests/inputs/the-bustle.txt
     1  The bustle in a house                  1  The bustle in a house
     2  The morning after death                2  The morning after death
     3  Is solemnest of industries             3  Is solemnest of industries
     4  Enacted upon earth,–                    4  Enacted upon earth,–
     5
     6  The sweeping up the heart,              5  The sweeping up the heart,
     7  And putting love away                   6  And putting love away
     8  We shall not want to use again          7  We shall not want to use again
     9  Until eternity.                         8  Until eternity.
```

Oddly, you can use -b and -n together, and the -b option takes precedence. The challenge program will allow only one or the other.

In the following example, I'm using *blargh* to represent a nonexistent file. I create the file *cant-touch-this* using the touch command and use the chmod command to set permissions that make it unreadable. (You'll learn more about what the 000 means in Chapter 14 when you write a Rust version of ls.) When cat encounters any file that does not exist or cannot be opened, it will print a message to STDERR and move to the next file:

```
$ touch cant-touch-this && chmod 000 cant-touch-this
$ cat tests/inputs/fox.txt blargh tests/inputs/spiders.txt cant-touch-this
The quick brown fox jumps over the lazy dog. ❶
cat: blargh: No such file or directory ❷
Don't worry, spiders, ❸
I keep house
casually.
cat: cant-touch-this: Permission denied ❹
```

❶ This is the output from the first file.

❷ This is the error for a nonexistent file.

❸ This is the output from the third file.

❹ This is the error for an unreadable file.

Finally, I'll run cat with all the files. Notice in the following output that the BSD version starts renumbering the lines for each file, which is the implementation expected by the tests. The GNU version of cat keeps incrementing the line counter over all the files.

```
$ cd tests/inputs ❶
$ cat -n empty.txt fox.txt spiders.txt the-bustle.txt ❷
     1  The quick brown fox jumps over the lazy dog.
     1  Don't worry, spiders,
     2  I keep house
     3  casually.
     1  The bustle in a house
     2  The morning after death
     3  Is solemnest of industries
     4  Enacted upon earth,—
     5
     6  The sweeping up the heart,
     7  And putting love away
```

```
      8  We shall not want to use again
      9  Until eternity.
```

❶   Change into the *tests/inputs* directory.

❷   Run cat with all the files and the -n option to number the lines.

If you look at the *mk-outs.sh* script used to generate the test cases, you'll see I execute cat with all these files, individually and together, as regular files and through STDIN, using no flags and with the -n and -b flags. I capture all the outputs to various files in the *tests/expected* directory to use in testing.

Getting Started

The challenge program you write should be called catr (pronounced *cat-er*) for a Rust version of cat. I suggest you begin with **cargo new catr** to start a new application. You'll use all the same external crates as in Chapter 2, plus the rand crate (*https://oreil.ly/HJOPg*) to create random values for testing. Update your *Cargo.toml* to add the following dependencies:

```
[dependencies]
anyhow = "1.0.79"
clap = { version = "4.5.0", features = ["derive"] }

[dev-dependencies]
assert_cmd = "2.0.13"
predicates = "3.0.4"
pretty_assertions = "1.4.0"
rand = "0.8.5"
```

You're going to write the whole challenge program yourself later, but first I'm going to coach you through the things you need to know.

Starting with Tests

So far in this book, I've shown you how to write tests after writing the programs to get you used to the idea of testing and to practice the basics of the Rust language. Starting with this chapter, I want you to think about the tests before you start writing the program. Tests force you to consider the program's requirements and how you will verify that the program works as expected. Ultimately, I want to draw your attention to *test-driven development* (TDD) as described in a book by that title (*https://oreil.ly/Aved3*) written by Kent Beck (Addison-Wesley). TDD advises we write the tests *before* writing the code, as shown in Figure 3-1. Technically, TDD involves writing tests as you add each feature, and I will demonstrate this technique in later chapters. Because I've written all the tests for the program, you might consider this more like *test-first development*. Regardless of how and when the tests are written, the point is to emphasize testing at the beginning of the process. Once your program passes the tests, you can use the tests to improve and refactor your code, perhaps by reducing the lines of code or by finding a faster implementation.

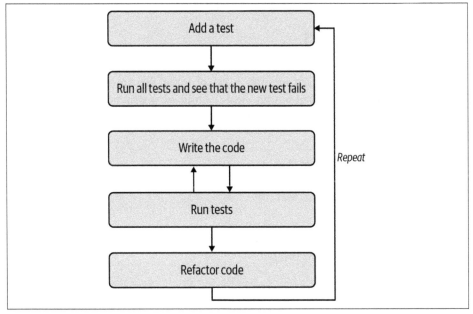

Figure 3-1. The test-driven development cycle starts with writing a test and then the code that passes it.

Copy the *03_catr/tests* directory into your new *catr* directory. Don't copy anything but the tests, as you will write the rest of the code yourself. On a Unix-type system, you can copy this directory and its contents using the cp command with the *recursive* -r option:

```
$ cd catr
$ cp -r ~/command-line-rust/03_catr/tests .
```

Your project directory should have a structure like this:

```
$ tree -L 2
.
├── Cargo.toml
├── src
│   └── main.rs
└── tests
    ├── cli.rs
    ├── expected
    └── inputs
```

Run `cargo test` to download the dependencies, compile your program, and run the tests, all of which should fail. Starting with this chapter, I'll get you started with the basics of setting up each program, give you the info you need to write the program, and let you finish writing it using the tests to guide you.

Defining the Parameters

Let's start by representing the command-line parameters for `catr` with a struct called `Args`. Specifically, the program requires a list of input filenames and two Boolean flags for numbering the lines of output. Add the following struct to *src/main.rs*. I recommend placing this near the top after any `use` statements:

```
#[derive(Debug)] ❶
struct Args { ❷
    files: Vec<String>, ❸
    number_lines: bool, ❹
    number_nonblank_lines: bool, ❺
}
```

❶ The `derive` macro (*https://oreil.ly/Lr8JE*) adds the `Debug` trait (*https://oreil.ly/cEl5P*) so the struct can be printed.

❷ Define a struct called `Args`.

❸ The `files` will be a vector of strings.

❹ This is a Boolean value to indicate whether or not to print the line numbers.

❺ This is a Boolean to control printing line numbers only for nonblank lines.

If you would like to use the `clap` derive pattern, then you can add the necessary annotations to the preceding struct. If you prefer the builder pattern, I suggest that you write a function called `get_args` with the following skeleton. Use what you learned from Chapter 2 to complete this function on your own:

```
fn get_args() -> Args { ❶
    let matches = Command::new("catr")
        .version("0.1.0")
        .author("Ken Youens-Clark <kyclark@gmail.com>")
        .about("Rust version of `cat`")
        // What goes here? ❷
        .get_matches();

    Args { ❸
        files: ...
        number_lines: ...
        number_nonblank_lines: ...
```

```
        }
    }
```

❶ This function returns an Args struct.

❷ Define the program's arguments here.

❸ Return an Args struct using the supplied values.

Update the main function to the following code:

```
fn main() {
    let args = get_args(); ❶
    println!("{args:#?}"); ❷
}
```

❶ Attempt to parse the command-line arguments.

❷ Pretty-print the arguments.

When run with the -h or --help flags, your program should print a usage like this:

```
$ cargo run -- --help
Rust version of `cat`

Usage: catr [OPTIONS] [FILE]...

Arguments:
  [FILE]...  Input file(s) [default: -]

Options:
  -n, --number            Number lines
  -b, --number-nonblank   Number non-blank lines
  -h, --help              Print help
  -V, --version           Print version
```

With no arguments, your program should print the Args like this:

```
$ cargo run
Args {
    files: [ ❶
        "-",
    ],
    number_lines: false, ❷
    number_nonblank_lines: false,
}
```

❶ The files argument should default to a vector containing a single dash (-) for STDIN.

❷ The Boolean arguments should both default to false.

Run it with some arguments and be sure the arguments are parsed correctly:

```
$ cargo run -- -n tests/inputs/fox.txt
Args {
    files: [
        "tests/inputs/fox.txt", ❶
    ],
    number_lines: true, ❷
    number_nonblank_lines: false,
}
```

❶ The positional file argument is parsed into the files.

❷ The -n option causes number_lines to be true.

While the BSD version will allow both -n and -b, the challenge program should consider these to be mutually exclusive and generate an error when they're used together:

```
$ cargo run -- -b -n tests/inputs/fox.txt
error: the argument '--number-nonblank' cannot be used with '--number'

Usage: catr --number-nonblank <FILE>...

For more information, try '--help'.
```

 Stop reading here and get your program working as described so far. Seriously! I want you to try writing your version of this before you read ahead. Your program should also pass **cargo test usage**. I'll wait here until you finish.

All set? Compare what you have to my get_args function. Be sure to add use clap::{Arg, ArgAction, Command} to your imports for the following code:

```
fn get_args() -> Args {
    let matches = Command::new("catr")
        .version("0.1.0")
        .author("Ken Youens-Clark <kyclark@gmail.com>")
        .about("Rust version of `cat`")
        .arg(
            Arg::new("files") ❶
                .value_name("FILE")
                .help("Input file(s)")
                .num_args(1..)
                .default_value("-"),
        )
        .arg(
            Arg::new("number") ❷
                .short('n')
                .long("number")
                .help("Number lines")
```

```
                .action(ArgAction::SetTrue)
                .conflicts_with("number_nonblank"),
        )
        .arg(
            Arg::new("number_nonblank") ❸
                .short('b')
                .long("number-nonblank")
                .help("Number non-blank lines")
                .action(ArgAction::SetTrue),
        )
        .get_matches();

    Args {
        files: matches.get_many("files").unwrap().cloned().collect(), ❹
        number_lines: matches.get_flag("number"), ❺
        number_nonblank_lines: matches.get_flag("number_nonblank"),
    }
}
```

❶ This positional argument is for the files and is required to have at least one value that defaults to a dash (-).

❷ This is an option that has a short name -n and a long name --number. When present, it will tell the program to print line numbers. It cannot occur in conjunction with -b.

❸ The -b|--number-nonblank flag controls whether or not to print line numbers for nonblank lines.

❹ Because at least one value is required, it should be safe to call Option::unwrap. Note that Iterator::collect returns a Vec due to type inference.

❺ The two Boolean options are set using ArgMatches::get_flag.

 Optional arguments have short and/or long names, but positional ones do not. You can define optional arguments before or after positional arguments.

For the clap derive pattern, update the Args struct as follows:

```
use clap::Parser;

#[derive(Debug, Parser)]
#[command(author, version, about)]
/// Rust version of `cat`
struct Args {
```

```
/// Input file(s)
#[arg(value_name = "FILE", default_value = "-")]
files: Vec<String>,

/// Number lines
#[arg(
    short('n'),
    long("number"),
    conflicts_with("number_nonblank_lines")
)]
number_lines: bool,

/// Number non-blank lines
#[arg(short('b'), long("number-nonblank"))]
number_nonblank_lines: bool,
}
```

Then change the main function to call Args::parse() instead of get_args():

```
fn main() {
    let args = Args::parse();
    println!("{args:#?}");
}
```

Execute **cargo test** to see the failing test output, but don't despair. You will soon rejoice in a fully passing test suite.

Iterating Through the File Arguments

Now that you have validated all the arguments, you are ready to process the files and create the correct output. Next, I suggest you write a function called run that will accept the Args struct and return a Result. There are two important reasons for this:

1. I want to separate the parsing of command-line arguments from their use in the logic of the program. This makes it easier for you to choose the derive or builder patterns of clap or replace it with some other code.

2. We are now moving into territory where code can fail. I want to use the ? operator to call other functions that return a Result and pass any errors back to the caller, which requires that my calling function also return a Result.

Add use anyhow::Result and the following code to *src/main.rs*:

```
fn run(_args: Args) -> Result<()> {  ❶
    Ok(())  ❷
}
```

❶ The function takes the Args struct and returns a Result.

❷ Implicitly return an Ok containing the unit type.

If you want to use the get_args builder pattern, change the main function to the following:

```
fn main() {
    if let Err(e) = run(get_args()) { ❶
        eprintln!("{e}"); ❷
        std::process::exit(1); ❸
    }
}
```

❶ Call run with the results of get_args and catch the Err variant.

❷ Print the error message e to STDERR.

❸ Exit the program with a nonzero value to indicate an error.

If you want to use the derive pattern, the code is almost identical:

```
fn main() {
    if let Err(e) = run(Args::parse()) { ❶
        eprintln!("{e}");
        std::process::exit(1);
    }
}
```

❶ Change get_args to Args::parse.

Next, modify the run function to print each filename:

```
fn run(args: Args) -> Result<()> {
    for filename in args.files { ❶
        println!("{filename}"); ❷
    }
    Ok(())
}
```

❶ Iterate through each filename.

❷ Print the filename.

Run the program with some input files. In the following example, the bash shell will expand the file glob[1] *.txt into all filenames that end with the extension *.txt*:

```
$ cargo run -- tests/inputs/*.txt
tests/inputs/empty.txt
tests/inputs/fox.txt
```

---

[1] *Glob* is short for *global*, an early Unix program that would expand wildcard characters into filepaths. Nowadays, the shell handles glob patterns directly.

```
tests/inputs/spiders.txt
tests/inputs/the-bustle.txt
```

Windows PowerShell can expand file globs using Get-ChildItem:

```
> cargo run -q -- -n (Get-ChildItem .\tests\inputs\*.txt)
C:\Users\kyclark\work\command-line-rust\03_catr\tests\inputs\empty.txt
C:\Users\kyclark\work\command-line-rust\03_catr\tests\inputs\fox.txt
C:\Users\kyclark\work\command-line-rust\03_catr\tests\inputs\spiders.txt
C:\Users\kyclark\work\command-line-rust\03_catr\tests\inputs\the-bustle.txt
```

Opening a File or STDIN

The next step is to try to open each filename. When the filename is a dash, you should open STDIN; otherwise, attempt to open the given filename and handle errors. For the following code, you will need to expand your imports with the following:

```
use std::fs::File;
use std::io::{self, BufRead, BufReader};
```

This next step is a bit tricky, so I will provide an open function for you to use. In the following code, I'm using the match keyword, which is similar to a switch statement in C. Specifically, I'm matching on whether the given filename is equal to a dash (-) or anything else, which is specified using the wildcard _:

```
fn open(filename: &str) -> Result<Box<dyn BufRead>> { ❶
    match filename {
        "-" => Ok(Box::new(BufReader::new(io::stdin()))), ❷
        _ => Ok(Box::new(BufReader::new(File::open(filename)?))), ❸
    }
}
```

❶ The function will accept a filename and will return either an error or a boxed value that implements the BufRead trait.

❷ When the filename is a dash (-), read from std::io::stdin (*https://oreil.ly/ TtQvx*).

❸ Otherwise, use File::open (*https://oreil.ly/Aj1pC*) to try to open the given file or propagate an error.

If File::open is successful, the result will be a *filehandle* of the type std::fs::File (*https://oreil.ly/S16cp*), which is a mechanism for reading the contents of a file. Both a filehandle and std::io::stdin implement the Read trait (*https://oreil.ly/2Dn3M*) that a BufReader struct (*https://oreil.ly/OUSJb*) will use to implement the BufRead trait (*https://oreil.ly/4tYrU*). This means the return value will, for instance, respond to the BufRead::lines function (*https://oreil.ly/KhmCp*) to produce lines of text. Note that this function will remove any line endings, such as \r\n on Windows and \n on Unix.

The return type includes the dyn (*https://oreil.ly/OobOp*) keyword to say that the return type's trait is dynamically dispatched. This allows us to abstract the idea of the input source. At the moment, we're reading from either a file or from STDIN, but we could expand this to include reading from some other source like a socket or a web page or the Mars rover, as long as that source that implements the trait BufRead.

The return type is placed into a Box (*https://oreil.ly/o8EdI*), which is a way to store a value on the heap. You may wonder if this is completely necessary. I could try to write the function without using Box:

```
// This will not compile
fn open(filename: &str) -> Result<dyn BufRead> {
    match filename {
        "-" => Ok(BufReader::new(io::stdin())),
        _ => Ok(BufReader::new(File::open(filename)?)),
    }
}
```

But if I try to compile this code, I get the following error:

```
error[E0277]: the size for values of type `(dyn BufRead + 'static)`
cannot be known at compilation time
  --> src/main.rs:70:28
   |
70 | fn open(filename: &str) -> Result<dyn BufRead> {
   |                            ^^^^^^^^^^^^^^^^^^^^ doesn't have a size
   |                                                known at compile-time
   |
   = help: the trait `Sized` is not implemented for `(dyn BufRead + 'static)`
note: required by a bound in `Result`
```

The compiler doesn't have enough information from dyn BufRead to know the size of the return type. If a variable doesn't have a fixed, known size, then Rust can't store it on the stack. The solution is to instead allocate memory on the heap by putting the return value into a Box, which is a pointer with a known size.

The preceding open function is dense. I can appreciate if you think that it's more than a little complicated; however, it handles almost any error you will encounter. To demonstrate this, change your run to the following:

```
fn run(args: Args) -> Result<()> {
    for filename in args.files { ❶
        match open(&filename) { ❷
            Err(err) => eprintln!("Failed to open {filename}: {err}"), ❸
            Ok(_) => println!("Opened {filename}"), ❹
        }
    }
    Ok(())
}
```

❶ Iterate through the filenames.

❷ Try to open the filename. Note the use of & to borrow the variable.

❸ Print an error message to STDERR when open fails.

❹ Print a success message when open works. The underscore for the variable tells the compiler that I do not intend to use it.

Try to run your program with the following:

1. A valid input file such as *tests/inputs/fox.txt*
2. A nonexistent file
3. An unreadable file

For the last option, you can create a file that cannot be read like so:

```
$ touch cant-touch-this && chmod 000 cant-touch-this
```

Run your program and verify your code gracefully prints error messages for bad input files and continues to process the valid ones:

```
$ cargo run -- blargh cant-touch-this tests/inputs/fox.txt
Failed to open blargh: No such file or directory (os error 2)
Failed to open cant-touch-this: Permission denied (os error 13)
Opened tests/inputs/fox.txt
```

At this point, you should be able to pass **cargo test skips_bad_file**. Now that you can open and read valid input files, I want you to finish the program on your own. Can you figure out how to read the opened file line by line? Start with *tests/inputs/fox.txt*, which has only one line. You should be able to see the following output:

```
$ cargo run -- tests/inputs/fox.txt
The quick brown fox jumps over the lazy dog.
```

Verify that you can read STDIN by default. In the following command, I use the | to pipe STDOUT from the first command to the STDIN of the second command:

```
$ cat tests/inputs/fox.txt | cargo run
The quick brown fox jumps over the lazy dog.
```

The output should be the same when providing a dash as the filename. In the following command, I will use the bash redirect operator < to take input from the given filename and provide it to STDIN:

```
$ cargo run -- - < tests/inputs/fox.txt
The quick brown fox jumps over the lazy dog.
```

Next, try an input file with more than one line and try to number the lines with -n:

```
$ cargo run -- -n tests/inputs/spiders.txt
     1  Don't worry, spiders,
     2  I keep house
     3  casually.
```

Then try to skip blank lines in the numbering with -b:

```
$ cargo run -- -b tests/inputs/the-bustle.txt
     1  The bustle in a house
     2  The morning after death
     3  Is solemnest of industries
     4  Enacted upon earth,–

     5  The sweeping up the heart,
     6  And putting love away
     7  We shall not want to use again
     8  Until eternity.
```

Run **cargo test** often to see which tests are failing.

Using the Test Suite

Now is a good time to examine the tests more closely so you can understand both how to write tests and what they expect of your program. The test structure in *tests/cli.rs* is similar to Chapter 2, starting with the imports:

```
use anyhow::Result; ❶
use assert_cmd::Command;
use predicates::prelude::*;
use pretty_assertions::assert_eq; ❷
use rand::{distributions::Alphanumeric, Rng}; ❸
use std::fs;
```

❶ All programs will use anyhow::Result over the default Result.

❷ All tests will use pretty_assertions::assert_eq over the default assert_eq! macro.

❸ The rand crate (*https://oreil.ly/HJOPg*) is used to generate random values at runtime.

I've also added a little more organization. For instance, I use the const keyword (*https://oreil.ly/CY0Hn*) to create several *constant* &str values at the top of that module that I use throughout the crate. I use a common convention of ALL_CAPS names to highlight the fact that they are *scoped* or visible throughout the crate:

```
const PRG: &str = "catr";
const EMPTY: &str = "tests/inputs/empty.txt";
const FOX: &str = "tests/inputs/fox.txt";
const SPIDERS: &str = "tests/inputs/spiders.txt";
const BUSTLE: &str = "tests/inputs/the-bustle.txt";
```

To test that the program will die when given a nonexistent file, I use the `rand` crate to generate a random filename that does not exist:

```
fn gen_bad_file() -> String { ❶
    loop { ❷
        let filename: String = rand::thread_rng() ❸
            .sample_iter(&Alphanumeric)
            .take(7)
            .map(char::from)
            .collect();

        if fs::metadata(&filename).is_err() { ❹
            return filename;
        }
    }
}
```

❶ The function will return a `String` (*https://oreil.ly/X32Yh*), which is a dynamically generated string closely related to the `str` struct I've been using.

❷ Start an infinite `loop`.

❸ Create a random string of seven alphanumeric characters.

❹ `fs::metadata` (*https://oreil.ly/VsRxb*) returns an error when the given filename does not exist, so return the nonexistent filename.

In the preceding function, I use `filename` two times after creating it. The first time I borrow it using `&filename`, and the second time I don't use the ampersand. Try removing the `&` and running the code. You should get an error message stating that ownership of the `filename` value is moved into `fs::metadata`:

```
error[E0382]: use of moved value: `filename`
  --> tests/cli.rs:37:20
   |
30 |         let filename: String = rand::thread_rng()
   |             -------- move occurs because `filename` has type `String`,
   |                      which does not implement the `Copy` trait
...
36 |         if fs::metadata(filename).is_err() {
   |                         -------- value moved here
37 |             return filename;
   |                    ^^^^^^^^ value used here after move
```

Effectively, the `fs::metadata` function consumes the `filename` variable, leaving it unusable. The & shows I only want to borrow a reference to the variable. Don't worry if you don't completely understand that yet. I'm only showing the following `gen_bad_file` function so that you understand how it is used in the `skips_bad_file` test:

```
#[test]
fn skips_bad_file() -> Result<()> {
    let bad = gen_bad_file(); ❶
    let expected = format!("{bad}: .* [(]os error 2[)]"); ❷
    Command::cargo_bin(PRG)? ❸
        .arg(&bad)
        .assert()
        .success() ❹
        .stderr(predicate::str::is_match(expected)?);
    Ok(())
}
```

❶ Generate the name of a nonexistent file.

❷ The expected error message should include the filename and the string *os error 2* on both Windows and Unix platforms.

❸ Run the program with the bad file and verify that STDERR matches the expected pattern.

❹ The program should not fail because bad files should only generate warnings and not kill the process.

 In the preceding function, I used the `format!` macro (*https://oreil.ly/rgrsJ*) to generate a new `String`. This macro works like `print!` except that it returns the value rather than printing it.

I created a helper function called `run` to run the program with input arguments and verify that the output matches the text in the file generated by *mk-outs.sh*:

```
fn run(args: &[&str], expected_file: &str) -> Result<()> { ❶
    let expected = fs::read_to_string(expected_file)?; ❷
    let output = Command::cargo_bin(PRG)?.args(args).output().unwrap(); ❸
    assert!(output.status.success()); ❹

    let stdout = String::from_utf8(output.stdout).expect("invalid UTF-8"); ❺
    assert_eq!(stdout, expected); ❻

    Ok(())
}
```

❶ The function accepts a slice of `&str` arguments and the filename with the expected output. The function returns a `Result` because some function calls within may fail.

❷ Try to read the expected output file.

❸ Execute the program with the arguments and obtain the output.

❹ Verify the program ran successfully.

❺ Attempt to convert the program's `STDOUT` to a string.

❻ Verify that the actual program output matches the expected output.

I use this function like so:

```
#[test]
fn bustle() -> Result<()> {
    run(&[BUSTLE], "tests/expected/the-bustle.txt.out") ❶
}
```

❶ Run the program with the `BUSTLE` input file and verify that the output matches the output produced by *mk-outs.sh*.

I also wrote a helper function to provide input via `STDIN`:

```
fn run_stdin(
    input_file: &str, ❶
    args: &[&str],
    expected_file: &str,
) -> Result {
    let input = fs::read_to_string(input_file)?; ❷
    let expected = fs::read_to_string(expected_file)?;
    let output = Command::cargo_bin(PRG)? ❸
        .write_stdin(input)
        .args(args)
        .output()
        .unwrap();
    assert!(output.status.success()); ❹

    let stdout = String::from_utf8(output.stdout).expect("invalid UTF-8"); ❺
    assert_eq!(stdout, expected);

    Ok(())
}
```

❶ The first argument is the filename containing the text that should be given to `STDIN`.

---

❷ Try to read the input and expected files.

❸ Try to run the program with the given arguments and STDIN.

❹ Verify that the program ran successfully.

❺ Check the program's output against the expected value.

This function is used similarly:

```
#[test]
fn bustle_stdin() -> Result<()> {
    run_stdin(BUSTLE, &["-"], "tests/expected/the-bustle.txt.stdin.out") ❶
}
```

❶ Run the program using the contents of the given filename as STDIN and a dash as the input filename. Verify the output matches the expected value.

 That should be enough for you to finish the rest of the program. Off you go! Come back when you're done.

Solution

I hope you found this an interesting and challenging program to write. I'll show you how to modify the program step by step to reach a final solution, which you can find in the book's repository.

Reading the Lines in a File

To start, I will print the lines of files that are opened successfully:

```
fn run(args: Args) -> Result<()> {
    for filename in args.files {
        match open(&filename) {
            Err(err) => eprintln!("Failed to open {filename}: {err}"), ❶
            Ok(file) => {
                for line_result in file.lines() { ❷
                    let line = line_result?; ❸
                    println!("{line}"); ❹
                }
            }
        }
    }
    Ok(())
}
```

❶ Print the filename and error when there is a problem opening a file.

❷ Iterate over each `line_result` value from `BufRead::lines`.

❸ Either unpack an `Ok` value from `line_result` or propagate an error.

❹ Print the line.

 When reading the lines from a file, you don't get the lines directly from the filehandle but instead get a `std::io::Result` (*https:// oreil.ly/kxFes*), which is a type "broadly used across `std::io` for any operation which may produce an error." The reading and writing of files falls into the category of I/O (input/output), which depends on external resources like the operating and filesystems. While it's unlikely that reading a line from a filehandle will fail, the point is that it *could* fail.

Run this code with an input file to see it in action:

```
$ cargo run -- tests/inputs/spiders.txt
Don't worry, spiders,
I keep house
casually.
```

If you run **cargo test** at this point, you should pass about half of the tests, which is not bad for so few lines of code.

Printing Line Numbers

Next is to add the printing of line numbers for the `-n|--number` option. One solution that will likely be familiar to C programmers would be something like this:

```
fn run(args: Args) -> Result<()> {
    for filename in args.files {
        match open(&filename) {
            Err(err) => eprintln!("Failed to open {filename}: {err}"),
            Ok(file) => {
                let mut line_num = 0; ❶
                for line_result in file.lines() {
                    let line = line_result?;
                    line_num += 1; ❷

                    if args.number_lines { ❸
                        println!("{line_num:>6}\t{line}"); ❹
                    } else {
                        println!("{line}"); ❺
                    }
                }
            }
```

```
                }
            }
        }
        Ok(())
    }
```

❶ Initialize a mutable counter variable to hold the line number.

❷ Add 1 to the line number.

❸ Check if the user wants line numbers.

❹ If so, print the current line number in a right-justified field six characters wide followed by a tab character and then the line of text.

❺ Otherwise, print the line.

Recall that all variables in Rust are immutable by default, so it's necessary to add mut to line_num, as I intend to change it. The += operator is a compound assignment that adds the righthand value 1 to line_num to increment it.[2] Of note, too, is the formatting syntax {:>6} that indicates the width of the field as six characters with the text aligned to the right. (You can use < for left-justified and ^ for centered text.) This syntax is similar to printf in C, Perl, and Python's string formatting.

If I run the program at this point, it looks pretty good:

```
$ cargo run -- tests/inputs/spiders.txt -n
     1  Don't worry, spiders,
     2  I keep house
     3  casually.
```

While this works adequately, I'd like to point out a more idiomatic solution using Iterator::enumerate (*https://oreil.ly/gXM7q*). This method will return a tuple (*https://oreil.ly/Cmywl*) containing the index position and value for each element in an *iterable*, which is something that can produce values until exhausted:

```
fn run(args: Args) -> Result<()> {
    for filename in args.files {
        match open(&filename) {
            Err(err) => eprintln!("Failed to open {filename}: {err}"),
            Ok(file) => {
                for (line_num, line_result) in file.lines().enumerate() { ❶
                    let line = line_result?;
                    if args.number_lines {
                        println!("{:>6}\t{line}", line_num + 1); ❷
                    } else {
```

---

2 Note that Rust does not have a unary ++ operator, so you cannot use line_num++ to increment a variable by 1.

```
                    println!("{line}");
                }
            }
        }
    }
    Ok(())
}
```

❶ The tuple values from `Iterator::enumerate` can be unpacked using pattern matching.

❷ Numbering from `enumerate` starts at 0, so add 1 to mimic `cat`, which starts at 1. Note that the expression `line_num + 1` may not be placed inside the `{}` placeholder and so is passed as an argument to `println!`.

This will create the same output as before, but now the code avoids using a mutable value. I can execute **cargo test fox** to run all the tests with the word *fox* in their name, and I find that two out of three pass. The program fails on the -b flag, so next I need to handle printing the line numbers only for nonblank lines. Notice in this version, I'm also going to remove `line_result` and shadow the `line` variable:

```
fn run(args: Args) -> Result<()> {
    for filename in args.files {
        match open(&filename) {
            Err(err) => eprintln!("Failed to open {filename}: {err}"),
            Ok(file) => {
                let mut prev_num = 0;  ❶
                for (line_num, line) in file.lines().enumerate() {
                    let line = line?;  ❷
                    if args.number_lines {  ❸
                        println!("{:>6}\t{line}", line_num + 1);
                    } else if args.number_nonblank_lines {  ❹
                        if line.is_empty() {
                            println!();  ❺
                        } else {
                            prev_num += 1;
                            println!("{prev_num:>6}\t{line}");  ❻
                        }
                    } else {
                        println!("{line}");  ❼
                    }
                }
            }
        }
    }
    Ok(())
}
```

❶ Initialize a mutable variable for the number of the last nonblank line.

❷ Shadow the `line` with the result of unpacking the `Result`.

❸ Handle printing line numbers.

❹ Handle printing line numbers for nonblank lines.

❺ If the line is empty, print a blank line.

❻ Otherwise, increment `prev_num` and print the output.

❼ If there are no numbering options, print the line.

 Shadowing a variable in Rust is when you reuse a variable's name and set it to a new value. Arguably the `line_result`/`line` code may be more explicit and readable, but reusing `line` in this context is more Rustic code you're likely to encounter.

If you run **cargo test**, you should pass all the tests.

Going Further

You have a working program now, but you don't have to stop there. If you're up for an additional challenge, try implementing the other options shown in the manual pages for both the BSD and GNU versions. For each option, use `cat` to create the expected output file, then expand the tests to check that your program creates this same output. I'd also recommend you check out `bat` (*https://oreil.ly/QgMnb*), which is another Rust clone of `cat` ("with wings"), for a more complete implementation.

The numbered lines output of `cat -n` is similar in ways to `nl`, a "line numbering filter." `cat` is also a bit similar to programs that will show you a *page* or screen full of text at a time, so-called *pagers* like `more` and `less`.[3] Consider implementing these programs. Read the manual pages, create the test output, and copy the ideas from this project to write and test your versions.

---

3 `more` shows you a page of text with "More" at the bottom to let you know you can continue. Obviously, someone decided to be clever and named their clone `less`, but it does the same thing.

Summary

You made big strides in this chapter, creating a much more complex program than in the previous chapters. Consider what you learned:

- You used a testing-first approach where all the tests exist before the program is even written. When the program passes all the tests, you can be confident your program meets all the specifications encoded in the tests.

- You saw how to use the rand crate to generate a random string for a nonexistent file.

- You learned about the const keyword to make constant values.

- You figured out how to read lines of text from both STDIN and regular files.

- You used the eprintln! macro to print to STDERR and format! to dynamically generate a new string.

- You used a for loop to visit each element in an iterable.

- You found that the Iterator::enumerate method will return both the index and the element as a tuple, which is useful for numbering the lines of text.

- You learned to use a Box that points to a filehandle to read STDIN or a regular file.

In the next chapter, you'll learn a good deal more about reading files by lines, bytes, or characters.

CHAPTER 4

Head Aches

Stand on your own head for a change / Give me some skin to call my own
— They Might Be Giants, "Stand on Your Own Head" (1988)

The challenge in this chapter is to implement the head program, which will print the first few lines or bytes of one or more files. This is a good way to peek at the contents of a regular text file and is often a much better choice than cat. When faced with a directory of something like output files from some process, using head can help you quickly scan for potential problems. It's particularly useful when dealing with extremely large files, as it will only read the first few bytes or lines of a file (as opposed to cat, which will always read the entire file).

In this chapter, you will learn how to do the following:

- Create optional command-line arguments that accept numeric values
- Convert between types using as
- Use take on an iterator or a filehandle
- Preserve line endings while reading a filehandle
- Read bytes versus characters from a filehandle
- Use the turbofish operator

How head Works

I'll start with an overview of head so you know what's expected of your program. There are many implementations of the original AT&T Unix operating system, such as Berkeley Standard Distribution (BSD), SunOS/Solaris, HP-UX, and Linux. Most of these operating systems have some version of a head program that will default to showing the first 10 lines of 1 or more files. Most will probably have options -n to control the number of lines shown and -c to instead show some number of bytes. The BSD version has only these two options, which I can see via **man head**:

```
HEAD(1)                      BSD General Commands Manual                      HEAD(1)

NAME
     head -- display first lines of a file

SYNOPSIS
     head [-n count | -c bytes] [file ...]

DESCRIPTION
     This filter displays the first count lines or bytes of each of the speci-
     fied files, or of the standard input if no files are specified.  If count
     is omitted it defaults to 10.

     If more than a single file is specified, each file is preceded by a
     header consisting of the string ''==> XXX <=='' where ''XXX'' is the name
     of the file.

EXIT STATUS
     The head utility exits 0 on success, and >0 if an error occurs.

SEE ALSO
     tail(1)

HISTORY
     The head command appeared in PWB UNIX.

BSD                               June 6, 1993                               BSD
```

With the GNU version, I can run **head --help** to read the usage:

```
Usage: head [OPTION]... [FILE]...
Print the first 10 lines of each FILE to standard output.
With more than one FILE, precede each with a header giving the file name.
With no FILE, or when FILE is -, read standard input.

Mandatory arguments to long options are mandatory for short options too.
  -c, --bytes=[-]K         print the first K bytes of each file;
                             with the leading '-', print all but the last
                             K bytes of each file
  -n, --lines=[-]K         print the first K lines instead of the first 10;
                             with the leading '-', print all but the last
                             K lines of each file
  -q, --quiet, --silent    never print headers giving file names
  -v, --verbose            always print headers giving file names
      --help     display this help and exit
      --version  output version information and exit

K may have a multiplier suffix:
```

```
b 512, kB 1000, K 1024, MB 1000*1000, M 1024*1024,
GB 1000*1000*1000, G 1024*1024*1024, and so on for T, P, E, Z, Y.
```

Note that the GNU version can specify negative numbers for -n and -c and with suffixes like K, M, etc., which the challenge program will not implement. In both the BSD and GNU versions, the files are optional positional arguments that will read STDIN by default or when a filename is a dash.

To demonstrate how head works, I'll use the files found in *04_headr/tests/inputs*:

- *empty.txt*: an empty file
- *one.txt*: a file with one line of text
- *two.txt*: a file with two lines of text
- *three.txt*: a file with three lines of text and Windows line endings
- *twelve.txt*: a file with 12 lines of text

Given an empty file, there is no output, which you can verify with **head tests/inputs/empty.txt**. As mentioned, head will print the first 10 lines of a file by default:

```
$ head tests/inputs/twelve.txt
one
two
three
four
five
six
seven
eight
nine
ten
```

The -n option allows you to control the number of lines that are shown. For instance, I can choose to show only the first two lines with the following command:

```
$ head -n 2 tests/inputs/twelve.txt
one
two
```

The -c option shows only the given number of bytes from a file. For instance, I can show just the first two bytes:

```
$ head -c 2 tests/inputs/twelve.txt
on
```

Oddly, the GNU version will allow you to provide both -n and -c and defaults to showing bytes. The BSD version will reject both arguments:

```
$ head -n 1 -c 2 tests/inputs/one.txt
head: can't combine line and byte counts
```

Any value for -n or -c that is not a positive integer will generate an error that will halt the program, and the error message will include the illegal value:

```
$ head -n 0 tests/inputs/one.txt
head: illegal line count -- 0
$ head -c foo tests/inputs/one.txt
head: illegal byte count -- foo
```

When there are multiple arguments, head adds a header and inserts a blank line between each file. Notice in the following output that the first character in *tests /inputs/one.txt* is an Ö, a silly multibyte character I inserted to force the program to discern between bytes and characters:

```
$ head -n 1 tests/inputs/*.txt
==> tests/inputs/empty.txt <==

==> tests/inputs/one.txt <==
Öne line, four words.

==> tests/inputs/three.txt <==
Three

==> tests/inputs/twelve.txt <==
one

==> tests/inputs/two.txt <==
Two lines.
```

With no file arguments, head will read from STDIN:

```
$ cat tests/inputs/twelve.txt | head -n 2
one
two
```

As with cat in Chapter 3, any nonexistent or unreadable file is skipped and a warning is printed to STDERR. In the following command, I will use *blargh* as a nonexistent file and will create an unreadable file called *cant-touch-this*:

```
$ touch cant-touch-this && chmod 000 cant-touch-this
$ head blargh cant-touch-this tests/inputs/one.txt
head: blargh: No such file or directory
head: cant-touch-this: Permission denied
==> tests/inputs/one.txt <==
Öne line, four words.
```

This is as much as this chapter's challenge program will need to implement.

Getting Started

You might have anticipated that the program I want you to write will be called headr (pronounced *head-er*). Start by running **cargo new headr**, then add the following dependencies to your *Cargo.toml*:

```
[dependencies]
anyhow = "1.0.79"
clap = { version = "4.5.0", features = ["derive"] }

[dev-dependencies]
assert_cmd = "2.0.13"
predicates = "3.0.4"
pretty_assertions = "1.4.0"
rand = "0.8.5"
```

Copy my *04_headr/tests* directory into your project directory, and then run **cargo test**. All the tests should fail. Your mission, should you choose to accept it, is to write a program that will pass these tests. I propose you begin *src/main.rs* with the following code to represent the program's three parameters with an Args struct:

```
#[derive(Debug)]
struct Args {
    files: Vec<String>,  ❶
    lines: u64,  ❷
    bytes: Option<u64>,  ❸
}
```

❶ files will be a vector of strings.

❷ The number of lines to print will be of the type u64 (*https://oreil.ly/fY3qc*).

❸ bytes will be an optional u64.

 All the command-line arguments for this program are optional because files should default to a dash (-), lines will default to 10, and bytes can be left out.

The primitive u64 is an unsigned integer that uses 8 bytes of memory and is similar to a usize, which is a pointer-sized unsigned integer type with a size that varies from 4 bytes on a 32-bit operating system to 8 bytes on a 64-bit system. Rust also has an isize type, which is a pointer-sized signed integer that you would need to represent negative numbers as the GNU version does. Since you only want to store positive numbers à la the BSD version, you can stick with an unsigned type. Note the other

Rust types of u32/i32 (unsigned/signed 32-bit integer) and u64/i64 (unsigned/signed 64-bit integer) if you want finer control over how large these values can be.

The lines and bytes parameters will be used in functions that expect the types usize and u64, so later we'll discuss how to convert between these types. Your program should use 10 as the default value for lines, but bytes will be an Option (*https:// oreil.ly/WkWZs*), which I first introduced in Chapter 2. This means that bytes will either be Some<u64> if the user provides a valid value or None if they do not.

I challenge you to parse the command-line arguments into this struct however you like. To use the derive pattern, annotate the preceding Args accordingly. If you prefer to follow the builder pattern, consider writing a get_args function with the following outline:

```
fn get_args() -> Args {
    let matches = Command::new("headr")
        .version("0.1.0")
        .author("Ken Youens-Clark <kyclark@gmail.com>")
        .about("Rust version of `head`")
        // What goes here?
        .get_matches();

    Args {
        files: ...
        lines: ...
        bytes: ...
    }
}
```

Update main to parse and pretty-print the arguments:

```
fn main() {
    let args = Args::parse();
    println!("{:#?}", args);
}
```

See if you can get your program to print a usage like the following. Note that I use the short and long names from the GNU version:

```
$ cargo run -- -h
Rust version of `head`

Usage: headr [OPTIONS] [FILE]...

Arguments:
  [FILE]...  Input file(s) [default: -]

Options:
  -n, --lines <LINES>  Number of lines [default: 10]
  -c, --bytes <BYTES>  Number of bytes
```

```
-h, --help          Print help
-V, --version       Print version
```

Run the program with no inputs and verify the defaults are correctly set:

```
$ cargo run
Args {
    files: [
        "-",    ❶
    ],
    lines: 10,  ❷
    bytes: None,  ❸
}
```

❶ files should default to a dash (-) as the filename.

❷ The number of lines should default to 10.

❸ bytes should be None.

Now run the program with arguments and ensure they are correctly parsed:

```
$ cargo run -- -n 3 tests/inputs/one.txt
Args {
    files: [
        "tests/inputs/one.txt",  ❶
    ],
    lines: 3,  ❷
    bytes: None,  ❸
}
```

❶ The positional argument *tests/inputs/one.txt* is parsed as one of the files.

❷ The -n option for lines sets this to 3.

❸ The -b option for bytes defaults to None.

If I provide more than one positional argument, they will all go into files, and the -c argument will go into bytes. In the following command, I'm again relying on the bash shell to expand the file glob *.txt into all the files ending in *.txt*. PowerShell users should refer to the equivalent use of Get-ChildItem shown in the section "Iterating Through the File Arguments" on page 56:

```
$ cargo run -- -c 4 tests/inputs/*.txt
Args {
    files: [
        "tests/inputs/empty.txt",  ❶
        "tests/inputs/one.txt",
        "tests/inputs/three.txt",
        "tests/inputs/twelve.txt",
        "tests/inputs/two.txt",
```

```
        ],
        lines: 10, ❷
        bytes: Some( ❸
            4,
        ),
    }
```

❶ There are four files ending in *.txt*.

❷ `lines` is still set to the default value of `10`.

❸ The `-c 4` results in the `bytes` now being `Some(4)`.

Any value for `-n` or `-c` that cannot be parsed into a positive integer should cause the program to halt with an error. Use `clap::value_parser` (*https://oreil.ly/GHQ9h*) to ensure that the integer arguments are valid and convert them to numbers:

```
$ cargo run -- -n blargh tests/inputs/one.txt
error: invalid value 'blargh' for '--lines <LINES>':
invalid digit found in string
$ cargo run -- -c 0 tests/inputs/one.txt
error: invalid value '0' for '--bytes <BYTES>':
0 is not in 1..18446744073709551615
```

The program should disallow the use of both `-n` and `-c`:

```
$ cargo run -- -n 1 -c 1 tests/inputs/one.txt
error: the argument '--lines <LINES>' cannot be used with '--bytes <BYTES>'

Usage: headr --lines <LINES> <FILE>...
```

 Just parsing and validating the arguments is a challenge, but I know you can do it. Stop reading here and get your program to pass all the tests included with **cargo test dies**:

```
running 3 tests
test dies_bad_lines ... ok
test dies_bad_bytes ... ok
test dies_bytes_and_lines ... ok
```

Defining the Arguments

Welcome back. I will first show the builder pattern with a `get_args` function as in the previous chapter. Note that the two optional arguments, `lines` and `bytes`, accept numeric values. This is different from the optional arguments implemented in Chapter 3 that are used as Boolean flags. Note that the following code requires `use clap::{Arg, Command}`:

```
fn get_args() -> Args {
    let matches = Command::new("headr")
```

```
            .version("0.1.0")
            .author("Ken Youens-Clark <kyclark@gmail.com>")
            .about("Rust version of `head`")
            .arg(
                Arg::new("lines") ❶
                    .short('n')
                    .long("lines")
                    .value_name("LINES")
                    .help("Number of lines")
                    .value_parser(clap::value_parser!(u64).range(1..))
                    .default_value("10"),
            )
            .arg(
                Arg::new("bytes") ❷
                    .short('c')
                    .long("bytes")
                    .value_name("BYTES")
                    .conflicts_with("lines")
                    .value_parser(clap::value_parser!(u64).range(1..))
                    .help("Number of bytes"),
            )
            .arg(
                Arg::new("files") ❸
                    .value_name("FILE")
                    .help("Input file(s)")
                    .num_args(0..)
                    .default_value("-"),
            )
            .get_matches();

    Args {
        files: matches.get_many("files").unwrap().cloned().collect(),
        lines: matches.get_one("lines").cloned().unwrap(),
        bytes: matches.get_one("bytes").cloned(),
    }
}
```

❶ The lines option takes a value and defaults to 10.

❷ The bytes option takes a value, and it conflicts with the lines parameter so that they are mutually exclusive.

❸ The files parameter is positional, takes zero or more values, and defaults to a dash (-).

Alternatively, the clap derive pattern requires annotating the Args struct:

```
#[derive(Parser, Debug)]
#[command(author, version, about)]
/// Rust version of `head`
struct Args {
```

```
/// Input file(s)
#[arg(default_value = "-", value_name = "FILE")]
files: Vec<String>,

/// Number of lines
#[arg(
    short('n'),
    long,
    default_value = "10",
    value_name = "LINES",
    value_parser = clap::value_parser!(u64).range(1..)
)]
lines: u64,

/// Number of bytes
#[arg(
    short('c'),
    long,
    value_name = "BYTES",
    conflicts_with("lines"),
    value_parser = clap::value_parser!(u64).range(1..)
)]
bytes: Option<u64>,
}
```

 In the derive pattern, the default Arg::long (*https://oreil.ly/uUZJN*) value will be the name of the struct field, for example, *lines* and *bytes*. The default value for Arg::short (*https://oreil.ly/fZl0Q*) will be the first letter of the struct field, so *l* or *b*. I specify the short names *n* and *c*, respectively, to match the original tool.

It's quite a bit of work to validate all the user input, but now I have some assurance that I can proceed with good data.

Processing the Input Files

I recommend that you have your main call a run function. Be sure to add use anyhow::Result for the following:

```
fn main() {
    if let Err(e) = run(Args::parse()) {
        eprintln!("{e}");
        std::process::exit(1);
    }
}

fn run(_args: Args) -> Result<()> {
    Ok(())
}
```

This challenge program should handle the input files as in Chapter 3, so I suggest you add the same open function:

```
fn open(filename: &str) -> Result<Box<dyn BufRead>> {
    match filename {
        "-" => Ok(Box::new(BufReader::new(io::stdin()))),
        _ => Ok(Box::new(BufReader::new(File::open(filename)?))),
    }
}
```

Be sure to add all these additional dependencies:

```
use std::fs::File;
use std::io::{self, BufRead, BufReader};
```

Expand your run function to try opening the files, printing errors as you encounter them:

```
fn run(args: Args) -> Result<()> {
    for filename in args.files {  ❶
        match open(&filename) {  ❷
            Err(err) => eprintln!("{filename}: {err}"),  ❸
            Ok(_) => println!("Opened {filename}"),  ❹
        }
    }
    Ok(())
}
```

❶ Iterate through each of the filenames.

❷ Attempt to open the given file.

❸ Print errors to STDERR.

❹ Print a message that the file was successfully opened.

Run your program with a good file and a bad file to ensure it seems to work. In the following command, *blargh* represents a nonexistent file:

```
$ cargo run -- blargh tests/inputs/one.txt
blargh: No such file or directory (os error 2)
Opened tests/inputs/one.txt
```

Without looking ahead to my solution, figure out how to read the lines and then the bytes of a given file. Next, add the headers separating multiple file arguments. Look closely at the error output from the original head program when handling invalid files, noticing that readable files have a header first and then the file output, but invalid files only print an error. Additionally, there is an extra blank line separating the output for the valid files:

```
$ head -n 1 tests/inputs/one.txt blargh tests/inputs/two.txt
==> tests/inputs/one.txt <==
Öne line, four words.
head: blargh: No such file or directory

==> tests/inputs/two.txt <==
Two lines.
```

I've specifically designed some challenging inputs for you to consider. To see what you face, use the file command to report file type information:

```
$ file tests/inputs/*.txt
tests/inputs/empty.txt:  empty ❶
tests/inputs/one.txt:    UTF-8 Unicode text ❷
tests/inputs/three.txt:  ASCII text, with CRLF, LF line terminators ❸
tests/inputs/twelve.txt: ASCII text ❹
tests/inputs/two.txt:    ASCII text ❺
```

❶ This is an empty file just to ensure your program doesn't fall over.

❷ This file contains Unicode, as I put an umlaut over the O in Öne to force you to consider the differences between bytes and characters.

❸ This file has Windows-style line endings.

❹ This file has 12 lines to ensure the default of 10 lines is shown.

❺ This file has Unix-style line endings.

 On Windows, the newline is the combination of the carriage return and the line feed, often shown as CRLF or \r\n. On Unix platforms, only the newline is used, so LF or \n. These line endings must be preserved in the output from your program, so you will have to find a way to read the lines in a file without removing the line endings.

Reading Bytes Versus Characters

Before continuing, you should understand the difference between reading *bytes* and *characters* from a file. In the early 1960s, the American Standard Code for Information Interchange (ASCII, pronounced *as-key*) table of 128 characters represented all possible text elements in computing. It takes only seven bits ($2^7 = 128$) to represent this many characters. Usually a byte consists of eight bits, so the notion of byte and character were interchangeable.

Since the creation of Unicode (Universal Coded Character Set) to represent all the writing systems of the world (and even emojis), some characters may require up to four bytes. The Unicode standard defines several ways to encode characters, including UTF-8 (Unicode Transformation Format using eight bits). As noted, the file *tests/inputs/one.txt* begins with the character Ő, which is two bytes long in UTF-8. If you want head to show you this one character, you must request two bytes:

```
$ head -c 2 tests/inputs/one.txt
Ö
```

If you ask head to select just the first byte from this file, you get the byte value 195, which is not a valid UTF-8 string. The output is a special character that indicates a problem converting a character into Unicode:

```
$ head -c 1 tests/inputs/one.txt
�
```

The challenge program is expected to re-create this behavior. This is not an easy program to write, but you should be able to use std::io (*https://oreil.ly/PpLCr*), std::fs::File (*https://oreil.ly/VtAdj*), and std::io::BufReader (*https://oreil.ly/bznCz*) to figure out how to read bytes and lines from each of the files. Note that in Rust, a String (*https://oreil.ly/X32Yh*) must be a valid UTF-8-encoded string, and so the method String::from_utf8_lossy (*https://oreil.ly/Bs4Zl*) might prove useful. I've included a full set of tests in *tests/cli.rs* that you should have copied into your source tree.

> Stop reading here and finish the program. Use **cargo test** frequently to check your progress. Do your best to pass all the tests before looking at my solution.

Solution

This challenge proved more interesting than I anticipated. I thought it would be little more than a variation on cat, but it turned out to be quite a bit more difficult. I'll walk you through how I arrived at my solution.

Reading a File Line by Line

After opening the valid files, I started by reading lines from the filehandle. I decided to modify some code from Chapter 3:

```
fn run(args: Args) -> Result<()> {
    for filename in args.files {
        match open(&filename) {
            Err(err) => eprintln!("{filename}: {err}"),
            Ok(file) => {
                for line in file.lines().take(args.lines as usize) { ❶
                    println!("{}", line?); ❷
```

```
                    }
                }
            }
        }
        Ok(())
    }
```

❶ Use `Iterator::take` (*https://oreil.ly/OjTMN*) to select the desired number of lines from the filehandle.

❷ Print the line to the console.

 The `Iterator::take` method expects its argument to be the type `usize`, but I have a `u64`. I *cast* or convert the value using the `as` keyword (*https://oreil.ly/X7cc9*).

I think this is a fun solution because it uses the `Iterator::take` method to select the desired number of lines. I can run the program to select one line from a file, and it appears to work well:

```
$ cargo run -- -n 1 tests/inputs/twelve.txt
one
```

If I run **cargo test**, the program passes almost half the tests, which seems pretty good for having implemented only a small portion of the specifications; however, it's failing all the tests that use the Windows-encoded input file. To fix this problem, I have a confession to make.

Preserving Line Endings While Reading a File

I hate to break it to you, dear reader, but the `catr` program in Chapter 3 does not completely replicate the original `cat` program because it uses `BufRead::lines` (*https://oreil.ly/KhmCp*) to read the input files. The documentation for that function says, "Each string returned will *not* have a newline byte (the 0xA byte) or CRLF (0xD, 0xA bytes) at the end." I hope you'll forgive me because I wanted to show you how easy it can be to read the lines of a file, but you should be aware that the `catr` program replaces Windows CRLF line endings with Unix-style newlines.

To fix this, I must instead use `BufRead::read_line` (*https://oreil.ly/aJFkc*), which, according to the documentation, "will read bytes from the underlying stream until the newline delimiter (the 0xA byte) or EOF is found. Once found, all bytes up to, and including, the delimiter (if found) will be appended to buf."[1] Following is a version that will preserve the original line endings. With these changes, the program will pass more tests than it fails:

```
fn run(args: Args) -> Result<()> {
    for filename in args.files {
        match open(&filename) {
            Err(err) => eprintln!("{filename}: {err}"),
            Ok(mut file) => { ❶
                let mut line = String::new(); ❷
                for _ in 0..args.lines { ❸
                    let bytes = file.read_line(&mut line)?; ❹
                    if bytes == 0 { ❺
                        break;
                    }
                    print!("{line}"); ❻
                    line.clear(); ❼
                }
            }
        };
    }
    Ok(())
}
```

❶ Accept the filehandle as a mutable value.

❷ Use String::new (https://oreil.ly/Lg0D2) to create a new, empty mutable string buffer to hold each line.

❸ Use for to iterate through a std::ops::Range (https://oreil.ly/gA0sx) to count up from zero to the requested number of lines. The variable name _ indicates I do not intend to use it.

❹ Use BufRead::read_line (https://oreil.ly/aJFkc) to read the next line into the string buffer.

❺ The filehandle will return zero bytes when it reaches the end of the file, so break (https://oreil.ly/UG54e) out of the loop.

❻ Print the line, including the original line ending.

❼ Use String::clear (https://oreil.ly/IpZ2x) to empty the line buffer.

---

1 EOF is an acronym for *end of file*.

If I run **cargo test** at this point, the program will pass almost all the tests for reading lines and will fail all those for reading bytes and handling multiple files.

Reading Bytes from a File

Next, I'll handle reading bytes from a file. After I attempt to open the file, I check to see if args.bytes is Some number of bytes; otherwise, I'll use the preceding code that reads lines. For the following code, be sure to add use std::io::Read to your imports:

```
for filename in args.files {
    match open(&filename) {
        Err(err) => eprintln!("{filename}: {err}"),
        Ok(mut file) => {
            if let Some(num_bytes) = args.bytes { ❶
                let mut buffer = vec![0; num_bytes as usize]; ❷
                let bytes_read = file.read(&mut buffer)?; ❸
                print!(
                    "{}",
                    String::from_utf8_lossy(&buffer[..bytes_read]) ❹
                );
            } else {
                ... // Same as before
            }
        }
    };
}
```

❶ Use pattern matching to check if args.bytes is Some number of bytes to read.

❷ Create a mutable buffer of a fixed length num_bytes filled with zeros to hold the bytes read from the file.

❸ Read bytes from the filehandle into the buffer. The value bytes_read will contain the number of bytes that were read, which may be fewer than the number requested.

❹ Convert the selected bytes into a string, which may not be valid UTF-8. Note the range operation to select only the bytes actually read.

As you saw in the case of selecting only part of a multibyte character, converting bytes to characters could fail because strings in Rust must be valid UTF-8. The String::from_utf8 function (*https://oreil.ly/Ps3jV*) will return an Ok only if the string is valid, but String::from_utf8_lossy (*https://oreil.ly/Bs4Zl*) will convert invalid UTF-8 sequences to the *unknown* or *replacement* character:

```
$ cargo run -- -c 1 tests/inputs/one.txt
◆
```

Let me show you another, much worse, way to read the bytes from a file. You can read the entire file into a string, convert that into a vector of bytes, and then select the first num_bytes:

```
let mut contents = String::new(); ❶
file.read_to_string(&mut contents)?; // Danger here ❷
let bytes = contents.as_bytes(); ❸
print!(
    "{}",
    String::from_utf8_lossy(&bytes[..num_bytes as usize]) // More danger ❹
);
```

❶ Create a new string buffer to hold the contents of the file.

❷ Read the entire file contents into the string buffer.

❸ Use str::as_bytes (*https://oreil.ly/JaIiI*) to convert the contents into bytes (u8 or unsigned 8-bit integers).

❹ Use String::from_utf8_lossy to turn a slice of bytes into a string.

As I've noted before, this approach can crash your program or computer if the file's size exceeds the amount of memory on your machine. Another serious problem with the preceding code is that it assumes the slice operation bytes[..num_bytes] will succeed. If you use this code with an empty file, for instance, you'll be asking for bytes that don't exist. This will cause your program to panic and exit immediately with an error message:

```
$ cargo run -- -c 1 tests/inputs/empty.txt
thread 'main' panicked at src/main.rs:53:55:
range end index 1 out of range for slice of length 0
note: run with `RUST_BACKTRACE=1` environment variable to display a backtrace
```

Following is a safe—and perhaps the shortest—way to read the desired number of bytes from a file. Be sure to add the trait use std::io::Read to your imports:

```
let bytes: Result<Vec<_>, _> = file.bytes().take(num_bytes as usize).collect();
print!("{}", String::from_utf8_lossy(&bytes?));
```

In the preceding code, the type annotation Result<Vec<_>, _> is necessary as the compiler infers the type of bytes as a slice, which has an unknown size. I must indicate I want a Vec, which is a smart pointer to heap-allocated memory. The underscores (_) indicate partial type annotation, causing the compiler to infer the types. Without any type annotation for bytes, the compiler complains thusly:

```
error[E0277]: the size for values of type `[u8]` cannot be known at
compilation time
 --> src/main.rs:50:59
   |
95 |                        print!("{}", String::from_utf8_lossy(&bytes?));
   |                                                              ^^^^^^^ doesn't
   |                                                 have a size known at compile-time
   |
   = help: the trait `Sized` is not implemented for `[u8]`
   = note: all local variables must have a statically known size
   = help: unsized locals are gated as an unstable feature
```

 You've now seen that the underscore (_) serves various functions. As the prefix or name of a variable, it shows the compiler you don't want to use the value. In a match arm, it is the wildcard for handling any case. When used in a type annotation, it tells the compiler to infer the type.

You can also indicate the type information on the righthand side of the expression using the *turbofish* (*https://turbo.fish*) operator (::<>). Often it's a matter of style whether you indicate the type on the lefthand or righthand side, but later you will see examples where the turbofish is required for some expressions. Here's what the previous example would look like with the type indicated with the turbofish instead:

```
let bytes = file
    .bytes()
    .take(num_bytes as usize)
    .collect::<Result<Vec<_>, _>>();
```

The unknown character produced by String::from_utf8_lossy (b'\xef\xbf\xbd') is not exactly the same output produced by the BSD head (b'\xc3'), making this somewhat difficult to test. If you look at the run helper function in *tests/cli.rs*, you'll see that I read the expected value (the output from head) and used the same function to convert what could be invalid UTF-8 so that I can compare the two outputs. The run_stdin function works similarly:

```
fn run(args: &[&str], expected_file: &str) -> Result {
    // Extra work here due to lossy UTF
    let mut file = File::open(expected_file)?;
    let mut buffer = Vec::new();
    file.read_to_end(&mut buffer)?;
    let expected = String::from_utf8_lossy(&buffer); ❶

    let output = Command::cargo_bin(PRG)?.args(args).output().expect("fail");
    assert!(output.status.success());
    assert_eq!(String::from_utf8_lossy(&output.stdout), expected); ❷

    Ok(())
}
```

❶ Handle any invalid UTF-8 in `expected_file`.

❷ Compare the output and expected values as lossy strings.

Printing the File Separators

The last piece to handle is the separators between multiple files. As noted before, valid files have a header that puts the filename inside ==> and <== markers. Files after the first have an additional newline at the beginning to visually separate the output. This means I will need to know the file number that I'm handling, which I can get by using the `Iterator::enumerate` method (*https://oreil.ly/gXM7q*). Following is the final version of my `run` function that will pass all the tests:

```
fn run(args: Args) -> Result<()> {
    let num_files = args.files.len(); ❶

    for (file_num, filename) in args.files.iter().enumerate() { ❷
        match open(filename) {
            Err(err) => eprintln!("{filename}: {err}"),
            Ok(mut file) => {
                if num_files > 1 { ❸
                    println!(
                        "{}==> {filename} <==",
                        if file_num > 0 { "\n" } else { "" }, ❹
                    );
                }

                if let Some(num_bytes) = args.bytes {
                    let mut buffer = vec![0; num_bytes as usize];
                    let bytes_read = file.read(&mut buffer)?;
                    print!(
                        "{}",
                        String::from_utf8_lossy(&buffer[..bytes_read])
                    );
                } else {
                    let mut line = String::new();
                    for _ in 0..args.lines {
                        let bytes = file.read_line(&mut line)?;
                        if bytes == 0 {
                            break;
                        }
                        print!("{line}");
                        line.clear();
                    }
                }
            }
        }
    }
}
```

```
    Ok(())
}
```

❶ Use the Vec::len method (*https://oreil.ly/e0wqL*) to get the number of files.

❷ Use the Iterator::enumerate method to track the file number and filenames.

❸ Only print headers when there are multiple files.

❹ Print a newline when file_num is greater than 0, which indicates the first file.

Going Further

There's no reason to stop this party now. Consider implementing how the GNU head handles numeric values with suffixes and negative values. For instance, -c=1K means print the first 1,024 bytes of the file, and -n=-3 means print all but the last three lines of the file. You'll need to change lines and bytes to signed integer values to store both positive and negative numbers. Be sure to run the GNU head with these arguments, capture the output to test files, and write tests to cover the new features you add.

You could also add an option for selecting characters in addition to bytes. You can use the String::chars function (*https://oreil.ly/Yohiw*) to split a string into characters. Finally, copy the test input file with the Windows line endings (*tests/inputs/three.txt*) to the tests for Chapter 3. Edit the *mk-outs.sh* for that program to incorporate this file, and then expand the tests and program to ensure that line endings are preserved.

Summary

This chapter dove into some fairly sticky subjects, such as converting types like string inputs to a u64 and then casting these to usize. If you still feel confused, just know that you won't always. If you keep reading the docs and writing more code, it will eventually make sense.

Here are some things you accomplished in this chapter:

- You learned to create optional parameters that can take values. Previously, the options were flags.
- You saw that all command-line arguments are strings and used clap to attempt the conversion of a string like "3" into the number 3.
- You learned to convert types using the as keyword.

- You found that using _ as the name or prefix of a variable is a way to indicate to the compiler that you don't intend to use the value. When used in a type annotation, it tells the compiler to infer the type.

- You learned how to use `BufRead::read_line` to preserve line endings while reading a filehandle.

- You found that the `take` method works on both iterators and filehandles to limit the number of elements you select.

- You learned to indicate type information on the lefthand side of an assignment or on the righthand side using the turbofish operator.

In the next chapter, you'll learn more about Rust iterators and how to break input into lines, bytes, and characters.

CHAPTER 5

Word to Your Mother

All hail the dirt bike / Philosopher dirt bike /
Silence as we gathered round / We saw the word and were on our way

    — They Might Be Giants, "Dirt Bike" (1994)

For this chapter's challenge, you will create a version of the venerable wc (*word count*) program, which dates back to version 1 of AT&T Unix. This program will display the number of lines, words, and bytes found in text from STDIN or one or more files. I often use it to count the number of lines returned by some other process.

In this chapter, you will learn how to do the following:

- Use the Iterator::all function
- Create a module for unit tests
- Fake a filehandle for testing
- Conditionally format and print a value
- Conditionally compile a module when testing
- Break a line of text into words, bytes, and characters

How wc Works

I'll start by showing how wc works so you know what is expected by the tests. Following is an excerpt from the BSD wc manual page that describes the elements that the challenge program will implement:

NAME
     wc -- word, line, character, and byte count

SYNOPSIS
     wc [-clmw] [file ...]

DESCRIPTION
     The wc utility displays the number of lines, words, and bytes contained
     in each input file, or standard input (if no file is specified) to the
     standard output. A line is defined as a string of characters delimited
     by a <newline> character. Characters beyond the final <newline> charac-
     ter will not be included in the line count.

     A word is defined as a string of characters delimited by white space
     characters. White space characters are the set of characters for which
     the iswspace(3) function returns true. If more than one input file is
     specified, a line of cumulative counts for all the files is displayed on
     a separate line after the output for the last file.

     The following options are available:

     -c   The number of bytes in each input file is written to the standard
             output. This will cancel out any prior usage of the -m option.

     -l   The number of lines in each input file is written to the standard
             output.

     -m   The number of characters in each input file is written to the
             standard output. If the current locale does not support multi-
             byte characters, this is equivalent to the -c option. This will
             cancel out any prior usage of the -c option.

     -w   The number of words in each input file is written to the standard
             output.

     When an option is specified, wc only reports the information requested by
     that option. The order of output always takes the form of line, word,
     byte, and file name. The default action is equivalent to specifying the
     -c, -l and -w options.

     If no files are specified, the standard input is used and no file name is
     displayed. The prompt will accept input until receiving EOF, or [^D] in
     most environments.

A picture is worth a kilobyte of words, so I'll show you some examples using the following test files in the *05_wcr/tests/inputs* directory:

- *empty.txt*: an empty file
- *fox.txt*: a file with one line of text

- *atlamal.txt*: a file with the first stanza from "Atlamál hin groenlenzku" or "The Greenland Ballad of Atli," an Old Norse poem

When run with an empty file, the program reports zero lines, words, and bytes in three right-justified columns eight characters wide:

```
$ cd 05_wcr
$ wc tests/inputs/empty.txt
       0       0       0 tests/inputs/empty.txt
```

Next, consider a file with one line of text with varying spaces between words and a tab character. Let's take a look at it before running wc on it. Here I'm using cat with the flag -t to display the tab character as ^I and -e to display $ for the end of the line:

```
$ cat -te tests/inputs/fox.txt
The  quick brown fox^Ijumps over   the lazy dog.$
```

This example is short enough that I can manually count all the lines, words, and bytes as shown in Figure 5-1, where spaces are noted with raised dots, the tab character with \t, and the end of the line as $.

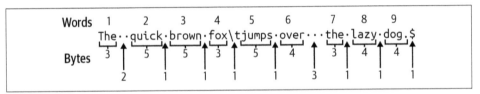

Figure 5-1. There is 1 line of text containing 9 words and 48 bytes.

I find that wc is in agreement:

```
$ wc tests/inputs/fox.txt
       1       9      48 tests/inputs/fox.txt
```

As mentioned in Chapter 4, bytes may equate to characters for ASCII, but Unicode characters may require multiple bytes. The file *tests/inputs/atlamal.txt* contains many such examples:[1]

```
$ cat tests/inputs/atlamal.txt
Frétt hefir öld óvu, þá er endr of gerðu
seggir samkundu, sú var nýt fæstum,
æxtu einmæli, yggr var þeim síðan
ok it sama sonum Gjúka, er váru sannráðnir.
```

According to wc, this file contains 4 lines, 29 words, and 177 bytes:

---

1 The text shown in this example translates to: "There are many who know how of old did men, in counsel gather / little good did they get / in secret they plotted, it was sore for them later / and for Gjuki's sons, whose trust they deceived."

```
$ wc tests/inputs/atlamal.txt
      4      29     177 tests/inputs/atlamal.txt
```

If I want only the number of *lines*, I can use the -l flag and only that column will be shown:

```
$ wc -l tests/inputs/atlamal.txt
      4 tests/inputs/atlamal.txt
```

I can similarly request only the number of *bytes* with -c and *words* with -w, and only those two columns will be shown:

```
$ wc -w -c tests/inputs/atlamal.txt
     29     177 tests/inputs/atlamal.txt
```

I can request the number of *characters* using the -m flag:

```
$ wc -m tests/inputs/atlamal.txt
    159 tests/inputs/atlamal.txt
```

The GNU version of wc will show both character and byte counts if you provide both the flags -m and -c, but the BSD version will show only one or the other, with the latter flag taking precedence:

```
$ wc -cm tests/inputs/atlamal.txt ❶
    159 tests/inputs/atlamal.txt
$ wc -mc tests/inputs/atlamal.txt ❷
    177 tests/inputs/atlamal.txt
```

❶   The -m flag comes last, so characters are shown.

❷   The -c flag comes last, so bytes are shown.

Note that no matter the order of the flags, like -wc or -cw, the output columns are always ordered by lines, words, and bytes/characters:

```
$ wc -cw tests/inputs/atlamal.txt
     29     177 tests/inputs/atlamal.txt
```

If no positional arguments are provided, wc will read from STDIN and will not print a filename:

```
$ cat tests/inputs/atlamal.txt | wc -lc
      4     177
```

The GNU version of wc will understand a filename consisting of a dash (-) to mean STDIN, and it also provides long flag names as well as some other options:

```
$ wc --help
Usage: wc [OPTION]... [FILE]...
  or:  wc [OPTION]... --files0-from=F
Print newline, word, and byte counts for each FILE, and a total line if
more than one FILE is specified.  With no FILE, or when FILE is -,
```

```
read standard input.  A word is a non-zero-length sequence of characters
delimited by white space.
The options below may be used to select which counts are printed, always in
the following order: newline, word, character, byte, maximum line length.
  -c, --bytes           print the byte counts
  -m, --chars           print the character counts
  -l, --lines           print the newline counts
      --files0-from=F   read input from the files specified by
                            NUL-terminated names in file F;
                            If F is - then read names from standard input
  -L, --max-line-length print the length of the longest line
  -w, --words           print the word counts
      --help      display this help and exit
      --version   output version information and exit
```

If processing more than one file, both versions will finish with a *total* line showing the number of lines, words, and bytes for all the inputs:

```
$ wc tests/inputs/*.txt
     4     29    177 tests/inputs/atlamal.txt
     0      0      0 tests/inputs/empty.txt
     1      9     48 tests/inputs/fox.txt
     5     38    225 total
```

Nonexistent files are noted with a warning to STDERR as the files are being processed. In the following example, *blargh* represents a nonexistent file:

```
$ wc tests/inputs/fox.txt blargh tests/inputs/atlamal.txt
     1      9     48 tests/inputs/fox.txt
wc: blargh: open: No such file or directory
     4     29    177 tests/inputs/atlamal.txt
     5     38    225 total
```

As I first showed in Chapter 2, I can redirect the STDERR filehandle 2 in bash to verify that wc prints the warnings to that channel:

```
$ wc tests/inputs/fox.txt blargh tests/inputs/atlamal.txt 2>err ❶
     1      9     48 tests/inputs/fox.txt
     4     29    177 tests/inputs/atlamal.txt
     5     38    225 total
$ cat err ❷
wc: blargh: open: No such file or directory
```

❶ Redirect output handle 2 (STDERR) to the file *err*.

❷ Verify that the error message is in the file.

There is an extensive test suite to verify that your program implements all these options.

Getting Started

The challenge program should be called wcr (pronounced *wick-er*) for our Rust version of wc. Use **cargo new wcr** to start, then modify your *Cargo.toml* to add the following dependencies:

```
[dependencies]
anyhow = "1.0.79"
clap = { version = "4.5.0", features = ["derive"] }

[dev-dependencies]
assert_cmd = "2.0.13"
predicates = "3.0.4"
pretty_assertions = "1.4.0"
rand = "0.8.5"
```

Copy the *05_wcr/tests* directory into your new project and run **cargo test** to perform an initial build and run the tests, all of which should fail. Open *src/main.rs* and add the following Args struct to represent the command-line parameters:

```
#[derive(Debug)]
struct Args {
    files: Vec<String>, ❶
    lines: bool, ❷
    words: bool, ❸
    bytes: bool, ❹
    chars: bool, ❺
}
```

❶ The files parameter will be a vector of strings.

❷ The lines parameter is a Boolean for whether or not to print the line count.

❸ The words parameter is a Boolean for whether or not to print the word count.

❹ The bytes parameter is a Boolean for whether or not to print the byte count.

❺ The chars parameter is a Boolean for whether or not to print the character count.

Choose your method of parsing the command-line arguments. If you prefer the derive pattern from clap, then add use clap::Parser and the necessary annotations to the Args struct. If you prefer the builder pattern, I suggest you create a get_args function from the following outline:

```
fn get_args() -> Args {
    let matches = Command::new("wcr")
        .version("0.1.0")
        .author("Ken Youens-Clark <kyclark@gmail.com>")
        .about("Rust version of `wc`")
        // What goes here?
        .get_matches();

    Args {
        files: ...,
        lines: ...,
        words: ...,
        bytes: ...,
        chars: ...,
    }
}
```

I suggest you use the same main structure from previous programs to pass the arguments to a run function:

```
fn main() {
    if let Err(e) = run(Args::parse()) {
        eprintln!("{e}");
        std::process::exit(1);
    }
}
```

Start by printing the Args structure. The default behavior should be to print lines, words, and bytes from STDIN, which means those values in the structure should be true when none have been explicitly requested by the user. Because the flags are set to false by default, you will need to alter the values after parsing. I recommend you pass the Args struct as mutable. Be sure to add use anyhow::Result for the following code:

```
fn run(mut args: Args) -> Result<()> {
    // Alter args as needed
    println!("{args:#?}");
    Ok(())
}
```

Try to get your program to generate --help output similar to the following:

```
$ cargo run -- --help
Rust version of `wc`

Usage: wcr [OPTIONS] [FILE]...

Arguments:
  [FILE]...  Input file(s) [default: -]

Options:
  -l, --lines    Show line count
```

```
-w, --words     Show word count
-c, --bytes     Show byte count
-m, --chars     Show character count
-h, --help      Print help
-V, --version   Print version
```

The challenge program will mimic the BSD wc in disallowing both the -m (character) and -c (bytes) flags:

```
$ cargo run -- -cm tests/inputs/fox.txt
error: the argument '--bytes' cannot be used with '--chars'

Usage: wcr --bytes <FILE>...
```

Get your program to print the following output when run with no arguments:

```
$ cargo run
Args {
    files: [
        "-", ❶
    ],
    lines: true, ❷
    words: true,
    bytes: true,
    chars: false,
}
```

❶ The default value for files should be a dash (-) for STDIN.

❷ The lines, words, and bytes flags should be true by default.

If any single flag is present, then all the other flags *not* mentioned should be false:

```
$ cargo run -- -l tests/inputs/*.txt ❶
Args {
    files: [
        "tests/inputs/atlamal.txt",
        "tests/inputs/empty.txt",
        "tests/inputs/fox.txt",
    ],
    lines: true, ❷
    words: false,
    bytes: false,
    chars: false,
}
```

❶ The -l flag indicates only the line count is wanted, and bash will expand the file glob tests/inputs/*.txt into all the filenames in that directory.

❷ Because the -l flag is present, the lines value is the only Boolean option that is true.

Stop here and get this much working. My dog needs a bath, so I'll
be right back.

Following is how I wrote `get_args` to use the builder pattern. There's nothing new to
how I declare the parameters, so I'll not comment on this. Be sure to add use `clap::`
`{Arg, ArgAction, Command}` for the following code:

```
fn get_args() -> Args {
    let matches = Command::new("wcr")
        .version("0.1.0")
        .author("Ken Youens-Clark <kyclark@gmail.com>")
        .about("Rust version of `wc`")
        .arg(
            Arg::new("files")
                .value_name("FILE")
                .help("Input file(s)")
                .default_value("-")
                .num_args(0..),
        )
        .arg(
            Arg::new("lines")
                .short('l')
                .long("lines")
                .action(ArgAction::SetTrue)
                .help("Show line count"),
        )
        .arg(
            Arg::new("words")
                .short('w')
                .long("words")
                .action(ArgAction::SetTrue)
                .help("Show word count"),
        )
        .arg(
            Arg::new("bytes")
                .short('c')
                .long("bytes")
                .action(ArgAction::SetTrue)
                .help("Show byte count"),
        )
        .arg(
            Arg::new("chars")
                .short('m')
                .long("chars")
                .action(ArgAction::SetTrue)
                .help("Show character count")
                .conflicts_with("bytes"),
        )
```

```
        .get_matches();

    Args {
        files: matches.get_many("files").unwrap().cloned().collect(),
        lines: matches.get_flag("lines"),
        words: matches.get_flag("words"),
        bytes: matches.get_flag("bytes"),
        chars: matches.get_flag("chars"),
    }
}
```

To use the derive pattern, add use `clap::Parser` and update the Args to the following:

```
#[derive(Debug, Parser)]
#[command(author, version, about)]
/// Rust version of `wc`
struct Args {
    /// Input file(s)
    #[arg(value_name = "FILE", default_value = "-")]
    files: Vec<String>,

    /// Show line count
    #[arg(short, long)]
    lines: bool,

    /// Show word count
    #[arg(short, long)]
    words: bool,

    /// Show byte count
    #[arg(short('c'), long)]
    bytes: bool,

    /// Show character count
    #[arg(short('m'), long, conflicts_with("bytes"))]
    chars: bool,
}
```

Inside the run function, I change the flags if needed:

```
fn run(mut args: Args) -> Result<()> {
    if [args.words, args.bytes, args.chars, args.lines] ❶
        .iter()
        .all(|v| v == &false)
    {
        args.lines = true;
        args.words = true;
        args.bytes = true;
    }
    println!("{args:#?}");
    Ok(())
}
```

❶ If all the flags are `false`, then set `lines`, `words`, and `bytes` to `true`.

I want to highlight how I create a temporary list using a `slice` (*https://oreil.ly/NHidS*) with all the flags. I then call the `slice::iter` method (*https://oreil.ly/hcprj*) to create an iterator so I can use the `Iterator::all` function (*https://oreil.ly/O8CL1*) to find if all the values are `false`. This method expects a closure (*https://oreil.ly/onL9M*), which is an anonymous function that can be passed as an argument to another function. Here, the closure is a *predicate* or a *test* that determines if an element is `false`. Because these values are references, I compare to `&false`, which is a reference to a Boolean value. If *all* the evaluations are `true`, then `Iterator::all` will return `true`.[2] A slightly shorter but possibly less obvious way to write this would be:

```
if [args.lines, args.words, args.bytes, args.chars].iter().all(|v| !v) { ❶
```

❶ Negate each Boolean value `v` using `std::ops::Not` (*https://oreil.ly/ZvixG*), which is written using a prefix exclamation point (`!`).

Iterator Methods That Take a Closure

You should take some time to read the `Iterator` documentation (*https://oreil.ly/CEdH5*) to note the other methods that take a closure as an argument to select, test, or transform the elements, including the following:

- `Iterator::any` (*https://oreil.ly/HvVrb*) will return `true` if even one evaluation of the closure for an item returns `true`.

- `Iterator::filter` (*https://oreil.ly/LDu90*) will find all elements for which the predicate is `true`.

- `Iterator::map` (*https://oreil.ly/cfevE*) will apply a closure to each element and return a `std::iter::Map` (*https://oreil.ly/PITID*) with the transformed elements.

- `Iterator::find` (*https://oreil.ly/7n1u5*) will return the first element of an iterator that satisfies the predicate as `Some(value)` or `None` if all elements evaluate to `false`.

- `Iterator::position` (*https://oreil.ly/TAlOW*) will return the index of the first element that satisfies the predicate as `Some(value)` or `None` if all elements evaluate to `false`.

---

2 When my youngest first started brushing his own teeth before bed, I would ask if he'd brushed and flossed. The problem was that he was prone to fibbing, so it was hard to trust him. In an actual exchange one night, I asked, "Did you brush and floss your teeth?" *Yes*, he replied. "Did you brush your teeth?" *Yes*, he replied. "Did you floss your teeth?" *No*, he replied. So clearly he failed to properly combine Boolean values because a `true` statement *and* a `false` statement should result in a `false` outcome.

- `Iterator::cmp` (*https://oreil.ly/7uabU*), `Iterator::min_by` (*https://oreil.ly/uEiqO*), and `Iterator::max_by` (*https://oreil.ly/mXDle*) have predicates that accept pairs of items for comparison or to find the minimum and maximum.

Iterating the Files

Now to work on the counting part of the program. This will require iterating over the file arguments and trying to open them, and I suggest you use the `open` function from Chapter 2 for this:

```
fn open(filename: &str) -> Result<Box<dyn BufRead>> {
    match filename {
        "-" => Ok(Box::new(BufReader::new(io::stdin()))),
        _ => Ok(Box::new(BufReader::new(File::open(filename)?))),
    }
}
```

Be sure to expand your imports to include the following:

```
use std::fs::File;
use std::io::{self, BufRead, BufReader};
```

Expand the `run` function to open the files:

```
fn run(mut args: Args) -> Result<()> {
    // Same as before

    for filename in &args.files {
        match open(filename) {
            Err(err) => eprintln!("{filename}: {err}"), ❶
            Ok(_) => println!("Opened {filename}"), ❷
        }
    }

    Ok(())
}
```

❶ When a file fails to open, print the filename and error message to STDERR.

❷ When a file is opened, print a message to STDOUT.

Run your program to verify it properly handles good and bad file inputs:

```
$ cargo run -- blargh tests/inputs/fox.txt
blargh: No such file or directory (os error 2)
Opened tests/inputs/fox.txt
```

Next, it's time to count the elements of the input files.

Writing and Testing a Function to Count File Elements

You are welcome to write your solution however you like, but I decided to create a function called count that would take a filehandle and possibly return a struct called FileInfo containing the number of lines, words, bytes, and characters, each represented as a usize. I put the following definition just after the Args struct. For reasons I will explain shortly, this must derive the PartialEq trait (*https://oreil.ly/kOB0D*) in addition to Debug:

```
#[derive(Debug, PartialEq)]
struct FileInfo {
    num_lines: usize,
    num_words: usize,
    num_bytes: usize,
    num_chars: usize,
}
```

My count function might succeed or fail because it will involve I/O, which could go sideways. Therefore, the function will return a Result<FileInfo>, meaning that on success it will have a FileInfo in the Ok variant or else will have an error. To start this function, I will initialize some mutable variables to count all the elements and will return a FileInfo struct:

```
fn count(mut file: impl BufRead) -> Result<FileInfo> { ❶
    let mut num_lines = 0; ❷
    let mut num_words = 0;
    let mut num_bytes = 0;
    let mut num_chars = 0;

    Ok(FileInfo {
        num_lines, ❸
        num_words,
        num_bytes,
        num_chars,
    })
}
```

❶ The count function will accept a mutable file value, and it might return a FileInfo struct.

❷ Initialize mutable variables to count the lines, words, bytes, and characters.

❸ For now, return a FileInfo with all zeros. Because my variable names match the struct fieldnames, I can use this shorthand syntax.

I'm introducing the impl keyword (*https://oreil.ly/BYApT*) to indicate that the file value must *implement* the BufRead trait. Recall that open returns a value that meets this criterion. You'll shortly see how this makes the function flexible.

Next, I will show you how to write a unit test for the count function and place it inside a module called tests. This is a tidy way to group unit tests, and I can use the #[cfg(test)] configuration option to tell Rust to compile the module only during testing. This is especially useful because I want to use std::io::Cursor (*https://oreil.ly/jQVVm*) in my test to fake a filehandle for the count function. According to the documentation, a Cursor is "used with in-memory buffers, anything implementing AsRef<[u8]>, to allow them to implement Read and/or Write, allowing these buffers to be used anywhere you might use a reader or writer that does actual I/O." Placing this dependency inside the tests module ensures that it will be included only when I test the program. Add the following code to your *src/main.rs* to create the tests module that will import and test the count function:

```
#[cfg(test)] ❶
mod tests { ❷
    use super::{count, FileInfo}; ❸
    use std::io::Cursor; ❹

    #[test]
    fn test_count() {
        let text = "I don't want the world.\nI just want your half.\r\n";
        let info = count(Cursor::new(text)); ❺
        assert!(info.is_ok()); ❻
        let expected = FileInfo {
            num_lines: 2,
            num_words: 10,
            num_chars: 48,
            num_bytes: 48,
        };
        assert_eq!(info.unwrap(), expected); ❼
    }
}
```

❶ The cfg (*https://oreil.ly/Fl3pU*) enables conditional compilation, so this module will be compiled only when testing.

❷ Define a new module (mod) called tests.

❸ Import the count function and FileInfo struct from the parent module super, meaning *next above* and referring to the module above tests that contains it.

❹ Import std::io::Cursor.

❺ Run count with the Cursor.

❻ Ensure the result is Ok.

❼ Compare the result to the expected value. This comparison requires FileInfo to implement the PartialEq trait, which is why I added derive(PartialEq) earlier.

Run this test using **cargo test test_count**. You will see lots of warnings from the Rust compiler about unused variables or variables that do not need to be mutable. The most important result is that the test fails:

```
running 1 test
test tests::test_count ... FAILED

failures:

---- tests::test_count stdout ----
thread 'tests::test_count' panicked at src/main.rs:103:9:
assertion `left == right` failed
  left: FileInfo { num_lines: 0, num_words: 0, num_bytes: 0, num_chars: 0 }
 right: FileInfo { num_lines: 1, num_words: 10, num_bytes: 48, num_chars: 48 }
note: run with `RUST_BACKTRACE=1` environment variable to display a backtrace
```

This is an example of test-driven development, where you write a test to define the expected behavior of your function and then write the function that passes the unit test. Your next task is to make this test pass. Then, call the count function in your run function and use the FileInfo to print the expected output. Start as simply as possible using the empty file, and make sure your program prints zeros for the three columns of lines, words, and bytes:

```
$ cargo run -- tests/inputs/empty.txt
       0       0       0 tests/inputs/empty.txt
```

Next, use *tests/inputs/fox.txt* and make sure you get the following counts. I specifically added various kinds and numbers of whitespace to challenge you on how to split the text into words:

```
$ cargo run -- tests/inputs/fox.txt
       1       9      48 tests/inputs/fox.txt
```

Be sure your program can handle the Unicode in *tests/inputs/atlamal.txt* correctly:

```
$ cargo run -- tests/inputs/atlamal.txt
       4      29     177 tests/inputs/atlamal.txt
```

And that you correctly count the characters:

```
$ cargo run -- tests/inputs/atlamal.txt -wml
       4      29     159 tests/inputs/atlamal.txt
```

Next, use multiple input files to check that your program prints the correct *total* column:

```
$ cargo run -- tests/inputs/*.txt
       4        29       177 tests/inputs/atlamal.txt
       0         0         0 tests/inputs/empty.txt
       1         9        48 tests/inputs/fox.txt
       5        38       225 total
```

When all that works correctly, try reading from STDIN:

```
$ cat tests/inputs/atlamal.txt | cargo run
       4        29       177
```

 Stop reading here and finish your program. Run **cargo test** often to see how you're progressing.

Solution

Now, I'll walk you through how I went about writing the wcr program. Bear in mind that you could have solved this in many different ways. As long as your code passes the tests and produces the same output as the BSD version of wc, then it works well and you should be proud of your accomplishments.

Counting the Elements of a File or STDIN

I left you with an unfinished count function, so I'll start there. As we discussed in Chapter 3, BufRead::lines (*https://oreil.ly/KhmCp*) will remove the line endings, and I don't want that because newlines in Windows files are two bytes (\r\n) but Unix newlines are just one byte (\n). I can copy some code from Chapter 3 that uses Buf Read::read_line (*https://oreil.ly/aJFkc*) to read each line into a buffer.

Conveniently, this function tells me how many bytes have been read from the file:

```
fn count(mut file: impl BufRead) -> Result<FileInfo> {
    let mut num_lines = 0;
    let mut num_words = 0;
    let mut num_bytes = 0;
    let mut num_chars = 0;
    let mut line = String::new(); ❶

    loop { ❷
        let line_bytes = file.read_line(&mut line)?; ❸
        if line_bytes == 0 { ❹
            break;
        }
```

```
            num_bytes += line_bytes; ❺
            num_lines += 1; ❻
            num_words += line.split_whitespace().count(); ❼
            num_chars += line.chars().count(); ❽
            line.clear(); ❾
        }

        Ok(FileInfo {
            num_lines,
            num_words,
            num_bytes,
            num_chars,
        })
    }
```

❶ Create a mutable buffer to hold each line of text.

❷ Create an infinite loop for reading the filehandle.

❸ Try to read a line from the filehandle.

❹ End of file (EOF) has been reached when zero bytes are read, so break out of the loop.

❺ Add the number of bytes from this line to the num_bytes variable.

❻ Each time through the loop is a line, so increment num_lines by one.

❼ Use the str::split_whitespace method (*https://oreil.ly/sCxGE*) to break the string on whitespace and use Iterator::count (*https://oreil.ly/Y7yPl*) to find the number of words.

❽ Use the str::chars method (*https://oreil.ly/u9LXa*) to break the string into Unicode characters and use Iterator::count to count the characters.

❾ Clear the line buffer for the next line of text.

With these changes, the test_count test will pass. To integrate this into my code, I will first change run to print the FileInfo struct or print a warning to STDERR when the file can't be opened:

```
fn run(mut args: Args) -> Result<()> {
    // Same as before

    for filename in &args.files {
        match open(filename) {
            Err(err) => eprintln!("{filename}: {err}"),
            Ok(file) => {
```

```
                    let info = count(file)?; ❶
                    println!("{:?}", info); ❷
                }
            }
        }

        Ok(())
    }
```

❶ Attempt to get the counts from a file.

❷ Print the counts.

When I run it on one of the test inputs, it appears to work for a valid file:

```
$ cargo run -- tests/inputs/fox.txt
FileInfo { num_lines: 1, num_words: 9, num_bytes: 48, num_chars: 48 }
```

It even handles reading from STDIN:

```
$ cat tests/inputs/fox.txt | cargo run
FileInfo { num_lines: 1, num_words: 9, num_bytes: 48, num_chars: 48 }
```

Next, I need to format the output to meet the specifications.

Formatting the Output

To create the expected output, I can start by changing run to always print the lines, words, and bytes followed by the filename:

```
fn run(mut args: Args) -> Result<()> {
    // Same as before

    for filename in &args.files {
        match open(filename) {
            Err(err) => eprintln!("{filename}: {err}"),
            Ok(file) => {
                let info = count(file)?;
                println!(
                    "{:>8}{:>8}{:>8} {filename}", ❶
                    info.num_lines, info.num_words, info.num_bytes
                );
            }
        }
    }

    Ok(())
}
```

❶ Format the number of lines, words, and bytes into a right-justified field eight characters wide.

If I run it with one input file, it's already looking pretty sweet:

```
$ cargo run -- tests/inputs/fox.txt
       1       9       48 tests/inputs/fox.txt
```

If I run **cargo test fox** to run all the tests with the word *fox* in the name, I pass one out of eight tests. Huzzah!

```
running 8 tests
test fox ... ok
test fox_bytes ... FAILED
test fox_chars ... FAILED
test fox_bytes_lines ... FAILED
test fox_words_bytes ... FAILED
test fox_words ... FAILED
test fox_words_lines ... FAILED
test fox_lines ... FAILED
```

I can inspect *tests/cli.rs* to see what the passing test looks like. Note that the tests reference constant values declared at the top of the module:

```
const PRG: &str = "wcr";
const EMPTY: &str = "tests/inputs/empty.txt";
const FOX: &str = "tests/inputs/fox.txt";
const ATLAMAL: &str = "tests/inputs/atlamal.txt";
```

Again I have a run helper function to run my tests:

```
fn run(args: &[&str], expected_file: &str) -> Result<()> {
    let expected = fs::read_to_string(expected_file)?; ❶
    let output = Command::cargo_bin(PRG)?.args(args).output().expect("fail");
    assert!(output.status.success()); ❷

    let stdout = String::from_utf8(output.stdout).expect("invalid UTF-8");
    assert_eq!(stdout, expected); ❸
    Ok(())
}
```

❶ Try to read the expected output for this command.

❷ Run the wcr program with the given arguments and assert that the program succeeds.

❸ Check that the program's output matches the expected value.

The fox test is running wcr with the FOX input file and no options, comparing it to the contents of the expected output file that was generated using *05_wcr/mk-outs.sh*:

```
#[test]
fn fox() -> Result<()> {
    run(&[FOX], "tests/expected/fox.txt.out")
}
```

Look at the next function in the file to see a failing test:

```
#[test]
fn fox_bytes() -> Result<()> {
    run(&["--bytes", FOX], "tests/expected/fox.txt.c.out") ❶
}
```

❶ Run the wcr program with the same input file and the --bytes option.

When run with --bytes, my program should print only that column, but it always prints lines, words, and bytes. To correct my program's output, I decided to write a function called format_field that would conditionally return a formatted string or the empty string depending on a Boolean value:

```
fn format_field(value: usize, show: bool) -> String { ❶
    if show { ❷
        format!("{value:>8}") ❸
    } else {
        "".to_string() ❹
    }
}
```

❶ The function accepts a usize value and a Boolean and returns a String.

❷ Check if the show value is true.

❸ Return a new string by formatting the number into a string eight characters wide.

❹ Otherwise, return the empty string.

 Why does this function return a String and not a str? They're both *strings*, but a str is an immutable, fixed-length string. The value that will be returned from the function is dynamically generated at runtime, so I must use String, which is a growable, heap-allocated structure.

I can expand my tests module to add a unit test for this:

```
#[cfg(test)]
mod tests {
    use super::{count, format_field, FileInfo}; ❶
    use std::io::Cursor;

    #[test]
    fn test_count() {} // Same as before

    #[test]
    fn test_format_field() {
        assert_eq!(format_field(1, false), ""); ❷
```

```
                assert_eq!(format_field(3, true), "       3"); ❸
                assert_eq!(format_field(10, true), "      10"); ❹
        }
    }
```

❶ Add `format_field` to the imports.

❷ The function should return the empty string when `show` is `false`.

❸ Check formatting for a single-digit number.

❹ Check formatting for a double-digit number.

Run **cargo test format** to ensure the function passes the test. Here is how I use the `format_field` function in context, where I also handle printing the empty string when reading from STDIN:

```
fn run(mut args: Args) -> Result<()> {
    // Same as before

    for filename in &args.files {
        match open(filename) {
            Err(err) => eprintln!("{filename}: {err}"),
            Ok(file) => {
                let info = count(file)?;
                println!(
                    "{}{}{}{}{}",  ❶
                    format_field(info.num_lines, args.lines),
                    format_field(info.num_words, args.words),
                    format_field(info.num_bytes, args.bytes),
                    format_field(info.num_chars, args.chars),
                    if filename == "-" {  ❷
                        "".to_string()
                    } else {
                        format!(" {filename}")
                    }
                );
            }
        }
    }

    Ok(())
}
```

❶ Format the output for each of the columns using the `format_field` function.

❷ When the filename is a dash, print the empty string; otherwise, print a space and the filename.

With these changes, all the tests for **cargo test fox** pass. But if I run the entire test suite, I see that my program is still failing the tests with names that include the word *all*:

```
failures:
    test_all
    test_all_bytes
    test_all_bytes_lines
    test_all_lines
    test_all_words
    test_all_words_bytes
    test_all_words_lines
```

Looking at the `test_all` function in *tests/cli.rs* confirms that the test is using all the input files as arguments:

```
#[test]
fn test_all() -> Result<()> {
    run(&[EMPTY, FOX, ATLAMAL], "tests/expected/all.out")
}
```

If I run my current program with all the input files, I can see that I'm missing the *total* line:

```
$ cargo run -- tests/inputs/*.txt
       4       29      177 tests/inputs/atlamal.txt
       0        0        0 tests/inputs/empty.txt
       1        9       48 tests/inputs/fox.txt
```

Here is my final `run` function that keeps a running total and prints those values when there is more than one input:

```
fn run(mut args: Args) -> Result<()> {
    if [args.words, args.bytes, args.chars, args.lines]
        .iter()
        .all(|v| v == &false)
    {
        args.lines = true;
        args.words = true;
        args.bytes = true;
    }

    let mut total_lines = 0; ❶
    let mut total_words = 0;
    let mut total_bytes = 0;
    let mut total_chars = 0;

    for filename in &args.files {
        match open(filename) {
            Err(err) => eprintln!("{filename}: {err}"),
            Ok(file) => {
                let info = count(file)?;
                println!(
```

```
                "{}{}{}{}{}",
                format_field(info.num_lines, args.lines),
                format_field(info.num_words, args.words),
                format_field(info.num_bytes, args.bytes),
                format_field(info.num_chars, args.chars),
                if filename.as_str() == "-" {
                    "".to_string()
                } else {
                    format!(" {}", filename)
                }
            );

            total_lines += info.num_lines;  ❷
            total_words += info.num_words;
            total_bytes += info.num_bytes;
            total_chars += info.num_chars;
        }
    }
}

if args.files.len() > 1 {  ❸
    println!(
        "{}{}{}{} total",
        format_field(total_lines, args.lines),
        format_field(total_words, args.words),
        format_field(total_bytes, args.bytes),
        format_field(total_chars, args.chars)
    );
}

Ok(())
}
```

❶ Create mutable variables to track the total number of lines, words, bytes, and characters.

❷ Update the totals using the values from this file.

❸ Print the totals if there is more than one input.

This appears to work well:

```
$ cargo run -- tests/inputs/*.txt
       4      29     177 tests/inputs/atlamal.txt
       0       0       0 tests/inputs/empty.txt
       1       9      48 tests/inputs/fox.txt
       5      38     225 total
```

I can count characters instead of bytes:

```
$ cargo run -- -m tests/inputs/atlamal.txt
     159 tests/inputs/atlamal.txt
```

And I can show and hide any columns I want:

```
$ cargo run -- -wc tests/inputs/atlamal.txt
      29       177 tests/inputs/atlamal.txt
```

Most importantly, **cargo test** shows all passing tests.

Going Further

Write a version that mimics the output from the GNU wc instead of the BSD version. If your system already has the GNU version, run the *mk-outs.sh* program to generate the expected outputs for the given input files. Modify the program to create the correct output according to the tests. Then expand the program to handle the additional options like `--files0-from` for reading the input filenames from a file and `--max-line-length` to print the length of the longest line. Add tests for the new functionality.

Next, ponder the mysteries of the iswspace function mentioned in the BSD manual page noted at the beginning of the chapter. What if you ran the program on the *spiders.txt* file of the Issa haiku from Chapter 2, but it used Japanese characters?[3]

隅の蜘案じな煤はとらぬぞよ

What would the output be? If I place this into a file called *spiders.txt*, BSD wc thinks there are three words:

```
$ wc spiders.txt
       1       3      40 spiders.txt
```

The GNU version says there is only one word:

```
$ wc spiders.txt
  1 1 40 spiders.txt
```

I didn't want to open that can of worms (or spiders?), but if you were creating a version of this program to release to the public, how could you replicate the BSD and GNU versions?

Summary

Well, that was certainly fun. In under 200 lines of Rust, we wrote a pretty passable replacement for one of my favorite Unix programs. Compare your version to the 1,000 lines of C in the GNU source code (*https://oreil.ly/Lzy0u*) and ponder which codebase you would prefer to extend and maintain. Reflect upon your progress in this chapter:

---

3 A more literal translation might be "Corner spider, rest easy, my soot-broom is idle."

- You learned that the `Iterator::all` function will return `true` if all the elements evaluate to `true` for the given predicate, which is a closure accepting an element. Many similar `Iterator` methods accept a closure as an argument for testing, selecting, and transforming the elements.

- You used the `str::split_whitespace` and `str::chars` methods to break text into words and characters.

- You used the `Iterator::count` method to count the number of items.

- You wrote a function to conditionally format a value or the empty string to support the printing or omission of information according to the flag arguments.

- You organized your unit tests into a `tests` module and imported functions from the parent module, called `super`.

- You used the `#[cfg(test)]` configuration option to tell Rust to compile the `tests` module only when testing.

- You saw how to use `std::io::Cursor` to create a fake filehandle for testing a function that expects something that implements `BufRead`.

You've learned quite a bit about reading files with Rust, and in the next chapter, you'll learn how to write files.

CHAPTER 6

Den of Uniquity

There's only one everything

— They Might Be Giants, "One Everything" (2008)

In this chapter, you will write a Rust version of the uniq program (pronounced *unique*), which will find the distinct lines of text from either a file or STDIN. Among its many uses, it is often employed to count how many times each unique string is found.

Along the way, you will learn how to do the following:

- Write to a file or STDOUT
- Use a closure to capture a variable
- Apply the don't repeat yourself (DRY) concept
- Use the Write trait and the write! and writeln! macros
- Use temporary files
- Indicate the lifetime of a variable

How uniq Works

As usual, I'll start by explaining how uniq works so that you understand what is expected of your program. Following is part of the manual page for the BSD version of uniq. The challenge program in this chapter will only implement the reading of a file or STDIN, writing to a file or STDOUT, and counting the lines for the -c flag, but I include more of the documentation so that you can see the full scope of the program:

NAME
     uniq -- report or filter out repeated lines in a file

SYNOPSIS
     uniq [-c | -d | -u] [-i] [-f num] [-s chars] [input_file [output_file]]

DESCRIPTION
     The uniq utility reads the specified input_file comparing adjacent lines,
     and writes a copy of each unique input line to the output_file. If
     input_file is a single dash ('-') or absent, the standard input is read.
     If output_file is absent, standard output is used for output. The second
     and succeeding copies of identical adjacent input lines are not written.
     Repeated lines in the input will not be detected if they are not adja-
     cent, so it may be necessary to sort the files first.

     The following options are available:

     -c   Precede each output line with the count of the number of times
             the line occurred in the input, followed by a single space.

     -d   Only output lines that are repeated in the input.

     -f num Ignore the first num fields in each input line when doing compar-
             isons. A field is a string of non-blank characters separated
             from adjacent fields by blanks. Field numbers are one based,
             i.e., the first field is field one.

     -s chars
             Ignore the first chars characters in each input line when doing
             comparisons. If specified in conjunction with the -f option, the
             first chars characters after the first num fields will be
             ignored. Character numbers are one based, i.e., the first char-
             acter is character one.

     -u   Only output lines that are not repeated in the input.

     -i   Case insensitive comparison of lines.

In the *06_uniqr/tests/inputs* directory of the book's Git repository, you will find the
following input files I'll use for testing:

- *empty.txt*: an empty file
- *one.txt*: a file with one line of text
- *two.txt*: a file with two lines of the same text
- *three.txt*: a file with 13 lines of 4 unique values
- *skip.txt*: a file with four lines of two unique values plus an empty line

The other files *t[1–6].txt* are examples from a Perl program (*https://oreil.ly/I9QA5*) used to test the GNU version. These are generated by the *mk-outs.sh* file:

```
$ cat mk-outs.sh
#!/usr/bin/env bash

ROOT="tests/inputs"
OUT_DIR="tests/expected"

[[ ! -d "$OUT_DIR" ]] && mkdir -p "$OUT_DIR"

# Cf https://github.com/coreutils/coreutils/blob/master/tests/misc/uniq.pl
echo -ne "a\na\n"     > $ROOT/t1.txt  ❶
echo -ne "a\na"       > $ROOT/t2.txt  ❷
echo -ne "a\nb"       > $ROOT/t3.txt  ❸
echo -ne "a\na\nb"    > $ROOT/t4.txt  ❹
echo -ne "b\na\na\n" > $ROOT/t5.txt  ❺
echo -ne "a\nb\nc\n" > $ROOT/t6.txt  ❻

for FILE in $ROOT/*.txt; do
    BASENAME=$(basename "$FILE")
    uniq       $FILE > ${OUT_DIR}/${BASENAME}.out
    uniq -c    $FILE > ${OUT_DIR}/${BASENAME}.c.out
    uniq     < $FILE > ${OUT_DIR}/${BASENAME}.stdin.out
    uniq -c < $FILE > ${OUT_DIR}/${BASENAME}.stdin.c.out
done
```

❶ Two lines each ending with a newline

❷ No trailing newline on last line

❸ Two different lines, no trailing newline

❹ Two lines the same; last is different with no trailing newline

❺ Two different values with newlines on each

❻ Three different values with newlines on each

To demonstrate uniq, note that it will print nothing when given an empty file:

```
$ uniq tests/inputs/empty.txt
```

Given a file with just one line, the one line will be printed:

```
$ uniq tests/inputs/one.txt
a
```

It will also print the number of times a line occurs before the line when run with the -c option. The count is right-justified in a field four characters wide and is followed by a single space and then the line of text:

```
$ uniq -c tests/inputs/one.txt
    1 a
```

The file *tests/inputs/two.txt* contains two duplicate lines:

```
$ cat tests/inputs/two.txt
a
a
```

Given this input, uniq will emit one line:

```
$ uniq tests/inputs/two.txt
a
```

With the -c option, uniq will also include the count of unique lines:

```
$ uniq -c tests/inputs/two.txt
    2 a
```

A longer input file shows that uniq only considers the lines in order and not globally. For example, the value *a* appears four times in this input file:

```
$ cat tests/inputs/three.txt
a
a
b
b
a
c
c
c
a
d
d
d
d
```

When counting, uniq starts over at 1 each time it sees a new string. Since *a* occurs in three different places in the input file, it will also appear three times in the output:

```
$ uniq -c tests/inputs/three.txt
    2 a
    2 b
    1 a
    3 c
    1 a
    4 d
```

If you want the actual unique values, you must first sort the input, which can be done with the aptly named sort command. In the following output, you'll finally see that *a* occurs a total of four times in the input file:

```
$ sort tests/inputs/three.txt | uniq -c
    4 a
    2 b
```

```
    3 c
    4 d
```

The file *tests/inputs/skip.txt* contains a blank line:

```
$ cat tests/inputs/skip.txt
a

a
b
```

The blank line acts just like any other value, and so it will reset the counter:

```
$ uniq -c tests/inputs/skip.txt
   1 a
   1
   1 a
   1 b
```

If you study the Synopsis of the usage closely, you'll see a very subtle indication of how to write the output to a file. Notice how input_file and output_file in the following are grouped inside square brackets to indicate that they are optional *as a pair*. That is, if you provide input_file, you may also optionally provide output_file:

```
uniq [-c | -d | -u] [-i] [-f num] [-s chars] [input_file [output_file]]
```

For example, I can count *tests/inputs/two.txt* and place the output into *out*:

```
$ uniq -c tests/inputs/two.txt out
$ cat out
   2 a
```

With no positional arguments, uniq will read from STDIN by default:

```
$ cat tests/inputs/two.txt | uniq -c
   2 a
```

If you want to read from STDIN *and* indicate the output filename, you must use a dash (-) for the input filename:

```
$ cat tests/inputs/two.txt | uniq -c - out
$ cat out
   2 a
```

The GNU version works basically the same while also providing many more options:

```
$ uniq --help
Usage: uniq [OPTION]... [INPUT [OUTPUT]]
Filter adjacent matching lines from INPUT (or standard input),
writing to OUTPUT (or standard output).

With no options, matching lines are merged to the first occurrence.

Mandatory arguments to long options are mandatory for short options too.
  -c, --count           prefix lines by the number of occurrences
```

```
    -d, --repeated         only print duplicate lines, one for each group
    -D, --all-repeated[=METHOD]  print all duplicate lines
                           groups can be delimited with an empty line
                           METHOD={none(default),prepend,separate}
    -f, --skip-fields=N    avoid comparing the first N fields
        --group[=METHOD]   show all items, separating groups with an empty line
                           METHOD={separate(default),prepend,append,both}
    -i, --ignore-case      ignore differences in case when comparing
    -s, --skip-chars=N     avoid comparing the first N characters
    -u, --unique           only print unique lines
    -z, --zero-terminated  end lines with 0 byte, not newline
    -w, --check-chars=N    compare no more than N characters in lines
        --help     display this help and exit
        --version  output version information and exit

A field is a run of blanks (usually spaces and/or TABs), then nonblank
characters.  Fields are skipped before chars.

Note: 'uniq' does not detect repeated lines unless they are adjacent.
You may want to sort the input first, or use 'sort -u' without 'uniq'.
Also, comparisons honor the rules specified by 'LC_COLLATE'.
```

As you can see, both the BSD and GNU versions have many more options, but this is as much as the challenge program is expected to implement.

Getting Started

This chapter's challenge program should be called uniqr (pronounced *you-neek-er*) for a Rust version of uniq. Start by running **cargo new uniqr**, then modify your *Cargo.toml* to add the following dependencies:

```
[dependencies]
anyhow = "1.0.79"
clap = { version = "4.5.0", features = ["derive"] }

[dev-dependencies]
assert_cmd = "2.0.13"
predicates = "3.0.4"
pretty_assertions = "1.4.0"
tempfile = "3.10.0" ❶
rand = "0.8.5"
```

❶ The tests will create temporary files using the tempfile crate (*https://oreil.ly/ AYcMa*).

Copy the book's *06_uniqr/tests* directory into your project, and then run **cargo test** to ensure that the program compiles and the tests run and fail.

Defining the Arguments

Update your *src/main.rs* to add the following `Args` structure to represent the program's arguments:

```
#[derive(Debug)]
struct Args {
    in_file: String, ❶
    out_file: Option<String>, ❷
    count: bool, ❸
}
```

❶ This is the input filename to read, which may be STDIN if the filename is a dash.

❷ The output will be written either to an optional output filename or STDOUT.

❸ count is a Boolean for whether or not to print the counts of each line.

If you want to use the derive pattern, then annotate the `Args` as needed. For the builder pattern, you can start from the following skeleton for `get_args`:

```
fn get_args() -> Args {
    let matches = Command::new("uniqr")
        .version("0.1.0")
        .author("Ken Youens-Clark <kyclark@gmail.com>")
        .about("Rust version of `uniq`")
        // What goes here?
        .get_matches();

    Args {
        in_file: ...
        out_file: ...
        count: ...
    }
}
```

You can start your `main` by printing the arguments, parsing them however you like as in previous chapters:

```
fn main() {
    let args = Args::parse();
    println!("{:?}", args);
}
```

Your program should be able to produce the following usage:

```
$ cargo run -- -h
Rust version of `uniq`

Usage: uniqr [OPTIONS] [IN_FILE] [OUT_FILE]

Arguments:
```

```
    [IN_FILE]   Input file [default: -] ❶
    [OUT_FILE]  Output file ❷

Options:
  -c, --count     Show counts ❸
  -h, --help      Print help
  -V, --version   Print version
```

❶   The input file is the first positional argument and defaults to a dash (-).

❷   The output file is the second positional argument and is optional.

❸   The -c|--count flag is optional.

By default the program will read from STDIN, which can be represented using a dash:

```
$ cargo run
Args { in_file: "-", out_file: None, count: false }
```

The first positional argument should be interpreted as the input file and the second positional argument as the output file.[1] Note that clap can handle options either before or after positional arguments:

```
$ cargo run -- tests/inputs/one.txt out --count
Args { in_file: "tests/inputs/one.txt", out_file: Some("out"), count: true }
```

 Take a moment to finish the parsing of your arguments before reading further.

I assume you are an upright and moral person who figured out the parsing code on your own, so I will now share my solution, starting with the builder pattern. The following code requires use clap::{Arg, ArgAction, Command} and is similar to previous versions, so I won't comment:

```
fn get_args() -> Args {
    let matches = Command::new("uniqr")
        .version("0.1.0")
        .author("Ken Youens-Clark <kyclark@gmail.com>")
        .about("Rust version of `uniq`")
        .arg(
            Arg::new("in_file")
                .value_name("IN_FILE")
```

---

1 While the goal is to mimic the original versions as much as possible, I would note that I do not like optional positional parameters. In my opinion, it would be better to create an -o|--output option that defaults to STDOUT and one optional positional argument for the input file that defaults to STDIN.

```
                .help("Input file")
                .default_value("-"),
        )
        .arg(
            Arg::new("out_file")
                .value_name("OUT_FILE")
                .help("Output file"),
        )
        .arg(
            Arg::new("count")
                .short('c')
                .long("count")
                .action(ArgAction::SetTrue)
                .help("Show counts"),
        )
        .get_matches();

    Args {
        in_file: matches.get_one("in_file").cloned().unwrap(),
        out_file: matches.get_one("out_file").cloned(),
        count: matches.get_flag("count"),
    }
}
```

The derive pattern requires use clap::Parser and is as follows:

```
#[derive(Debug, Parser)]
#[command(author, version, about)]
/// Rust version of `uniq`
struct Args {
    /// Input file
    #[arg(value_name = "IN_FILE", default_value = "-")]
    in_file: String,

    /// Output file
    #[arg(value_name = "OUT_FILE")]
    out_file: Option<String>,

    /// Show counts
    #[arg(short, long)]
    count: bool,
}
```

Testing the Program

The test suite in *tests/cli.rs* is fairly large, containing 78 tests that check the program under the following conditions:

- Input file as the only positional argument, check STDOUT
- Input file as a positional argument with --count option, check STDOUT
- Input from STDIN with no positional arguments, check STDOUT

- Input from STDIN with --count and no positional arguments, check STDOUT
- Input and output files as positional arguments, check the output file
- Input and output files as positional arguments with --count, check the output file
- Input from STDIN and output files as positional arguments with --count, check the output file

Given how large and complicated the tests became, you may be interested to see how I structured *tests/cli.rs*, which starts with the following:

```
use anyhow::Result;
use assert_cmd::Command;
use predicates::prelude::*;
use pretty_assertions::assert_eq;
use rand::{distributions::Alphanumeric, Rng};
use std::fs;
use tempfile::NamedTempFile; ❶

struct Test { ❷
    input: &'static str,
    out: &'static str,
    out_count: &'static str,
}
```

❶ This is used to create temporary output files.

❷ A struct to define the input files and expected output values with and without the counts.

Note the use of 'static to denote the lifetime of the values. The *lifetime* refers to how long a value is valid for borrowing throughout a program. I want to define structs with &str values, and the Rust compiler would like to know exactly how long the values are expected to stick around relative to one another. The 'static annotation shows that this data will live for the entire lifetime of the program. If you remove it and run the tests, you'll see errors from the compiler along with a suggestion of how to fix it:

```
error[E0106]: missing lifetime specifier
  --> tests/cli.rs:10:12
   |
10 |     input: &str,
   |            ^ expected named lifetime parameter
   |
help: consider introducing a named lifetime parameter
```

Next, I define some constant values I need for testing:

```
const PRG: &str = "uniqr"; ❶

const EMPTY: Test = Test {
    input: "tests/inputs/empty.txt", ❷
    out: "tests/inputs/empty.txt.out", ❸
    out_count: "tests/inputs/empty.txt.c.out", ❹
};
```

❶ The name of the program being tested

❷ The location of the input file for this test

❸ The location of the output file without the counts

❹ The location of the output file with the counts

After the declaration of EMPTY, there are many more Test structures followed by several helper functions. The run function will use Test.input as an input file and will compare STDOUT to the contents of the Test.out file:

```
fn run(test: &Test) -> Result<()> { ❶
    let expected = fs::read_to_string(test.out)?; ❷
    let output = Command::cargo_bin(PRG)? ❸
        .arg(test.input)
        .output()
        .expect("fail");
    assert!(output.status.success());

    let stdout = String::from_utf8(output.stdout).expect("invalid UTF-8");
    assert_eq!(stdout, expected); ❹
    Ok(())
}
```

❶ The function accepts a Test and returns a Result.

❷ Try to read the expected output file.

❸ Try to run the program with the input file as an argument, and verify it ran successfully.

❹ Compare STDOUT to the expected value.

The run_count helper function works very similarly, but this time it tests for the counting:

```
fn run_count(test: &Test) -> Result<()> {
    let expected = fs::read_to_string(test.out_count)?; ❶
    let output = Command::cargo_bin(PRG)?
```

```
            .args([test.input, "-c"])  ❷
            .output()
            .expect("fail");
    assert!(output.status.success());

    let stdout = String::from_utf8(output.stdout).expect("invalid UTF-8");
    assert_eq!(stdout, expected);
    Ok(())
}
```

❶ Read the Test.out_count file for the expected output.

❷ Pass both the Test.input value and the flag -c to count the lines.

The run_stdin function will supply the input to the program through STDIN:

```
fn run_stdin(test: &Test) -> Result<()> {
    let input = fs::read_to_string(test.input)?;  ❶
    let expected = fs::read_to_string(test.out)?;  ❷
    let output = Command::cargo_bin(PRG)?  ❸
        .write_stdin(input)
        .output()
        .expect("fail");
    assert!(output.status.success());

    let stdout = String::from_utf8(output.stdout).expect("invalid UTF-8");
    assert_eq!(stdout, expected);  ❹
    Ok(())
}
```

❶ Try to read the Test.input file.

❷ Try to read the Test.out file.

❸ Pass the input through STDIN.

❹ Verify that STDOUT is the expected value.

The run_stdin_count function tests both reading from STDIN and counting the lines:

```
fn run_stdin_count(test: &Test) -> Result<()> {
    let input = fs::read_to_string(test.input)?;
    let expected = fs::read_to_string(test.out_count)?;
    let output = Command::cargo_bin(PRG)?  ❶
        .arg("--count")
        .write_stdin(input)
        .output()
        .expect("fail");
    assert!(output.status.success());

    let stdout = String::from_utf8(output.stdout).expect("invalid UTF-8");
```

```
        assert_eq!(stdout, expected); ❷
        Ok(())
    }
```

❶ Run the program with the long --count flag, feed the input to STDIN.

❷ Verify that STDOUT is correct.

The run_outfile function checks that the program accepts both the input and output files as positional arguments. This is somewhat more interesting as I needed to use temporary files in the testing because Rust will run the tests in parallel. If I were to use the same dummy filename like *blargh* to write all the output files, the tests would overwrite one another's output. To get around this, I use the tempfile::Name dTempFile (*https://oreil.ly/BnbCk*) to get a dynamically generated temporary filename that will automatically be removed when I finish:

```
fn run_outfile(test: &Test) -> Result<()> {
    let expected = fs::read_to_string(test.out)?;
    let outfile = NamedTempFile::new()?; ❶
    let outpath = &outfile.path().to_str().unwrap(); ❷

    Command::cargo_bin(PRG)? ❸
        .args(&[test.input, outpath])
        .assert()
        .success()
        .stdout("");
    let contents = fs::read_to_string(&outpath)?; ❹
    assert_eq!(&expected, &contents); ❺

    Ok(())
}
```

❶ Try to get a named temporary file.

❷ Get the path (*https://oreil.ly/BBq4n*) to the file.

❸ Run the program with the input and output filenames as arguments, then verify there is nothing in STDOUT.

❹ Try to read the output file.

❺ Check that the contents of the output file match the expected value.

The next two functions are variations on what I've already shown, adding in the --count flag and finally asking the program to read from STDIN when the input filename is a dash. The rest of the module calls these helpers using the various structs to run all the tests.

Processing the Input Files

As in previous chapters, I recommend you have your `main` pass the `Args` structure to a `run` function and handle errors. Be sure to add `use anyhow::Result` for the following code:

```
fn main() {
    if let Err(e) = run(Args::parse()) {
        eprintln!("{e}");
        std::process::exit(1);
    }
}

fn run(_args: Args) -> Result<()> {
    Ok(())
}
```

Your program will need to read the input file, so it makes sense to use the `open` function from previous chapters:

```
fn open(filename: &str) -> Result<Box<dyn BufRead>> {
    match filename {
        "-" => Ok(Box::new(BufReader::new(io::stdin()))),
        _ => Ok(Box::new(BufReader::new(File::open(filename)?))),
    }
}
```

Be sure you expand your imports to include the following:

```
use std::{ ❶
    fs::File,
    io::{self, BufRead, BufReader},
};
```

❶ This syntax will group imports by common prefixes, so all the following come from `std`.

You can borrow quite a bit of code from Chapter 3 that reads lines of text from an input file or `STDIN` while preserving the line endings. Note that the following code requires importing the `anyhow::anyhow` (*https://oreil.ly/AMqFU*) macro. I use this rather than `format!` to create the error message when the input file cannot be opened:

```
fn run(args: Args) -> Result<()> {
    let mut file = open(&args.in_file)
        .map_err(|e| anyhow!("{}: {e}", args.in_file))?; ❶
    let mut line = String::new(); ❷
    loop { ❸
        let bytes = file.read_line(&mut line)?; ❹
        if bytes == 0 { ❺
            break;
```

```
        }
        print!("{line}"); ❻
        line.clear(); ❼
    }
    Ok(())
}
```

❶ Either read STDIN if the input file is a dash or open the given filename. Create an informative error message when this fails.

❷ Create a new, empty mutable String buffer to hold each line.

❸ Create an infinite loop.

❹ Read a line of text while preserving the line endings.

❺ If no bytes were read, break out of the loop.

❻ Print the line buffer.

❼ Clear the line buffer.

Run your program with an input file to ensure it works:

```
$ cargo run -- tests/inputs/one.txt
a
```

It should also work for reading STDIN:

```
$ cargo run -- - < tests/inputs/one.txt
a
```

Next, make your program iterate the lines of input and count each unique run of lines, then print the lines with and without the counts. Once you can create the correct output, you will need to handle printing it either to STDOUT or a given filename. I suggest that you copy ideas from the open function and use File::create (*https://oreil.ly/QPy35*).

 Stop reading here and finish your program. Remember that you can run just a subset of tests with a command like **cargo test empty** to run all the tests with the string *empty* in the name.

Solution

I'll step you through how I arrived at a solution. Your version may be different, but it's fine as long as it passes the test suite. I decided to create two additional mutable variables to hold the previous line of text and the running count. For now, I will always print the count to make sure it's working correctly:

```
fn run(args: Args) -> Result<()> {
    let mut file =
        open(&args.in_file).map_err(|e| anyhow!("{}: {e}", args.in_file))?;
    let mut line = String::new();
    let mut previous = String::new(); ❶
    let mut count: u64 = 0; ❷

    loop {
        let bytes = file.read_line(&mut line)?;
        if bytes == 0 {
            break;
        }

        if line.trim_end() != previous.trim_end() { ❸
            if count > 0 { ❹
                print!("{count:>4} {previous}"); ❺
            }
            previous = line.clone(); ❻
            count = 0; ❼
        }

        count += 1; ❽
        line.clear();
    }

    if count > 0 { ❾
        print!("{count:>4} {previous}");
    }

    Ok(())
}
```

❶ Create a mutable variable to hold the previous line of text.

❷ Create a mutable variable to hold the count.

❸ Compare the current line to the previous line, both trimmed of any possible trailing whitespace.

❹ Print the output only when count is greater than 0.

❺ Print the count right-justified in a column four characters wide followed by a space and the `previous` value.

❻ Set the `previous` variable to a copy of the current `line`.

❼ Reset the counter to 0.

❽ Increment the counter by 1.

❾ Handle the last line of the file.

 I didn't have to indicate the type `u64` for the `count` variable. Rust will happily infer a type. On a 32-bit system, Rust would use an `i32`, which would limit the maximum number of duplicates to `i32::MAX` (*https://oreil.ly/sE2YC*), or 2,147,483,647. That's a big number that's likely to be adequate, but I think it's better to have the program work consistently by specifying `u64`.

If I run **cargo test**, this will pass a fair number of tests. This code is clunky, though. I don't like having to check `if count > 0` twice, as it violates the *don't repeat yourself* (DRY) principle, where you isolate a common idea into a single abstraction like a function rather than copying and pasting the same lines of code throughout a program. Also, my code always prints the count, but it should print the count only when `args.count` is `true`. I can put all of this logic into a function, and I will specifically use a closure to *close around* the `args.count` value. Add this inside the `run` function:

```
let print = |num: u64, text: &str| { ❶
    if num > 0 { ❷
        if args.count { ❸
            print!("{num:>4} {text}"); ❹
        } else {
            print!("{text}"); ❺
        }
    };
};
```

❶ The `print` closure will accept `num` and `text` values.

❷ Print only if `num` is greater than 0.

❸ Check if the `args.count` value is `true`.

❹ Use the `print!` macro to print the `num` and `text` to STDOUT.

❺ Otherwise, print the `text` to STDOUT.

Closures Versus Functions

A closure is a function, so you might be tempted to write `print` as a function inside the `run` function:

```
fn run(args: Args) -> Result<()> {
    ...
    fn print(num: u64, text: &str) {
        if num > 0 {
            if args.count {
                print!("{num:>4} {text}");
            } else {
                print!("{text}");
            }
        }
    }
    ...
```

This is a common way to write a closure in other languages, and Rust does allow you to declare a function inside another function; however, the Rust compiler specifically disallows capturing a dynamic value from the environment:

```
error[E0434]: can't capture dynamic environment in a fn item
  --> src/main.rs:40:16
   |
40 |                 if args.count {
   |                    ^^^^
   |
   = help: use the `|| { ... }` closure form instead
```

I can update the rest of the function to use this closure:

```
loop {
    let bytes = file.read_line(&mut line)?;
    if bytes == 0 {
        break;
    }

    if line.trim_end() != previous.trim_end() {
        print(count, &previous);
        previous = line.clone();
        count = 0;
    }

    count += 1;
    line.clear();
}

print(count, &previous);
```

At this point, the program will pass several more tests. All the failed test names have the string *outfile* because the program fails to write a named output file. To add this last feature, you can open the output file in the same way as the input file, either by creating a named output file using `File::create` or by using `std::io::stdout`. Be sure to add `use std::io::Write` for the following code, which you can place just after the `file` variable:

```
let mut out_file: Box<dyn Write> = match &args.out_file {  ❶
    Some(out_name) => Box::new(File::create(out_name)?),  ❷
    _ => Box::new(io::stdout()),  ❸
};
```

❶ The mutable `out_file` will be a boxed value that implements the `std::io::Write` trait (*https://oreil.ly/Hlk6A*).

❷ When `args.out_file` is `Some` filename, use `File::create` (*https://oreil.ly/QPy35*) to try to create the file.

❸ Otherwise, use `std::io::stdout` (*https://oreil.ly/gjxor*).

If you look at the documentation for `File::create` and `io::stdout`, you'll see both have a "Traits" section showing the various traits they implement. Both show that they implement `Write`, so they satisfy the type requirement `Box<dyn Write>`, which says that the value inside the `Box` must implement this trait.

The second change I need to make is to use `out_file` for the output. I will replace the `print!` macro with `write!` (*https://oreil.ly/oiJaM*) to write the output to a stream like a filehandle or STDOUT. The first argument to `write!` must be a mutable value that implements the `Write` trait. The documentation shows that `write!` will return a `std::io::Result` because it might fail. As such, I changed my `print` closure to return `Result`. Here is the final version of my `run` function that passes all the tests:

```
fn run(args: Args) -> Result<()> {
    let mut file =
        open(&args.in_file).map_err(|e| anyhow!("{}: {e}", args.in_file))?;  ❶

    let mut out_file: Box<dyn Write> = match &args.out_file {  ❷
        Some(out_name) => Box::new(File::create(out_name)?),
        _ => Box::new(io::stdout()),
    };

    let mut print = |num: u64, text: &str| -> Result<()> {  ❸
        if num > 0 {
            if args.count {
                write!(out_file, "{num:>4} {text}")?;
            } else {
                write!(out_file, "{text}")?;
            }
```

```
            };
            Ok(())
        };


        let mut line = String::new();
        let mut previous = String::new();
        let mut count: u64 = 0;
        loop {
            let bytes = file.read_line(&mut line)?;
            if bytes == 0 {
                break;
            }

            if line.trim_end() != previous.trim_end() {
                print(count, &previous)?;     ❹
                previous = line.clone();
                count = 0;
            }

            count += 1;
            line.clear();
        }
        print(count, &previous)?;     ❺

        Ok(())
    }
```

❶ Open either STDIN or the given input filename.

❷ Open either STDOUT or the given output filename.

❸ Create a mutable print closure to format the output.

❹ Use the print closure to possibly print output. Use ? to propagate potential
   errors.

❺ Handle the last line of the file.

Note that the print closure must be declared with the mut keyword because the
out_file filehandle is borrowed as a mutable value. Without this, the compiler will
show the following error:

```
error[E0596]: cannot borrow `print` as mutable, as it is not declared as mutable
  --> src/main.rs:41:9
   |
41 |      let print = |num: u64, text: &str| -> Result<()> {
   |          ^^^^^ not mutable
...
44 |                  write!(out_file, "{num:>4} {text}")?;
```

```
|        -------- calling `print` requires mutable binding
|                 due to mutable borrow of `out_file`
```

Again, it's okay if your solution is different from mine, as long as it passes the tests. Part of what I like about writing with tests is that there is an objective determination of when a program meets some level of specifications. As Louis Srygley once said, "Without requirements or design, programming is the art of adding bugs to an empty text file."[2] I would say that tests are the requirements made incarnate. Without tests, you simply have no way to know when a change to your program strays from the requirements or breaks the design.

Going Further

Can you find other ways to write this algorithm? For instance, I tried another method that read all the lines of the input file into a vector and used Vec::windows (*https://oreil.ly/vudZO*) to look at pairs of lines. This was interesting but could fail if the size of the input file exceeded the available memory on my machine. The solution presented here will only ever allocate memory for the current and previous lines and so should scale to any size file.

As usual, the BSD and GNU versions of uniq both have many more features than I chose to include in the challenge. I would encourage you to add all the features you would like to have in your version. Be sure to add tests for each feature, and always run the entire test suite to verify that all previous features still work.

In my mind, uniq is closely tied with sort, as I often use them together. Consider implementing a Rust version of sort, at least to the point of sorting values lexicographically (in dictionary order) or numerically.

Summary

In about 80 lines of Rust, the uniqr program manages to replicate a reasonable subset of features from the original uniq program. Compare this to the GNU C source code (*https://oreil.ly/X8ipY*), which has more than 600 lines of code. I would feel much more confident extending uniqr than I would using C due to the Rust compiler's use of types and useful error messages.

---

2 Programming Wisdom (@CodeWisdom), "'Without requirements or design, programming is the art of adding bugs to an empty text file.' - Louis Srygley," Twitter, January 24, 2018, 1:00 p.m., *https://oreil.ly/FC6aS*.

Let's review some of the things you learned in this chapter:

- You can now open a new file for writing or print to STDOUT.
- DRY says that any duplicated code should be moved into a single abstraction like a function or a closure.
- A closure must be used to capture values from the enclosing scope.
- When a value implements the Write trait, it can be used with the write! and writeln! macros.
- The tempfile crate helps you create and remove temporary files.
- The Rust compiler may sometimes require you to indicate the lifetime of a variable, which is how long it lives in relation to other variables.

In the next chapter, I'll show how to create Rust's enumerated enum type and how to use regular expressions.

CHAPTER 7

Finders Keepers

Then / Is when I maybe should have wrote it down /
But when I looked around to find a pen /
And then I tried to think of what you said / We broke in two

    — They Might be Giants, "Broke in Two" (2004)

In this chapter, you will write a Rust version of the `find` utility, which will, unsurprisingly, find files and directories for you. If you run `find` with no restrictions, it will recursively search one or more paths for entries such as files, symbolic links, sockets, and directories. You can add myriad matching restrictions, such as for names, file sizes, file types, modification times, permissions, and more. The challenge program will locate files, directories, or links in one or more directories having names that match one or more *regular expressions*, or patterns of text.

You will learn how to do the following:

- Use `clap` to constrain possible values for command-line arguments
- Use a regular expression to find a pattern of text
- Create an enumerated type with an implementation
- Recursively search filepaths using the `walkdir` crate
- Use the `Iterator::any` function
- Chain multiple `filter`, `map`, and `filter_map` operations
- Compile code conditionally when on Windows or not
- Refactor code

How find Works

Let's begin by exploring what find can do by consulting the manual page, which goes on for about 500 lines detailing dozens of options. The challenge program for this chapter will be required to find entries in one or more paths, and these entries can be filtered by files, links, and directories as well as by names that match an optional pattern. I'll show the beginning of the BSD find manual page that shows part of the requirements for the challenge:

```
FIND(1)                    BSD General Commands Manual                    FIND(1)

NAME
     find -- walk a file hierarchy

SYNOPSIS
     find [-H | -L | -P] [-EXdsx] [-f path] path ... [expression]
     find [-H | -L | -P] [-EXdsx] -f path [path ...] [expression]

DESCRIPTION
     The find utility recursively descends the directory tree for each path
     listed, evaluating an expression (composed of the ''primaries'' and
     ''operands'' listed below) in terms of each file in the tree.
```

The GNU find is similar:

```
$ find --help
Usage: find [-H] [-L] [-P] [-Olevel]
[-D help|tree|search|stat|rates|opt|exec] [path...] [expression]

default path is the current directory; default expression is -print
expression may consist of: operators, options, tests, and actions:

operators (decreasing precedence; -and is implicit where no others are given):
      ( EXPR )   ! EXPR   -not EXPR   EXPR1 -a EXPR2   EXPR1 -and EXPR2
      EXPR1 -o EXPR2   EXPR1 -or EXPR2   EXPR1 , EXPR2

positional options (always true): -daystart -follow -regextype

normal options (always true, specified before other expressions):
      -depth --help -maxdepth LEVELS -mindepth LEVELS -mount -noleaf
      --version -xautofs -xdev -ignore_readdir_race -noignore_readdir_race

tests (N can be +N or -N or N): -amin N -anewer FILE -atime N -cmin N
      -cnewer FILE -ctime N -empty -false -fstype TYPE -gid N -group NAME
      -ilname PATTERN -iname PATTERN -inum N -iwholename PATTERN
      -iregex PATTERN -links N -lname PATTERN -mmin N -mtime N
      -name PATTERN -newer FILE -nouser -nogroup -path PATTERN
      -perm [-/]MODE -regex PATTERN -readable -writable -executable
      -wholename PATTERN -size N[bcwkMG] -true -type [bcdpflsD] -uid N
      -used N -user NAME -xtype [bcdpfls] -context CONTEXT
```

```
actions: -delete -print0 -printf FORMAT -fprintf FILE FORMAT -print
        -fprint0 FILE -fprint FILE -ls -fls FILE -prune -quit
        -exec COMMAND ; -exec COMMAND {} + -ok COMMAND ;
        -execdir COMMAND ; -execdir COMMAND {} + -okdir COMMAND ;
```

As usual, the challenge program will attempt to implement only a subset of these options that I'll demonstrate forthwith using the files in *07_findr/tests/inputs*. In the following output from `tree` showing the directory and the file structure of that directory, the symbol -> indicates that *d/b.csv* is a symbolic link to the file *a/b/b.csv*:

```
$ cd 07_findr/tests/inputs/
$ tree
.
├── a
│   ├── a.txt
│   └── b
│       ├── b.csv
│       └── c
│           └── c.mp3
├── d
│   ├── b.csv -> ../a/b/b.csv
│   ├── d.tsv
│   ├── d.txt
│   └── e
│       └── e.mp3
├── f
│   └── f.txt
└── g.csv

6 directories, 9 files
```

 A *symbolic link* is a pointer or a shortcut to a file or directory. Windows does not have symbolic links (aka *symlinks*), so the output will be different on that platform because the path *tests\inputs\d \b.csv* will exist as a regular file. I recommend Windows users also explore writing and testing this program in Windows Subsystem for Linux.

Next, I will demonstrate the features of `find` that the challenge program is expected to implement. To start, `find` must have one or more positional arguments that indicate the paths to search. For each path, `find` will recursively search for all files and directories found therein. If I am in the *tests/inputs* directory and indicate . for the current working directory, `find` will list all the contents. The ordering of the output from the BSD `find` on macOS differs from the GNU version on Linux, which I show on the left and right, respectively:

```
$ find .                        $ find .
.                               .
./g.csv                         ./d
./a                             ./d/d.txt
./a/a.txt                       ./d/d.tsv
./a/b                           ./d/e
./a/b/b.csv                     ./d/e/e.mp3
./a/b/c                         ./d/b.csv
./a/b/c/c.mp3                   ./f
./f                             ./f/f.txt
./f/f.txt                       ./g.csv
./d                             ./a
./d/b.csv                       ./a/a.txt
./d/d.txt                       ./a/b
./d/d.tsv                       ./a/b/c
./d/e                           ./a/b/c/c.mp3
./d/e/e.mp3                     ./a/b/b.csv
```

I can use the -type option[1] to specify f and find only *files*:

```
$ find . -type f
./g.csv
./a/a.txt
./a/b/b.csv
./a/b/c/c.mp3
./f/f.txt
./d/d.txt
./d/d.tsv
./d/e/e.mp3
```

I can use l to find only *links*:

```
$ find . -type l
./d/b.csv
```

I can also use d to find only *directories*:

```
$ find . -type d
.
./a
./a/b
./a/b/c
./f
./d
./d/e
```

---

1 This is one of those odd programs that have no short flags and in which the long flags start with a single dash.

While the challenge program will try to find only these types, find will accept several more -type values per the manual page:

```
-type t
     True if the file is of the specified type.  Possible file types
     are as follows:

     b          block special
     c          character special
     d          directory
     f          regular file
     l          symbolic link
     p          FIFO
     s          socket
```

If you give a -type value not found in this list, find will stop with an error:

```
$ find . -type x
find: -type: x: unknown type
```

The -name option can locate items matching a file glob pattern, such as *.csv for any entry ending with *.csv*. In bash, the asterisk (*) must be escaped with a backslash so that it is passed as a literal character and not interpreted by the shell:

```
$ find . -name \*.csv
./g.csv
./a/b/b.csv
./d/b.csv
```

I can also put the pattern in quotes:

```
$ find . -name "*.csv"
./g.csv
./a/b/b.csv
./d/b.csv
```

I can search for multiple -name patterns by chaining them with -o, for *or*:

```
$ find . -name "*.txt" -o -name "*.csv"
./g.csv
./a/a.txt
./a/b/b.csv
./f/f.txt
./d/b.csv
./d/d.txt
```

I can combine -type and -name options. For instance, I can search for files or links matching *.csv:

```
$ find . -name "*.csv" -type f -o -type l
./g.csv
./a/b/b.csv
./d/b.csv
```

I must use parentheses to group the `-type` arguments when the `-name` condition follows an *or* expression:

```
$ find . \( -type f -o -type l \) -name "*.csv"
./g.csv
./a/b/b.csv
./d/b.csv
```

I can also list multiple search paths as positional arguments:

```
$ find a/b d -name "*.mp3"
a/b/c/c.mp3
d/e/e.mp3
```

If the given search path does not exist, `find` will print an error. In the following command, *blargh* represents a nonexistent path:

```
$ find blargh
find: blargh: No such file or directory
```

If an argument is the name of an existing file, `find` will print it:

```
$ find a/a.txt
a/a.txt
```

When `find` encounters an unreadable directory, it will print a message to STDERR and move on. You can verify this on a Unix platform by creating a directory called *cant-touch-this* and using `chmod 000` to remove all permissions:

```
$ mkdir cant-touch-this && chmod 000 cant-touch-this
$ find . -type d
.
./a
./a/b
./a/b/c
./f
./cant-touch-this
find: ./cant-touch-this: Permission denied
./d
./d/e
```

Windows does not have a permissions system that would render a directory unreadable, so this will work only on Unix. Be sure to remove the directory so that this will not interfere with the tests:

```
$ chmod 700 cant-touch-this && rmdir cant-touch-this
```

While `find` can do much more, this is as much as you will implement in this chapter.

Getting Started

The program you write will be called `findr` (pronounced *find-er*), and I recommend you run **cargo new findr** to start. Update *Cargo.toml* with the following:

```
[dependencies]
anyhow = "1.0.79"
clap = { version = "4.5.0", features = ["derive"] }
regex = "1.10.3"
walkdir = "2.4.0" ❶

[dev-dependencies]
assert_cmd = "2.0.13"
predicates = "3.0.4"
pretty_assertions = "1.4.0"
rand = "0.8.5"
```

❶ The `walkdir` crate (*https://oreil.ly/d8DsV*) will be used to recursively search the paths for entries.

At this point, I normally suggest that you copy the *tests* directory (*07_findr/tests*) into your project; however, in this case, special care must be taken to preserve the symlink in the *tests/inputs* directory or your tests will fail. In Chapter 3, I showed you how to use the `cp` (*copy*) command with the `-r` (*recursive*) option to copy the *tests* directory into your project. On both macOS and Linux, you can change `-r` to `-R` to recursively copy the directory and maintain symlinks. I've also provided a `bash` script in the *07_findr* directory that will copy *tests* into a destination directory and create the symlink manually. Run this with no arguments to see the usage:

```
$ ./cp-tests.sh
Usage: cp-tests.sh DEST_DIR
```

Assuming you created your new project in *~/rust-solutions/findr*, you can use the program like this:

```
$ ./cp-tests.sh ~/rust-solutions/findr
Copying "tests" to "/Users/kyclark/rust-solutions/findr"
Fixing symlink
Done.
```

Run **cargo test** to build the program and run the tests, all of which should fail.

Defining the Arguments

Before I get you started writing code, I want to show the expected command-line interface as it will affect how you define the arguments to `clap`:

```
$ cargo run -- --help
Rust version of `find`

Usage: findr [OPTIONS] [PATH]...

Arguments:
  [PATH]...  Search paths [default: .] ❶

Options:
```

```
-n, --name [<NAME>...]  Name ❷
-t, --type [<TYPE>...]  Entry type [possible values: d, f, l] ❸
-h, --help              Print help
-V, --version           Print version
```

❶ Zero or more directories can be supplied as positional arguments, and the default
should be a dot (.) for the current working directory.

❷ The -n|--name option can specify one or more patterns.

❸ The -t|--type option will be constrained to one or more of the values f for files,
d for directories, or l for links.

You can model this however you like, but I suggest you update *src/main.rs* to model
the program's argument as follows:

```
use regex::Regex; ❶

#[derive(Debug)]
struct Args {
    paths: Vec<String>, ❷
    names: Vec<Regex>, ❸
    entry_types: Vec<EntryType>, ❹
}
```

❶ The regex::Regex (*https://oreil.ly/8PrIh*) struct will represent a compiled regular
expression.

❷ paths will be a vector of strings and may name files or directories.

❸ names will be a vector of regular expressions.

❹ entry_types will be a vector of EntryType variants.

> Regular expressions use a unique syntax to describe patterns of
> text. The name comes from the concept of a *regular language* in
> linguistics. Often the name is shortened to *regex*, and you will
> find them used in many command-line tools and programming
> languages.

In the following code, I'm introducing enum (*https://oreil.ly/SGi2B*), which is a type
that can be one of several variants. You've already been using enum types such as
Option, which has the variants Some<T> or None, and Result, which has the variants
Ok<T> and Err<E>. In a language without such a type, you'd probably have to use literal strings in your code like "dir", "file", and "link". In Rust, you can create a
new enum called EntryType with exactly three possibilities: Dir, File, or Link. You

can use these values in pattern matching with much more precision than matching strings, which might be misspelled. Additionally, Rust will not allow you to match on EntryType values without considering all the variants, which adds yet another layer of safety in using them.

```
#[derive(Debug, Eq, PartialEq, Clone)]
enum EntryType {
    Dir,
    File,
    Link,
}
```

 Per Rust naming conventions (*https://oreil.ly/2tok7*), types, structs, traits, and enum variants use UpperCamelCase, also called Pascal Case.

If you are interested in using clap to constrain the entry types from the user, you will need to write an implementation for the clap::ValueEnum trait (*https://oreil.ly/ RhN_g*) to define clap::builder::PossibleValue (*https://oreil.ly/dXhAa*). You've encountered the impl keyword (*https://oreil.ly/1Hz3j*) in Chapter 5. In the following code, I'm using it to extend EntryType to implement the two required methods for the trait ValueEnum. Be sure to add use clap::{builder::PossibleValue, ValueEnum}:

```
impl ValueEnum for EntryType {
    fn value_variants<'a>() -> &'a [Self] { ❶
        &[EntryType::Dir, EntryType::File, EntryType::Link]
    }

    fn to_possible_value<'a>(&self) -> Option<PossibleValue> { ❷
        Some(match self {
            EntryType::Dir => PossibleValue::new("d"),
            EntryType::File => PossibleValue::new("f"),
            EntryType::Link => PossibleValue::new("l"),
        })
    }
}
```

❶ The value_variants method returns the allowed variants.

❷ The to_possible_value converts one of the enum variants to strings.

Try removing one of the preceding functions to see how Rust prevents you from compiling the code with an error message "not all trait items implemented."

You can annotate the `Args` struct for the derive function or you could start a `get_args` function like so:

```
fn get_args() -> Args {
    let matches = Command::new("findr")
        .version("0.1.0")
        .author("Ken Youens-Clark <kyclark@gmail.com>")
        .about("Rust version of `find`")
        // What goes here?
        .get_matches()

    Args {
        paths: ...
        names: ...
        entry_types: ...
    }
}
```

Start the `main` function by printing the arguments:

```
fn main() {
    let args = Args::parse();
    println!("{:?}", args);
}
```

When run with no arguments, the default `Args` values should look like this:

```
$ cargo run
Args { paths: ["."], names: [], entry_types: [] }
```

The `entry_types` should include the `File` variant when given a `--type` argument of `f`:

```
$ cargo run -- --type f
Args { paths: ["."], names: [], entry_types: [File] }
```

or `Dir` when the value is `d`:

```
$ cargo run -- --type d
Args { paths: ["."], names: [], entry_types: [Dir] }
```

or `Link` when the value is `l`:

```
$ cargo run -- --type l
Args { paths: ["."], names: [], entry_types: [Link] }
```

Any other value should be rejected:

```
$ cargo run -- --type x
error: invalid value 'x' for '--type [<TYPE>...]'
  [possible values: d, f, l]

For more information, try '--help'.
```

I'll be using the regex crate (*https://oreil.ly/VYPhC*) to match file and directory names, which means that the --name value must be a valid regular expression. Regular expression syntax differs slightly from file glob patterns, as shown in Figure 7-1. For instance, the dot has no special meaning in a file glob,[2] and the asterisk (*) in the glob *.txt means *zero or more of any character*, so this will match files that end in *.txt*. In regex syntax, however, the dot (.) is a metacharacter that means *any one character*, and the asterisk means *zero or more of the previous character*, so .* is the equivalent regex.

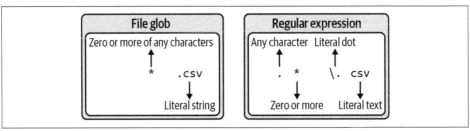

Figure 7-1. The dot (.) and asterisk (*) have different meanings in file globs and regular expressions.

This means that the equivalent regex should use a backslash to escape the literal dot, as in .*\.txt, and the backslash must itself be backslash-escaped on the command line:

```
$ cargo run -- --name .*\\.txt
Args { paths: ["."], names: [Regex(".*\\.txt")], entry_types: [] }
```

Alternatively, you can place the dot inside a character class like [.], where it is no longer a metacharacter:

```
$ cargo run -- --name .*[.]txt
Args { paths: ["."], names: [Regex(".*[.]txt")], entry_types: [] }
```

Technically, the regular expression will match anywhere in the string, even at the beginning, because .* means *zero* or more of anything:

```
let re = Regex::new(".*[.]csv").unwrap();
assert!(re.is_match("foo.csv"));
assert!(re.is_match(".csv.foo"));
```

---

2 Sometimes a dot is just a dot.

If I want to insist that the regex matches at the end of the string, I can add $ at the end of the pattern to indicate the end of the string:

```
let re = Regex::new(".*[.]csv$").unwrap();
assert!(re.is_match("foo.csv"));
assert!(!re.is_match(".csv.foo"));
```

 The converse of using $ to anchor a pattern to the end of a string is to use ^ to indicate the beginning of the string. For instance, the pattern ^foo would match *foobar* and *football* because those strings start with *foo*, but it would not match *barefoot*.

If I try to use the same file glob pattern that find expects, it should be rejected as invalid syntax:

```
$ cargo run -- --name \*.txt
error: invalid value '*.txt' for '--name [<NAME>...]': regex parse error:
    *.txt
    ^
error: repetition operator missing expression
```

Finally, all the Args fields should accept multiple values. I will pretty-print the structure so it's easier for you to see:

```
$ cargo run -- -t f l -n txt mp3 -- tests/inputs/a tests/inputs/d
Args {
    paths: [
        "tests/inputs/a",
        "tests/inputs/d",
    ],
    names: [
        Regex(
            "txt",
        ),
        Regex(
            "mp3",
        ),
    ],
    entry_types: [
        File,
        Link,
    ],
}
```

Stop reading and get this much working before attempting to solve the rest of the program. Don't proceed until your program can replicate the preceding output and can pass at least **cargo test dies**:

```
running 2 tests
test dies_bad_type ... ok
test dies_bad_name ... ok
```

Validating the Arguments

Following is my `get_args` function, so that we can regroup on the task at hand. First, bring in the following dependencies:

```
use clap::{builder::PossibleValue, Arg, ArgAction, Command, ValueEnum};
```

Following is how I wrote the function:

```
fn get_args() -> Args {
    let matches = Command::new("findr")
        .version("0.1.0")
        .author("Ken Youens-Clark <kyclark@gmail.com>")
        .about("Rust version of `find`")
        .arg(
            Arg::new("paths") ❶
                .value_name("PATH")
                .help("Search paths")
                .default_value(".")
                .num_args(0..),
        )
        .arg(
            Arg::new("names") ❷
                .value_name("NAME")
                .short('n')
                .long("name")
                .help("Name")
                .value_parser(Regex::new)
                .action(ArgAction::Append)
                .num_args(0..),
        )
        .arg(
            Arg::new("types")
                .value_name("TYPE")
                .short('t')
                .long("type")
                .help("Entry type")
                .value_parser(clap::value_parser!(EntryType)) ❸
                .action(ArgAction::Append)
                .num_args(0..),
        )
        .get_matches();
```

❶ The `paths` argument requires at least one value and defaults to a dot (`.`).

❷ The names option accepts zero or more values that must parse to a valid regex.

❸ The types option accepts zero or more values restricted to the values f, d, or l.

I finish by returning the Args structure:

```
Args {
    paths: matches.get_many("paths").unwrap().cloned().collect(),
    names: matches
        .get_many("names")
        .unwrap_or_default() ❶
        .cloned()
        .collect(),
    entry_types: matches
        .get_many("types")
        .unwrap_or_default()
        .cloned()
        .collect(),
    }
}
```

❶ The Option::unwrap_or_default (*https://oreil.ly/juX-y*) will return the default value for the underlying Vec type, which will be an empty vector.

Following is how you can use the derive pattern. Be sure to add use clap::{ArgAction, Parser} for the following code:

```
#[derive(Debug, Parser)]
#[command(author, version, about)]
/// Rust version of `find`
struct Args {
    /// Search path(s)
    #[arg(value_name = "PATH", default_value = ".")]
    paths: Vec<String>,

    /// Names
    #[arg(
        short('n'),
        long("name"),
        value_name = "NAME",
        value_parser(Regex::new),
        action(ArgAction::Append),
        num_args(0..)
    )]
    names: Vec<Regex>,

    /// Entry types
    #[arg(
        short('t'),
        long("type"),
        value_name = "TYPE",
```

```
            value_parser(clap::value_parser!(EntryType)),
            action(ArgAction::Append),
            num_args(0..)
        )]
        entry_types: Vec<EntryType>,
}
```

Finding All the Things

Now that you have validated the arguments from the user, it's time to look for the items that match the conditions. Start by passing these arguments to a run function as in previous chapters:

```
fn main() {
    if let Err(e) = run(Args::parse()) {
        eprintln!("{e}");
        std::process::exit(1);
    }
}
```

You might start by iterating over the given paths and trying to find all the files contained in each. You can use the walkdir crate for this. Be sure to add use anyhow::Result and use walkdir::WalkDir for the following code, which shows how to print all the entries:

```
fn run(args: Args) -> Result<()> {
    for path in args.paths {
        for entry in WalkDir::new(path) {
            match entry { ❶
                Err(e) => eprintln!("{e}"), ❷
                Ok(entry) => println!("{}", entry.path().display()), ❸
            }
        }
    }
    Ok(())
}
```

❶ Each directory entry is returned as a Result.

❷ Print errors to STDERR.

❸ Print the display name of Ok values.

To see if this works, list the contents of *tests/inputs/a/b*. Note that this is the order I see on macOS:

```
$ cargo run -- tests/inputs/a/b
tests/inputs/a/b
tests/inputs/a/b/b.csv
tests/inputs/a/b/c
tests/inputs/a/b/c/c.mp3
```

On Linux, I see the following output:

```
$ cargo run -- tests/inputs/a/b
tests/inputs/a/b
tests/inputs/a/b/c
tests/inputs/a/b/c/c.mp3
tests/inputs/a/b/b.csv
```

On Windows/PowerShell, I see this output:

```
> cargo run -- tests/inputs/a/b
tests/inputs/a/b
tests/inputs/a/b\b.csv
tests/inputs/a/b\c
tests/inputs/a/b\c\c.mp3
```

The test suite checks the output irrespective of order. It also includes output files for Windows to ensure the backslashes are correct and to deal with the fact that symlinks don't exist on that platform. Note that this program skips nonexistent directories such as *blargh*:

```
$ cargo run -- blargh tests/inputs/a/b
IO error for operation on blargh: No such file or directory (os error 2)
tests/inputs/a/b
tests/inputs/a/b/b.csv
tests/inputs/a/b/c
tests/inputs/a/b/c/c.mp3
```

This means that the program passes **cargo test skips_bad_dir** at this point:

```
running 1 test
test skips_bad_dir ... ok
```

It will also handle unreadable directories, printing a message to STDERR:

```
$ mkdir tests/inputs/hammer && chmod 000 tests/inputs/hammer
$ cargo run -- tests/inputs 1>/dev/null
IO error for operation on tests/inputs/cant-touch-this:
Permission denied (os error 13)
$ chmod 700 tests/inputs/hammer && rmdir tests/inputs/hammer
```

A quick check with **cargo test** shows that this simple version of the program already passes several tests.

 Now it's your turn. Take what I've shown you so far and build the rest of the program. Iterate over the contents of the directory and show files, directories, or links when args.entry_types contains the appropriate EntryType. Next, filter out entry names that fail to match any of the given regular expressions when they are present. I would encourage you to read the tests in *tests/cli.rs* to ensure you understand what the program should be able to handle.

Solution

Remember, you may have solved this differently from me, but a passing test suite is all that matters. I will walk you through how I arrived at a solution, starting with how I filter for entry types:

```
fn run(args: Args) -> Result<()> {
    for path in args.paths {
        for entry in WalkDir::new(path) {
            match entry {
                Err(e) => eprintln!("{e}"),
                Ok(entry) => {
                    if args.entry_types.is_empty() ❶
                        || args.entry_types.iter().any(|entry_type| {
                            match entry_type { ❷
                                EntryType::Link => {
                                    entry.file_type().is_symlink()
                                }
                                EntryType::Dir => entry.file_type().is_dir(),
                                EntryType::File => {
                                    entry.file_type().is_file()
                                }
                            }
                        })
                    {
                        println!("{}", entry.path().display()); ❸
                    }
                }
            }
        }
    }
    Ok(())
}
```

❶ Check if no entry types are indicated.

❷ If there are entry types, use Iterator::any (*https://oreil.ly/HvVrb*) to see if any of the desired types match the given entry type.

❸ Print only those entries matching the selection criteria.

Recall that I used Iterator::all in Chapter 5 to return true if *all* of the elements in a vector passed some predicate. In the preceding code, I'm using Iterator::any to return true if *at least one* of the elements proves true for the predicate, which in this case is whether the entry's type matches one of the desired types. When I check the output, it seems to be finding, for instance, all the directories:

```
$ cargo run -- tests/inputs/ -t d
tests/inputs/
tests/inputs/a
```

```
tests/inputs/a/b
tests/inputs/a/b/c
tests/inputs/f
tests/inputs/d
tests/inputs/d/e
```

I can run **cargo test type** to verify that I'm now passing all of the tests that check for types alone. The failures are for a combination of type and name, so next I also need to check the filenames with the given regular expressions:

```
fn run(args: Args) -> Result<()> {
    for path in args.paths {
        for entry in WalkDir::new(path) {
            match entry {
                Err(e) => eprintln!("{e}"),
                Ok(entry) => {
                    if (args.entry_types.is_empty() ❶
                        || args.entry_types.iter().any(|entry_type| {
                            match entry_type {
                                EntryType::Link => {
                                    entry.file_type().is_symlink()
                                }
                                EntryType::Dir => entry.file_type().is_dir(),
                                EntryType::File => {
                                    entry.file_type().is_file()
                                }
                            }
                        }))
                        && (args.names.is_empty() ❷
                            || args.names.iter().any(|re| { ❸
                                re.is_match(
                                    &entry.file_name().to_string_lossy(),
                                )
                            }))
                    {
                        println!("{}", entry.path().display());
                    }
                }
            }
        }
    }
    Ok(())
}
```

❶ Check the entry type as before.

❷ Combine the entry type check using && with a similar check on the given names.

❸ Use Iterator::any again to check if any of the provided regexes match the current filename.

In the preceding code, I'm using `Boolean::and` (*https://oreil.ly/ WWDcU*) (`&&`) and `Boolean::or` (*https://oreil.ly/NjWlZ*) (`||`) to combine two Boolean values according to the standard truth tables shown in the documentation. The parentheses are necessary to group the evaluations in the correct order.

I can use this to find, for instance, any regular file matching *mp3*, and it seems to work:

```
$ cargo run -- tests/inputs/ -t f -n mp3
tests/inputs/a/b/c/c.mp3
tests/inputs/d/e/e.mp3
```

If I run **cargo test** at this point, all tests pass. Huzzah! I could stop now, but I feel my code could be more elegant. There are several *smell tests* that fail for me. I don't like how the code continues to march to the right—there's just too much indentation. All the Boolean operations and parentheses also make me nervous. This looks like it would be a difficult program to expand if I wanted to add more selection criteria.

I want to *refactor* this code, which means I want to restructure it without changing the way it works. Refactoring is only possible once I have a working solution, and tests help ensure that any changes I make still work as expected. Specifically, I want to find a less convoluted way to select the entries to display. These are *filter* operations, so I'd like to use `Iterator::filter` (*https://oreil.ly/LDu90*), and I'll show you why. Following is my final run that still passes all the tests. Be sure you add use `walk dir::DirEntry` to your code for this:

```
fn run(args: Args) -> Result<()> {
    let type_filter = |entry: &DirEntry| { ❶
        args.entry_types.is_empty()
            || args.entry_types.iter().any(|entry_type| match entry_type {
                EntryType::Link => entry.file_type().is_symlink(),
                EntryType::Dir => entry.file_type().is_dir(),
                EntryType::File => entry.file_type().is_file(),
            })
    };

    let name_filter = |entry: &DirEntry| { ❷
        args.names.is_empty()
            || args
                .names
                .iter()
                .any(|re| re.is_match(&entry.file_name().to_string_lossy()))
    };

    for path in &args.paths {
        let entries = WalkDir::new(path)
            .into_iter()
            .filter_map(|e| match e { ❸
```

```
                    Err(e) => {
                        eprintln!("{e}");
                        None
                    }
                    Ok(entry) => Some(entry),
                })
                .filter(type_filter) ❹
                .filter(name_filter) ❺
                .map(|entry| entry.path().display().to_string()) ❻
                .collect::<Vec<_>>(); ❼

            println!("{}", entries.join("\n")); ❽
        }

        Ok(())
    }
```

❶ Create a closure to filter entries on any of the regular expressions.

❷ Create a similar closure to filter entries by any of the types.

❸ Turn WalkDir into an iterator and use Iterator::filter_map (*https://oreil.ly/ nZ8Yi*) to remove and print bad results to STDERR while allowing Ok results to pass through.

❹ Filter out unwanted types.

❺ Filter out unwanted names.

❻ Turn each DirEntry (*https://oreil.ly/F0xri*) into a string to display.

❼ Use Iterator::collect (*https://oreil.ly/Xn28H*) to create a vector.

❽ Join the found entries on newlines and print.

In the preceding code, I create two closures to use with filter operations. I chose to use closures because I wanted to capture values from the args. The first closure checks if any of the args.entry_types match the DirEntry::file_type (*https:// oreil.ly/9PU5P*):

```
let type_filter = |entry: &DirEntry| {
    args.entry_types.is_empty() ❶
        || args.entry_types.iter().any(|entry_type| match entry_type { ❷
            EntryType::Link => entry.file_type().is_symlink(), ❸
            EntryType::Dir => entry.file_type().is_dir(), ❹
            EntryType::File => entry.file_type().is_file(), ❺
        })
};
```

❶ Return `true` immediately if no entry types have been indicated.

❷ Otherwise, iterate over the `args.entry_types` to compare to the given entry type.

❸ When the entry type is `Link`, use the `DirEntry::file_type` function to call `File Type::is_symlink` (*https://oreil.ly/6_XUV*).

❹ When the entry type is `Dir`, similarly use `FileType::is_dir` (*https://oreil.ly/Cmkjx*).

❺ When the entry type is `File`, similarly use `FileType::is_file` (*https://oreil.ly/hUsYz*).

The preceding `match` takes advantage of the Rust compiler's ability to ensure that all variants of `EntryType` have been covered. For instance, comment out one arm like so:

```
let type_filter = |entry: &DirEntry| {
    args.entry_types.is_empty()
            || args.entry_types.iter().any(|entry_type| match entry_type {
            EntryType::Link => entry.file_type().is_symlink(),
            EntryType::Dir => entry.file_type().is_dir(),
            //EntryType::File => entry.file_type().is_file(), // Error!
        })
};
```

The compiler stops and politely explains that you have not handled the case of the `EntryType::File` variant. You will not get this kind of safety if you use strings to model this. The `enum` type makes your code far safer and easier to verify and modify:

```
error[E0004]: non-exhaustive patterns: `&EntryType::File` not covered
 --> src/main.rs:68:63
   |
68 |             || args.entry_types.iter().any(|entry_type| match entry_type {
   |                                                         ^^^^^^^^^^
   |
   |                                 pattern `&EntryType::File` not covered
```

The second closure is used to remove filenames that don't match one of the given regular expressions:

```
let name_filter = |entry: &DirEntry| {
    args.names.is_empty() ❶
        || args
            .names
            .iter()
            .any(|re| re.is_match(&entry.file_name().to_string_lossy())) ❷
};
```

❶ Return `true` immediately if no name regexes are present.

❷ Use `Iterator::any` to check if the `DirEntry::file_name` (*https://oreil.ly/3LGTA*) matches any one of the regexes.

The last thing I'll highlight is the multiple operations I can chain together with iterators in the following code. As with reading lines from a file or entries in a directory, each value in the iterator is a `Result` that might yield a `DirEntry` value. I use `Iterator::filter_map` to map each `Result` into a closure that prints errors to `STDERR` and removes by them by returning `None`; otherwise, the `Ok` values are allowed to pass by turning them into `Some` values. The valid `DirEntry` values are then passed to the filters for types and names before being shunted to the `map` operation to transform them into `String` values:

```
let entries = WalkDir::new(path)
    .into_iter()
    .filter_map(|e| match e {
        Err(e) => {
            eprintln!("{}", e);
            None
        }
        Ok(entry) => Some(entry),
    })
    .filter(type_filter)
    .filter(name_filter)
    .map(|entry| entry.path().display().to_string())
    .collect::<Vec<_>>();
```

Although this is fairly lean, compact code, I find it expressive. I appreciate how much these functions are doing for me and how well they fit together. Most importantly, I can clearly see a way to expand this code with additional filters for file size, modification time, ownership, and so forth, which would have been much more difficult without refactoring the code to use `Iterator::filter`. You are free to write code however you like so long as it passes the tests, but this is my preferred solution.

Conditionally Testing on Unix Versus Windows

It's worth taking a moment to talk about how I wrote tests that pass on both Windows and Unix. On Windows, the symlinked file becomes a regular file, so nothing will be found for `--type l`. This also means there will be an additional regular file found when searching with `--type f`. You will find all the tests in *tests/cli.rs*. As in previous tests, I wrote a helper function called `run` to run the program with various arguments and compare the output to the contents of a file:

```
fn run(args: &[&str], expected_file: &str) -> Result<()> { ❶
    let file = format_file_name(expected_file); ❷
    let contents = fs::read_to_string(file.as_ref())?; ❸
    let mut expected: Vec<&str> =
        contents.split("\n").filter(|s| !s.is_empty()).collect();
```

```
expected.sort();

let cmd = Command::cargo_bin(PRG)?.args(args).assert().success(); ❹
let out = cmd.get_output();
let stdout = String::from_utf8(out.stdout.clone())?;
let mut lines: Vec<&str> =
    stdout.split("\n").filter(|s| !s.is_empty()).collect();
lines.sort();

assert_eq!(lines, expected); ❺
Ok(())
}
```

❶   The function accepts the command-line arguments and the file containing the expected output.

❷   Decide whether to use the file for Unix or Windows, which will be explained shortly.

❸   Read the contents of the expected file, then split and sort the lines.

❹   Run the program with the arguments, assert it runs successfully, then split and sort the lines of output.

❺   Assert that the output is equal to the expected values.

If you look in the *tests/expected* directory, you'll see there are pairs of files for each test. That is, the test name_a has two possible output files, one for Unix and another for Windows:

```
$ ls tests/expected/name_a.txt*
tests/expected/name_a.txt           tests/expected/name_a.txt.windows
```

The name_a test looks like this:

```
#[test]
fn name_a() -> Result<()> {
    run(&["tests/inputs", "-n", "a"], "tests/expected/name_a.txt")
}
```

The run function uses the format_file_name function to create the appropriate filename. I use conditional compilation (*https://oreil.ly/AnpGk*) to decide which version of the function is compiled. Note that these functions require use std::borrow::Cow. When the program is compiled on Windows, the following function will be used to append the string *.windows* to the expected filename:

```
#[cfg(windows)]
fn format_file_name(expected_file: &str) -> Cow<str> {
    // Equivalent to: Cow::Owned(format!("{}.windows", expected_file))
```

```
        format!("{}.windows", expected_file).into()
    }
```

When the program is *not* compiled on Windows, this version will use the given file-name:

```
#[cfg(not(windows))]
fn format_file_name(expected_file: &str) -> Cow<str> {
    // Equivalent to: Cow::Borrowed(expected_file)
    expected_file.into()
}
```

Using `std::borrow::Cow` (*https://oreil.ly/f88Lq*) means that on Unix systems the string is not cloned, and on Windows, the modified filename is returned as an owned string.

Lastly, there is an `unreadable_dir` test that will run only on a non-Windows platform:

```
#[test]
#[cfg(not(windows))]
fn unreadable_dir() -> Result<()> {
    let dirname = "tests/inputs/cant-touch-this"; ❶
    if !Path::new(dirname).exists() {
        fs::create_dir(dirname)?;
    }

    std::process::Command::new("chmod") ❷
        .args(&["000", dirname])
        .status()
        .expect("failed");

    let cmd = Command::cargo_bin(PRG)? ❸
        .arg("tests/inputs")
        .assert()
        .success();
    fs::remove_dir(dirname)?; ❹

    let out = cmd.get_output(); ❺
    let stdout = String::from_utf8(out.stdout.clone())?;
    let lines: Vec<&str> =
        stdout.split("\n").filter(|s| !s.is_empty()).collect();

    assert_eq!(lines.len(), 17); ❻

    let stderr = String::from_utf8(out.stderr.clone())?; ❼
    assert!(stderr.contains("cant-touch-this: Permission denied"));
    Ok(())
}
```

❶ Define and create the directory.

❷ Set the permissions to make the directory unreadable.

❸ Run findr and assert that it does not fail.

❹ Remove the directory so that it does not interfere with future tests.

❺ Split the lines of STDOUT.

❻ Verify there are 17 lines.

❼ Check that STDERR contains the expected warning.

Going Further

As with all the previous programs, I challenge you to implement all of the other features in find. For instance, two very useful options of find are -max_depth and -min_depth to control how deeply into the directory structure it should search. There are WalkDir::min_depth (*https://oreil.ly/J5iea*) and WalkDir::max_depth (*https://oreil.ly/kpO18*) options you might use.

Next, perhaps try to find files by size. The find program has a particular syntax for indicating files less than, greater than, or exactly equal to the specified size:

```
-size n[ckMGTP]
    True if the file's size, rounded up, in 512-byte blocks is n.    If
    n is followed by a c, then the primary is true if the file's size
    is n bytes (characters).   Similarly if n is followed by a scale
    indicator then the file's size is compared to n scaled as:

    k       kilobytes (1024 bytes)
    M       megabytes (1024 kilobytes)
    G       gigabytes (1024 megabytes)
    T       terabytes (1024 gigabytes)
    P       petabytes (1024 terabytes)
```

The find program can also take action on the results. For instance, there is a -delete option to remove an entry. This is useful for finding and removing empty files:

```
$ find . -size 0 -delete
```

I've often thought it would be nice to have a -count option to tell me how many items are found, like uniqr -c did in the last chapter. I can, of course, pipe this into wc -l (or, even better, wcr), but consider adding such an option to your program.

Write a Rust version of the tree program that I've shown several times. This program recursively searches a path for entries and creates a visual representation of the file and directory structure. It also has many options to customize the output; for instance, you can display only directories using the -d option:

```
$ tree -d
.
├── a
│   └── b
│       └── c
├── d
│   └── e
└── f

6 directories
```

tree also allows you to use a file glob to display only entries matching a given pattern, with the -P option:

```
$ tree -P \*.csv
.
├── a
│   └── b
│       ├── b.csv
│       └── c
├── d
│   ├── b.csv -> ../a/b/b.csv
│   └── e
├── f
└── g.csv

6 directories, 3 files
```

Finally, compare your version to fd (*https://oreil.ly/ralqD*), another Rust replacement for find, to see how someone else has solved these problems.

Summary

I hope you have an appreciation now for how complex real-world programs can become. For instance, find can combine multiple comparisons to help you locate the large files eating up your disk or files that haven't been modified in a long time that can be removed.

Consider the skills you learned in this chapter:

- You can use clap to constrain argument values to a limited set of strings, saving you time in validating user input.
- You learned to create an implementation block for an enum, which is an enumeration of possible values.

- You saw how to use a regular expression to find a pattern of text. You also learned that the caret (^) anchors the pattern to the beginning of the search string and the dollar sign ($) anchors the expression to the end.

- You can use `WalkDir` to recursively search through a directory structure and evaluate the `DirEntry` values to find files, directories, and links.

- You learned how to chain multiple operations like `any`, `filter`, `map`, and `filter_map` with iterators.

- You can use `#[cfg(windows)]` to compile code conditionally if on Windows or `#[cfg(not(windows))]` if not on Windows.

- You saw a case for refactoring code to simplify the logic while using tests to ensure that the program still works.

In Chapter 8 you will learn to read delimited text files, and in Chapter 9 you will use regular expressions to find lines of text that match a given pattern.

Shave and a Haircut

I'm a mess / Since you cut me out / But Chucky's arm keeps me company
— They Might Be Giants, "Cyclops Rock" (2001)

For the next challenge program, you will create a Rust version of cut, which will excise text from a file or STDIN. The selected text could be some range of bytes or characters or might be fields denoted by a delimiter like a comma or tab that creates field boundaries. You learned how to select a contiguous range of characters or bytes in Chapter 4, while working on the headr program, but this challenge goes further as the selections may be noncontiguous and in any order. For example, the selection 3,1,5-7 should cause the challenge program to print the third, first, and fifth through seventh bytes, characters, or fields, in that order. The challenge program will capture the spirit of the original but will not strive for complete fidelity, as I will suggest a few changes that I feel are improvements.

In this chapter, you will learn how to do the following:

- Read and write a delimited text file using the csv crate
- Deference a value using *
- Use Iterator::flatten to remove nested structures from iterators
- Use Iterator::flat_map to combine Iterator::map and Iterator::flatten

How cut Works

I will start by reviewing the portion of the BSD cut manual page that describes the features of the program you will write:

```
CUT(1)                    BSD General Commands Manual                    CUT(1)

NAME
     cut -- cut out selected portions of each line of a file

SYNOPSIS
     cut -b list [-n] [file ...]
     cut -c list [file ...]
     cut -f list [-d delim] [-s] [file ...]

DESCRIPTION
     The cut utility cuts out selected portions of each line (as specified by
     list) from each file and writes them to the standard output.  If no file
     arguments are specified, or a file argument is a single dash ('-'), cut
     reads from the standard input.  The items specified by list can be in
     terms of column position or in terms of fields delimited by a special
     character.  Column numbering starts from 1.

     The list option argument is a comma or whitespace separated set of num-
     bers and/or number ranges.  Number ranges consist of a number, a dash
     ('-'), and a second number and select the fields or columns from the
     first number to the second, inclusive.  Numbers or number ranges may be
     preceded by a dash, which selects all fields or columns from 1 to the
     last number.  Numbers or number ranges may be followed by a dash, which
     selects all fields or columns from the last number to the end of the
     line.  Numbers and number ranges may be repeated, overlapping, and in any
     order.  If a field or column is specified multiple times, it will appear
     only once in the output.  It is not an error to select fields or columns
     not present in the input line.
```

The original tool offers quite a few options, but the challenge program will implement only the following:

```
-b list
     The list specifies byte positions.

-c list
     The list specifies character positions.

-d delim
     Use delim as the field delimiter character instead of the tab
     character.

-f list
     The list specifies fields, separated in the input by the field
     delimiter character (see the -d option.)  Output fields are sepa-
     rated by a single occurrence of the field delimiter character.
```

As usual, the GNU version offers both short and long flags for these options:

```
NAME
       cut - remove sections from each line of files

SYNOPSIS
       cut OPTION... [FILE]...

DESCRIPTION
       Print selected parts of lines from each FILE to standard output.

       Mandatory  arguments  to  long  options are mandatory for short options
       too.

       -b, --bytes=LIST
             select only these bytes

       -c, --characters=LIST
             select only these characters

       -d, --delimiter=DELIM
             use DELIM instead of TAB for field delimiter

       -f, --fields=LIST
             select only these fields;  also print any line that contains  no
             delimiter character, unless the -s option is specified
```

Both tools implement the selection ranges in similar ways, where numbers can be selected individually, in closed ranges like 1-3, or in partially defined ranges like -3 to indicate 1 through 3 or 5- to indicate 5 to the end, but the challenge program will support only closed ranges. I'll use some of the files found in the book's *08_cutr/tests /inputs* directory to show the features that the challenge program will implement. You should change into this directory if you want to execute the following commands:

```
$ cd 08_cutr/tests/inputs
```

First, consider a file of *fixed-width text* where each column occupies a fixed number of characters:

```
$ cat books.txt
Author              Year Title
Émile Zola          1865 La Confession de Claude
Samuel Beckett      1952 Waiting for Godot
Jules Verne         1870 20,000 Leagues Under the Sea
```

The *Author* column takes the first 20 characters:

```
$ cut -c 1-20 books.txt
Author
Émile Zola
Samuel Beckett
Jules Verne
```

The publication *Year* column spans the next five characters:

```
$ cut -c 21-25 books.txt
Year
1865
1952
1870
```

The *Title* column fills the remainder of the line, where the longest title is 28 characters. Note here that I intentionally request a larger range than exists to show that this is not considered an error:

```
$ cut -c 26-70 books.txt
Title
La Confession de Claude
Waiting for Godot
20,000 Leagues Under the Sea
```

The program does not allow me to rearrange the output by requesting the range 26-55 for the *Title* followed by the range 1-20 for the *Author*. Instead, the selections are placed in their original, ascending order:

```
$ cut -c 26-55,1-20 books.txt
Author              Title
Émile Zola          La Confession de Claude
Samuel Beckett      Waiting for Godot
Jules Verne         20,000 Leagues Under the Sea
```

I can use the option -c 1 to select the first character, like so:

```
$ cut -c 1 books.txt
A
É
S
J
```

As you've seen in previous chapters, bytes and characters are not always interchangeable. For instance, the *É* in *Émile Zola* is a Unicode character that is composed of two bytes, so asking for just one byte will result in invalid UTF-8 that is represented with the Unicode replacement character:

```
$ cut -b 1 books.txt
A
◆
S
J
```

In my experience, fixed-width datafiles are less common than those where the columns of data are delimited by a character such as a comma or a tab. Consider the same data in the file *books.tsv*, where the file extension *.tsv* stands for *tab-separated values* (TSV), and the columns are delimited by the tab:

```
$ cat books.tsv
Author   Year    Title
Émile Zola    1865       La Confession de Claude
Samuel Beckett   1952    Waiting for Godot
Jules Verne      1870    20,000 Leagues Under the Sea
```

By default, cut will assume the tab character is the field delimiter, so I can use the -f option to select, for instance, the publication year in the second column and the title in the third column, like so:

```
$ cut -f 2,3 books.tsv
Year     Title
1865     La Confession de Claude
1952     Waiting for Godot
1870     20,000 Leagues Under the Sea
```

The comma is another common delimiter, and such files often have the extension *.csv* for *comma-separated values* (CSV). Following is the same data as a CSV file:

```
$ cat books.csv
Author,Year,Title
Émile Zola,1865,La Confession de Claude
Samuel Beckett,1952,Waiting for Godot
Jules Verne,1870,"20,000 Leagues Under the Sea"
```

To parse a CSV file, I must indicate the delimiter with the -d option. Note that I'm still unable to reorder the fields in the output, as I indicate 2,1 for the second column followed by the first, but I get the columns back in their original order:

```
$ cut -d , -f 2,1 books.csv
Author,Year
Émile Zola,1865
Samuel Beckett,1952
Jules Verne,1870
```

You may have noticed that the third title contains a comma in *20,000* and so the title has been enclosed in quotes to indicate that this comma is not a field delimiter. This is a way to *escape* the delimiter, or to tell the parser to ignore it. Unfortunately, neither the BSD nor the GNU version of cut recognizes this and so will truncate the title prematurely:

```
$ cut -d , -f 1,3 books.csv
Author,Title
Émile Zola,La Confession de Claude
Samuel Beckett,Waiting for Godot
Jules Verne,"20
```

Noninteger values for any of the list option values are rejected:

```
$ cut -f foo,bar books.tsv
cut: [-cf] list: illegal list value
```

Any error opening a file is handled in the course of processing, printing a message to STDERR. In the following example, *blargh* represents a nonexistent file:

```
$ cut -c 1 books.txt blargh movies1.csv
A
É
S
J
cut: blargh: No such file or directory
t
T
L
```

Finally, the program will read STDIN by default or if the given input filename is a dash (-):

```
$ cat books.tsv | cut -f 2
Year
1865
1952
1870
```

The challenge program is expected to implement just this much, with the following changes:

- Ranges must indicate both start and stop values (inclusive).
- Selection ranges should be printed in the order specified by the user.
- Ranges may include repeated values.
- The parsing of delimited text files should respect escaped delimiters.

Getting Started

The name of the challenge program should be cutr (pronounced *cut-er*) for a Rust version of cut. I recommend you begin with **cargo new cutr** and then copy the *08_cutr/tests* directory into your project. My solution will use the following crates, which you should add to your *Cargo.toml*:

```
[dependencies]
anyhow = "1.0.79"
clap = { version = "4.5.0", features = ["derive"] }
csv = "1.3.0"  ❶
regex = "1.10.3"

[dev-dependencies]
assert_cmd = "2.0.13"
predicates = "3.0.4"
pretty_assertions = "1.4.0"
rand = "0.8.5"
```

❶ The csv crate (*https://oreil.ly/cE8fC*) will be used to parse delimited files such as CSV files.

Run **cargo test** to download the dependencies and run the tests, all of which should fail.

Defining the Arguments

Following is the expected usage for the program:

```
$ cargo run -- --help
Rust version of `cut`

Usage: cutr [OPTIONS] <--fields <FIELDS>|--bytes <BYTES>|--chars <CHARS>> ❶
       [FILES]...

Arguments:
  [FILES]...  Input file(s) [default: -] ❷

Options:
  -d, --delimiter <DELIMITER>  Field delimiter [default: "\t"] ❸
  -f, --fields <FIELDS>        Selected fields
  -b, --bytes <BYTES>          Selected bytes
  -c, --chars <CHARS>          Selected chars
  -h, --help                   Print help
  -V, --version                Print version
```

❶ Exactly one of `--fields`, `--bytes`, or `--chars` is required.

❷ The input files are optional, and the default is STDIN as denoted by a dash.

❸ The default record delimiter is the tab character.

To have clap require one of `--fields`, `--bytes`, or `--chars` when using the derive pattern, I will create an ArgGroup (*https://oreil.ly/1h53Z*) using following structures for the program's arguments:

```
#[derive(Debug)]
struct Args {
    files: Vec<String>, ❶
    delimiter: String, ❷
    extract: ArgsExtract, ❸
}

#[derive(Debug)]
struct ArgsExtract { ❹
    fields: Option<String>,
    bytes: Option<String>,
    chars: Option<String>,
}
```

❶ The `files` parameter is a vector of strings.

❷ The `delimiter` is the character separating the columns.

❸ The `extract` field points to a separate struct.

❹ The `ArgsExtract` struct is used by `clap` to group these arguments.

If you prefer the derive pattern, annotate the preceding structs to produce the expected usage statement. If you prefer to use the builder pattern, you can start your `get_args` by expanding on the following skeleton. Note that defining an `ArgGroup` using the builder pattern does not require any separation of structures, but for the sake of consistency, I will use the preceding structs for both versions of the program:

```
fn get_args() -> Args {
    let matches = Command::new("cutr")
        .version("0.1.0")
        .author("Ken Youens-Clark <kyclark@gmail.com>")
        .about("Rust version of `cut`")
        // What goes here?
        .get_matches();

    Args {
        files: ...
        delimiter: ...
        extract: ...
    }
}
```

The first order of business is pretty-printing the runtime values in `main`:

```
fn main() {
    let args = get_args();
    println!("{:#?}", args);
}
```

When run with no arguments, your program should fail as follows:

```
$ cargo run
error: the following required arguments were not provided:
  <--fields <FIELDS>|--bytes <BYTES>|--chars <CHARS>>

Usage: cutr <--fields <FIELDS>|--bytes <BYTES>|--chars <CHARS>> [FILES]...
```

When run with one of the required arguments, it should print a struct as follows:

```
$ cargo run -- -f 1
Args {
    files: [ ❶
        "-",
    ],
    delimiter: "\t", ❷
```

```
        extract: ArgsExtract {
            fields: Some( ❸
                "1",
            ),
            bytes: None,
            chars: None,
        },
    }
```

❶ The default file input is a dash.

❷ The default delimiter is a tab.

❸ The --fields value of 1 is part of the ArgsExtract struct.

Verify that the other arguments are parsed correctly:

```
$ cargo run -- -b 4 -d , tests/inputs/movies1.csv
Args {
    files: [
        "tests/inputs/movies1.csv", ❶
    ],
    delimiter: ",", ❷
    extract: ArgsExtract {
        fields: None,
        bytes: Some( ❸
            "4",
        ),
        chars: None,
    },
}
```

❶ The positional argument is parsed into the files field.

❷ The -d argument is parsed into the delimiter field.

❸ The -b argument is parsed into the bytes field.

The options for -f|--fields, -b|--bytes, and -c|--chars should all be mutually exclusive:

```
$ cargo run -- -f 1 -b 8-9 tests/inputs/movies1.tsv
error: the argument '--fields <FIELDS>' cannot be used with '--bytes <BYTES>'

Usage: cutr <--fields <FIELDS>|--bytes <BYTES>|--chars <CHARS>> [FILES]...
```

Stop reading and get your program to match the preceding behavior. It should pass five tests for bad inputs when you run **cargo test dies**.

If you chose the builder pattern, your `get_args` function probably looks like the following. Be sure to add use `clap::{Arg, ArgGroup, Command}` for the following code:

```
fn get_args() -> Args {
    let matches = Command::new("cutr")
        .version("0.1.0")
        .author("Ken Youens-Clark <kyclark@gmail.com>")
        .about("Rust version of `cut`")
        .arg(
            Arg::new("files") ❶
                .value_name("FILES")
                .help("Input file(s)")
                .num_args(0..)
                .default_value("-"),
        )
        .arg(
            Arg::new("delimiter") ❷
                .value_name("DELIMITER")
                .short('d')
                .long("delim")
                .help("Field delimiter")
                .default_value("\t"),
        )
        .arg(
            Arg::new("fields") ❸
                .value_name("FIELDS")
                .short('f')
                .long("fields")
                .help("Selected fields"),
        )
        .arg(
            Arg::new("bytes") ❹
                .value_name("BYTES")
                .short('b')
                .long("bytes")
                .help("Selected bytes"),
        )
        .arg(
            Arg::new("chars") ❺
                .value_name("CHARS")
                .short('c')
                .long("chars")
                .help("Selected characters"),
        )
        .group(
            ArgGroup::new("extract")
                .args(["fields", "bytes", "chars"]) ❻
                .required(true)
                .multiple(false),
        )
        .get_matches();
```

```
        Args {
            files: matches.get_many("files").unwrap().cloned().collect(),
            delimiter: matches.get_one("delimiter").cloned().unwrap(),
            extract: ArgsExtract { ❼
                fields: matches.get_one("fields").cloned(),
                bytes: matches.get_one("bytes").cloned(),
                chars: matches.get_one("chars").cloned(),
            },
        }
    }
```

❶ The files argument is positional, not required, and defaults to a dash.

❷ The delimiter option defaults to a tab.

❸ fields is optional.

❹ bytes is optional.

❺ chars is optional.

❻ This creates an argument group that requires exactly one of the members.

❼ A struct can contain another struct.

The derive pattern requires use clap::Parser and looks like the following:

```
#[derive(Debug, Parser)]
#[command(author, version, about)]
/// Rust version of `cut`
struct Args {
    /// Input file(s)
    #[arg(default_value = "-")]
    files: Vec<String>,

    /// Field delimiter
    #[arg(short, long, value_name = "DELIMITER", default_value = "\t")]
    delimiter: String,

    #[command(flatten)] ❶
    extract: ArgsExtract,
}

#[derive(Debug, clap::Args)] ❷
#[group(required = true, multiple = false)] ❸
struct ArgsExtract {
    /// Selected fields
    #[arg(short, long, value_name = "FIELDS")]
    fields: Option<String>,
```

```
/// Selected bytes
#[arg(short, long, value_name = "BYTES")]
bytes: Option<String>,

/// Selected chars
#[arg(short, long, value_name = "CHARS")]
chars: Option<String>,
}
```

❶ The flatten will merge the ArgsExtract into the Args struct.

❷ Note that I derive from the fully qualified clap::Args to avoid namespace colli-
sions with my own Args.

❸ The group annotation creates the ArgGroup.

Next, it's time to go further in validating the arguments.

Validating the Delimiter

I first suggest you introduce a run function as in previous chapters. Add
use anyhow::Result and the following:

```
fn main() {
    if let Err(e) = run(Args::parse()) {
        eprintln!("{e}");
        std::process::exit(1);
    }
}

fn run(_args: Args) -> Result<()> {
    Ok(())
}
```

Later in the program, I'll be using the csv crate (*https://oreil.ly/B3F6c*) to parse the
input file, which requires the delimiter to be a single unsigned 8-bit integer u8
(*https://oreil.ly/P5d3b*). The program currently fails the test **cargo test
dies_bad_delimiter** that ensures the delimiter input is correct. I can look at the
source code in *tests/cli.rs* to see the expected error message:

```
#[test]
fn dies_bad_delimiter() -> Result<()> {
    dies(
        &[CSV, "-f", "1", "-d", ",,"], ❶
        r#"--delim ",," must be a single byte"#, ❷
    )
}
```

❶ The program is run with two commas for the delimiter.

❷ The error should echo the given delimiter along with how to fix the input.

 Stop reading and write the code necessary to pass this test. Be aware that I added use anyhow::bail to include the bail (*https://oreil.ly/wCanm*) macro to return from run with an error message.

Following is how I ensure that the delimiter is a single byte:

```
fn run(args: Args) -> Result<()> {
    let delim_bytes = args.delimiter.as_bytes(); ❶
    if delim_bytes.len() != 1 { ❷
        bail!(r#"--delim "{}" must be a single byte"#, args.delimiter); ❸
    }
    let delimiter: u8 = *delim_bytes.first().unwrap(); ❹
    println!("{delimiter}");
    Ok(())
}
```

❶ Use String::as_bytes (*https://oreil.ly/e-MWZ*) to break the string into a vector of u8.

❷ Check if the vector's length is any value other than one.

❸ Return an error using a *raw* string so the contained double quotes do not require escaping.

❹ Use Vec::first (*https://oreil.ly/rFrS8*) to select the first element of the vector. Because I have verified that this vector has exactly one byte, it is safe to call Option::unwrap.

In the preceding code, I use the Deref::deref (*https://oreil.ly/VCe9J*) operator * in the expression *delim_bytes to dereference the variable, which is a &u8. The code will not compile without the asterisk, and the error message shows exactly where to add the dereference operator:

```
error[E0308]: mismatched types
  --> src/main.rs:59:25
   |
59 |     let delimiter: u8 = delim_bytes.first().unwrap();
   |                    --   ^^^^^^^^^^^^^^^^^^^^^^^^^^^^^ expected `u8`,
   |                    |                                 found `&u8`
   |                    |
   |                    expected due to this
   |
help: consider dereferencing the borrow
   |
```

```
59 |      let delimiter: u8 = *delim_bytes.first().unwrap();
  |                          +
```

Requirements for Parsing the Position List

I will define a type alias PositionList to describe the fields, bytes, or characters that I
want to display from the input files. This is a Vec<Range<usize>> or a vector of
std::ops::Range structs (*https://oreil.ly/gA0sx*) to represent spans of positive integer
values. I will then use this type in a new enum to say which of Fields, Bytes, or Chars
I should extract:

```
type PositionList = Vec<Range<usize>>; ❶

#[derive(Debug)] ❷
pub enum Extract {
    Fields(PositionList),
    Bytes(PositionList),
    Chars(PositionList),
}
```

❶   A PositionList is a vector of Range<usize> values.

❷   Define an enum to hold the variants for extracting fields, bytes, or characters.

Unlike the original cut tool, the challenge program will allow only for the input
ranges to be a comma-separated list of either single numbers or closed ranges like
2-4. Also, the challenge program will use the selections in the given order rather than
rearranging them in ascending order.

To parse and validate the range values for the byte, character, and field arguments, I
wrote a function called parse_pos. Here is how you might start it:

```
fn parse_pos(range: String) -> Result<PositionList> { ❶
    unimplemented!(); ❷
}
```

❶   This function accepts a String and will either return a PositionList or an error.

❷   The unimplemented! macro (*https://oreil.ly/hqKK8*) will cause the program to
     panic or prematurely terminate with the message *not implemented*.

To help you along, I have written an extensive unit test for the numbers and number
ranges that should be accepted or rejected. The numbers may have leading zeros but
may not have any nonnumeric characters, and number ranges must be denoted with
a dash (-). Multiple numbers and ranges can be separated with commas. In this chapter, I will create a unit_tests module so that **cargo test unit** will run all the unit
tests. Note that my implementation of parse_pos uses index positions where I

---

subtract one from each value for zero-based indexing, but you may prefer to handle this differently. Add the following to your source code:

```
#[cfg(test)]
mod unit_tests {
    use super::parse_pos;

    #[test]
    fn test_parse_pos() {
        // The empty string is an error
        assert!(parse_pos("".to_string()).is_err());

        // Zero is an error
        let res = parse_pos("0".to_string());
        assert!(res.is_err());
        assert_eq!(
            res.unwrap_err().to_string(),
            r#"illegal list value: "0""#
        );

        let res = parse_pos("0-1".to_string());
        assert!(res.is_err());
        assert_eq!(
            res.unwrap_err().to_string(),
            r#"illegal list value: "0""#
        );

        // A leading "+" is an error
        let res = parse_pos("+1".to_string());
        assert!(res.is_err());
        assert_eq!(
            res.unwrap_err().to_string(),
            r#"illegal list value: "+1""#,
        );

        let res = parse_pos("+1-2".to_string());
        assert!(res.is_err());
        assert_eq!(
            res.unwrap_err().to_string(),
            r#"illegal list value: "+1-2""#,
        );

        let res = parse_pos("1-+2".to_string());
        assert!(res.is_err());
        assert_eq!(
            res.unwrap_err().to_string(),
            r#"illegal list value: "1-+2""#,
        );

        // Any non-number is an error
        let res = parse_pos("a".to_string());
        assert!(res.is_err());
```

```rust
    assert_eq!(
        res.unwrap_err().to_string(),
        r#"illegal list value: "a""#
    );

    let res = parse_pos("1,a".to_string());
    assert!(res.is_err());
    assert_eq!(
        res.unwrap_err().to_string(),
        r#"illegal list value: "a""#
    );

    let res = parse_pos("1-a".to_string());
    assert!(res.is_err());
    assert_eq!(
        res.unwrap_err().to_string(),
        r#"illegal list value: "1-a""#,
    );

    let res = parse_pos("a-1".to_string());
    assert!(res.is_err());
    assert_eq!(
        res.unwrap_err().to_string(),
        r#"illegal list value: "a-1""#,
    );

    // Wonky ranges
    let res = parse_pos("-".to_string());
    assert!(res.is_err());

    let res = parse_pos(",".to_string());
    assert!(res.is_err());

    let res = parse_pos("1,".to_string());
    assert!(res.is_err());

    let res = parse_pos("1-".to_string());
    assert!(res.is_err());

    let res = parse_pos("1-1-1".to_string());
    assert!(res.is_err());

    let res = parse_pos("1-1-a".to_string());
    assert!(res.is_err());

    // First number must be less than second
    let res = parse_pos("1-1".to_string());
    assert!(res.is_err());
    assert_eq!(
        res.unwrap_err().to_string(),
        "First number in range (1) must be lower than second number (1)"
    );
```

```
let res = parse_pos("2-1".to_string());
assert!(res.is_err());
assert_eq!(
    res.unwrap_err().to_string(),
    "First number in range (2) must be lower than second number (1)"
);

// All the following are acceptable
let res = parse_pos("1".to_string());
assert!(res.is_ok());
assert_eq!(res.unwrap(), vec![0..1]);

let res = parse_pos("01".to_string());
assert!(res.is_ok());
assert_eq!(res.unwrap(), vec![0..1]);

let res = parse_pos("1,3".to_string());
assert!(res.is_ok());
assert_eq!(res.unwrap(), vec![0..1, 2..3]);

let res = parse_pos("001,0003".to_string());
assert!(res.is_ok());
assert_eq!(res.unwrap(), vec![0..1, 2..3]);

let res = parse_pos("1-3".to_string());
assert!(res.is_ok());
assert_eq!(res.unwrap(), vec![0..3]);

let res = parse_pos("0001-03".to_string());
assert!(res.is_ok());
assert_eq!(res.unwrap(), vec![0..3]);

let res = parse_pos("1,7,3-5".to_string());
assert!(res.is_ok());
assert_eq!(res.unwrap(), vec![0..1, 6..7, 2..5]);

let res = parse_pos("15,19-20".to_string());
assert!(res.is_ok());
assert_eq!(res.unwrap(), vec![14..15, 18..20]);
    }
}
```

Some of the preceding tests check for a specific error message to help you write the parse_pos function; however, these could prove troublesome if you were trying to internationalize the error messages. An alternative way to check for specific errors would be to use enum variants that would allow the user interface to customize the output while still testing for specific errors.

At this point, I expect you can read the preceding code well enough to understand how the function should work. I recommend you stop reading at this point and write the code that will pass this test.

After **cargo test unit** passes, incorporate the parse_pos function into run so that your program will reject invalid arguments and print an error message like the following:

```
$ cargo run -- -f foo,bar tests/inputs/books.tsv
illegal list value: "foo"
```

The program should also reject invalid ranges:

```
$ cargo run -- -f 3-2 tests/inputs/books.tsv
First number in range (3) must be lower than second number (2)
```

When given valid arguments, your program should be able to print the Extract argument like so:

```
$ cargo run -- -f 4-8 tests/inputs/movies1.csv ❶
Fields([3..8])
```

❶ The -f 4-8 one-based input creates the Extract::Fields variant that holds a single range of zero-offset numbers, 3..8.

Stop here and get your program working as described. The program should be able to pass all the tests that validate the inputs, which you can run with **cargo test dies**:

```
running 10 tests
test dies_bad_delimiter ... ok
test dies_chars_fields ... ok
test dies_chars_bytes_fields ... ok
test dies_bytes_fields ... ok
test dies_chars_bytes ... ok
test dies_not_enough_args ... ok
test dies_empty_delimiter ... ok
test dies_bad_digit_field ... ok
test dies_bad_digit_bytes ... ok
test dies_bad_digit_chars ... ok
```

If you find you need more guidance on writing the parse_pos function, I'll provide that in the next section.

Solution for Parsing the Position List

The parse_pos function I will show relies on a parse_index function that attempts to parse a string into a positive index value one less than the given number, because the user will provide one-based values but Rust needs zero-offset indexes. The given string may not start with a plus sign, and the parsed value must be greater than zero. Note that closures normally accept arguments inside pipes (||), but the following function uses two closures that accept no arguments, which is why the pipes are empty. Both closures instead reference the provided input value. For the following code, be sure to use anyhow::anyhow and std::num::NonZeroUsize:

```rust
fn parse_index(input: &str) -> Result<usize> {
    let value_error = || anyhow!(r#"illegal list value: "{input}""#); ❶
    input
        .starts_with('+') ❷
        .then(|| Err(value_error())) ❸
        .unwrap_or_else(|| { ❹
            input
                .parse::<NonZeroUsize>() ❺
                .map(|n| usize::from(n) - 1) ❻
                .map_err(|_| value_error()) ❼
        })
}
```

❶ Create a closure that accepts no arguments and formats an error string.

❷ Check if the input value starts with a plus sign.

❸ If so, create an error.

❹ Otherwise, continue with the following closure, which accepts no arguments.

❺ Use str::parse to parse the input value, and use the turbofish to indicate the return type of std::num::NonZeroUsize (*https://oreil.ly/ec44d*), which is a positive integer value.

❻ If the input value parses successfully, cast the value to a usize and decrement the value to a zero-based offset.

❼ If the value does not parse, generate an error by calling the value_error closure.

The following is how parse_index is used in the parse_pos function. Add use regex::Regex to your imports for this:

```rust
fn parse_pos(range: String) -> Result<PositionList> {
    let range_re = Regex::new(r"^(\d+)-(\d+)$").unwrap(); ❶
    range
        .split(',') ❷
        .into_iter()
        .map(|val| { ❸
            parse_index(val).map(|n| n..n + 1).or_else(|e| { ❹
                range_re.captures(val).ok_or(e).and_then(|captures| { ❺
```

```
                let n1 = parse_index(&captures[1])?;  ❻
                let n2 = parse_index(&captures[2])?;
                if n1 >= n2 {  ❼
                    bail!(
                        "First number in range ({}) \
                        must be lower than second number ({})",
                        n1 + 1,
                        n2 + 1
                    );
                }
                Ok(n1..n2 + 1)  ❽
            })
        })
    })
    .collect::<Result<_, _>>()  ❾
    .map_err(From::from)  ❿
}
```

❶ Create a regular expression to match two integers separated by a dash, using parentheses to capture the matched numbers.

❷ Split the provided range value on the comma and turn the result into an iterator. In the event there are no commas, the provided value itself will be used.

❸ Map each split value into the closure.

❹ If parse_index parses a single number, then create a Range for the value. Otherwise, note the error value e and continue trying to parse a range.

❺ If the Regex matches the value, the numbers in parentheses will be available through Regex::captures (*https://oreil.ly/O6frw*).

❻ Parse the two captured numbers as index values.

❼ If the first value is greater than or equal to the second, return an error.

❽ Otherwise, create a Range from the lower number to the higher number, adding 1 to ensure the upper number is included.

❾ Use Iterator::collect (*https://oreil.ly/Xn28H*) to gather the values as a Result.

❿ Map any problems through From::from (*https://oreil.ly/sXlWa*) to create an error.

The regular expression in the preceding code is represented using a raw string to prevent Rust from interpreting backslash-escaped values in the string. For instance, you've seen that Rust will interpret \n as a newline. Without this, the compiler complains that \d is an *unknown character escape*:

```
error: unknown character escape: `d`
  --> src/main.rs:146:35
   |
146 |     let range_re = Regex::new("^(\d+)-(\d+)$").unwrap();
   |                                   ^ unknown character escape
   |
   = help: for more information, visit
   <https://doc.rust-lang.org/reference/tokens.html#literals>
help: if you meant to write a literal backslash (perhaps escaping in a
regular expression), consider a raw string literal
```

I would like to highlight the parentheses in the regular expression ^(\d+)-(\d+)$ to indicate one or more digits followed by a dash followed by one or more digits, as shown in Figure 8-1. If the regular expression matches the given string, then I can use Regex::captures to extract the digits that are surrounded by the parentheses. Note that they are available in one-based counting, so the contents of the first capturing parentheses are available in position 1 of the captures.

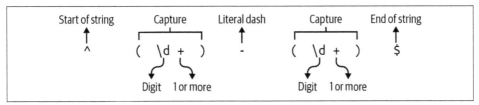

Figure 8-1. *The parentheses in the regular expression will capture the values they surround.*

Now that you have a way to parse and validate the numeric ranges, incorporate this into your run function to transform your ArgsExtract into an Extract enum before reading further.

Following is how I incorporate the parse_pos function into my run to figure out which Extract variant to create or generate an error if the user fails to select bytes, characters, or fields:

```
fn run(args: Args) -> Result<()> {
    // Same as before

    let extract = if let Some(fields) =
        args.extract.fields.map(parse_pos).transpose()? ❶
    {
        Extract::Fields(fields)
    } else if let Some(bytes) =
        args.extract.bytes.map(parse_pos).transpose()?
    {
        Extract::Bytes(bytes)
```

```
} else if let Some(chars) =
    args.extract.chars.map(parse_pos).transpose()?
{
    Extract::Chars(chars)
} else {
    unreachable!("Must have --fields, --bytes, or --chars"); ❷
};

println!("{extract:?}");

Ok(())
}
```

❶ Attempt to call `parse_pos` through `Option::map` (*https://oreil.ly/DOpks*) on `args.extract.fields`, using `Result::transpose` (*https://oreil.ly/HIxb_*) to turn the `Result` of an `Option` into an `Option` of a `Result`.

❷ Logically, this line should never be executed, so call the `unreachable!` (*https://oreil.ly/pwSIv*) macro to cause a panic.

Next, you will need to figure out how you will use this information to extract the desired bits from the inputs.

Extracting Characters or Bytes

In Chapters 4 and 5, you learned how to process lines, bytes, and characters in a file. You should draw on those programs to help you select characters and bytes in this challenge. One difference is that line endings need not be preserved, so you may use `BufRead::lines` (*https://oreil.ly/KhmCp*) to read the lines of input text. To start, you might consider bringing in the open function to open each file:

```
fn open(filename: &str) -> Result<Box<dyn BufRead>> {
    match filename {
        "-" => Ok(Box::new(BufReader::new(io::stdin()))),
        _ => Ok(Box::new(BufReader::new(File::open(filename)?))),
    }
}
```

The preceding function will require some additional imports from the `std` namespace:

```
use std::{
    fs::File,
    io::{self, BufRead, BufReader},
    num::NonZeroUsize,
    ops::Range,
};
```

You can expand your run to handle good and bad files:

```
fn run(args: Args) -> Result<()> {
    // Same as before

    for filename in &args.files {
        match open(filename) {
            Err(err) => eprintln!("{filename}: {err}"),
            Ok(_) => println!("Opened {filename}"),
        }
    }
    Ok(())
}
```

At this point, the program should pass **cargo test skips_bad_file**, and you can
manually verify that it skips invalid files such as the nonexistent *blargh*:

```
$ cargo run -- -c 1 tests/inputs/books.csv blargh
Opened tests/inputs/books.csv
blargh: No such file or directory (os error 2)
```

Now consider how you might extract ranges of characters from each line of a filehandle. I wrote a function called extract_chars that will return a new string composed
of the characters at the given index positions:

```
fn extract_chars(line: &str, char_pos: &[Range<usize>]) -> String {
    unimplemented!();
}
```

 I originally wrote the preceding function with the type annotation
&PositionList for char_pos, but the type &[Range<usize>] is
more flexible for callers, especially for writing tests.

The following is a test you can add to the unit_tests module. Be sure to add
extract_chars to the module's imports:

```
#[test]
fn test_extract_chars() {
    assert_eq!(extract_chars("", &[0..1]), "".to_string());
    assert_eq!(extract_chars("ábc", &[0..1]), "á".to_string());
    assert_eq!(extract_chars("ábc", &[0..1, 2..3]), "ác".to_string());
    assert_eq!(extract_chars("ábc", &[0..3]), "ábc".to_string());
    assert_eq!(extract_chars("ábc", &[2..3, 1..2]), "cb".to_string());
    assert_eq!(
        extract_chars("ábc", &[0..1, 1..2, 4..5]),
        "áb".to_string()
    );
}
```

I also wrote a similar `extract_bytes` function to parse out bytes:

```
fn extract_bytes(line: &str, byte_pos: &[Range<usize>]) -> String {
    unimplemented!();
}
```

For the following unit test, be sure to add `extract_bytes` to the module's imports:

```
#[test]
fn test_extract_bytes() {
    assert_eq!(extract_bytes("ábc", &[0..1]), "�".to_string()); ❶
    assert_eq!(extract_bytes("ábc", &[0..2]), "á".to_string());
    assert_eq!(extract_bytes("ábc", &[0..3]), "áb".to_string());
    assert_eq!(extract_bytes("ábc", &[0..4]), "ábc".to_string());
    assert_eq!(extract_bytes("ábc", &[3..4, 2..3]), "cb".to_string());
    assert_eq!(extract_bytes("ábc", &[0..2, 5..6]), "á".to_string());
}
```

❶ Note that selecting one byte from the string *ábc* should break the multibyte *á* and result in the Unicode replacement character.

Once you have written these two functions so that they pass tests, incorporate them into your main program so that you pass the integration tests for printing bytes and characters. The failing tests that include *tsv* and *csv* in the names involve reading text delimited by tabs and commas, which I'll discuss in the next section.

Parsing Delimited Text Files

Next, you will need to learn how to parse delimited text files. Technically, all the files you've read to this point were delimited in some manner, such as with newlines to denote the end of a line. In this case, a delimiter like a tab or a comma is used to separate the fields of a record, which is terminated with a newline. Sometimes the delimiting character may also be part of the data, as when the title *20,000 Leagues Under the Sea* occurs in a CSV file. In this case, the field should be enclosed in quotes to escape the delimiter. As noted in the chapter's introduction, neither the BSD nor the GNU version of `cut` respects this escaped delimiter, but the challenge program will. The easiest way to properly parse delimited text is to use something like the `csv` crate. I highly recommend that you first read the tutorial (*https://oreil.ly/Wcapp*), which explains the basics of working with delimited text files and how to use the `csv` module effectively.

Consider the following example that shows how you can use this crate to parse delimited data. If you would like to compile and run this code, start a new project, add the `csv = "1.3.0"` dependency to your *Cargo.toml*, and copy the *tests/inputs /books.csv* file into the root directory of the new project. Use the following for *src /main.rs*:

```
use csv::{ReaderBuilder, StringRecord};
use std::fs::File;

fn main() -> std::io::Result<()> {
    let mut reader = ReaderBuilder::new()        ❶
        .delimiter(b',')                          ❷
        .from_reader(File::open("books.csv")?);   ❸

    println!("{}", fmt(reader.headers()?));       ❹
    for record in reader.records() {              ❺
        println!("{}", fmt(&record?));            ❻
    }

    Ok(())
}

fn fmt(rec: &StringRecord) -> String {
    rec.into_iter().map(|v| format!("{:20}", v)).collect()  ❼
}
```

❶ Use `csv::ReaderBuilder` (*https://oreil.ly/aJ-kp*) to parse a file.

❷ The `delimiter` (*https://oreil.ly/cDuGF*) must be a single u8 byte.

❸ The `from_reader` method (*https://oreil.ly/nHl5R*) accepts a value that implements the `Read` trait (*https://oreil.ly/wDxvY*).

❹ The `Reader::headers` method (*https://oreil.ly/BtSg8*) will return the column names in the first row as a `StringRecord` (*https://oreil.ly/7UOCm*).

❺ The `Reader::records` method (*https://oreil.ly/SDfZC*) provides access to an iterator over `StringRecord` values.

❻ Print a formatted version of the record.

❼ Use `Iterator::map` (*https://oreil.ly/cfevE*) to format the values into fields 20 characters wide and collect the values into a new `String`.

If you run this program, you will see that the comma in *20,000 Leagues Under the Sea* was not used as a field delimiter because it was found within quotes, which themselves are metacharacters that have been removed:

```
$ cargo run
Author            Year          Title
Émile Zola        1865          La Confession de Claude
Samuel Beckett    1952          Waiting for Godot
Jules Verne       1870          20,000 Leagues Under the Sea
```

In addition to `csv::ReaderBuilder`, you should use `csv::Writer` `Builder` (*https://oreil.ly/uXNbn*) in your solution to escape the input delimiter in the output of the program.

Think about how you might use some of the ideas I just demonstrated in your challenge program. For example, you could write a function like `extract_fields` that accepts a `csv::StringRecord` and pulls out the fields found in the `PositionList`. For the following function, add `use csv::StringRecord`:

```
fn extract_fields(
    record: &StringRecord,
    field_pos: &[Range<usize>]
) -> Vec<String> {
    unimplemented!();
}
```

Following is a unit test for this function that you can add to the `unit_tests` module:

```
#[test]
fn test_extract_fields() {
    let rec = StringRecord::from(vec!["Captain", "Sham", "12345"]);
    assert_eq!(extract_fields(&rec, &[0..1]), &["Captain"]);
    assert_eq!(extract_fields(&rec, &[1..2]), &["Sham"]);
    assert_eq!(
        extract_fields(&rec, &[0..1, 2..3]),
        &["Captain", "12345"]
    );
    assert_eq!(extract_fields(&rec, &[0..1, 3..4]), &["Captain"]);
    assert_eq!(extract_fields(&rec, &[1..2, 0..1]), &["Sham", "Captain"]);
}
```

At this point, the `unit_tests` module will need all of the following imports:

```
use super::{extract_bytes, extract_chars, extract_fields, parse_pos};
use csv::StringRecord;
```

Once you can pass this last unit test, you should use all of the `extract_*` functions to print the desired bytes, characters, and fields from the input files. Be sure to run **cargo test** to see what is and is not working. This is a challenging program, so don't give up too quickly. Fear is the mind-killer.

Solution

I'll show you my solution now, but I would again stress that there are many ways to write this program. Any version that passes the test suite is acceptable. I'll begin by showing how I evolved `extract_chars` to select the characters.

Selecting Characters from a String

In this first version of `extract_chars`, I initialize a mutable vector to accumulate the results and then use an imperative approach to select the desired characters:

```
fn extract_chars(line: &str, char_pos: &[Range<usize>]) -> String {
    let chars: Vec<_> = line.chars().collect(); ❶
    let mut selected: Vec<char> = vec![]; ❷

    for range in char_pos.iter().cloned() { ❸
        for i in range { ❹
            if let Some(val) = chars.get(i) { ❺
                selected.push(*val) ❻
            }
        }
    }
    selected.iter().collect() ❼
}
```

❶ Use `str::chars` (*https://oreil.ly/u9LXa*) to split the line of text into characters. The `Vec` type annotation is required by Rust because `Iterator::collect` (*https://oreil.ly/Xn28H*) can return many different types of collections.

❷ Initialize a mutable vector to hold the selected characters.

❸ Iterate over each `Range` of indexes.

❹ Iterate over each value in the `Range`.

❺ Use `Vec::get` (*https://oreil.ly/7xsI8*) to select the character at the index. This might fail if the user has requested positions beyond the end of the string, but a failure to select a character should not generate an error.

❻ If it's possible to select the character, use `Vec::push` (*https://oreil.ly/TQlnN*) to add it to the `selected` characters. Note the use of `*` to dereference `&val`.

❼ Use `Iterator::collect` to create a `String` from the characters.

I can simplify the selection of the characters by using `Iterator::filter_map` (*https://oreil.ly/nZ8Yi*), which yields only the values for which the supplied closure returns `Some(value)`:

```
fn extract_chars(line: &str, char_pos: &[Range<usize>]) -> String {
    let chars: Vec<_> = line.chars().collect();
    let mut selected: Vec<char> = vec![];

    for range in char_pos.iter().cloned() {
        selected.extend(range.filter_map(|i| chars.get(i)));
```

```
        }
        selected.iter().collect()
}
```

The preceding versions both initialize a variable to collect the results. In this next version, an iterative approach avoids mutability and leads to a shorter function by using `Iterator::map` and `Iterator::flatten`, which, according to the documentation (*https://oreil.ly/RzXDz*), "is useful when you have an iterator of iterators or an iterator of things that can be turned into iterators and you want to remove one level of indirection":

```
fn extract_chars(line: &str, char_pos: &[Range<usize>]) -> String {
    let chars: Vec<_> = line.chars().collect();
    char_pos
        .iter()
        .cloned()
        .map(|range| range.filter_map(|i| chars.get(i)))  ❶
        .flatten()  ❷
        .collect()
}
```

❶ Use `Iterator::map` (*https://oreil.ly/cfevE*) to process each `Range` to select the characters.

❷ Use `Iterator::flatten` to remove nested structures.

Without `Iterator::flatten`, Rust will show the following error:

```
error[E0277]: a value of type `std::string::String` cannot be built from an
iterator over elements of type `FilterMap<std::ops::Range<usize>`
```

In the `findr` program from Chapter 7, I used `Iterator::filter_map` to combine the operations of `filter` and `map`. Similarly, the operations of `flatten` and `map` can be combined with `Iterator::flat_map` (*https://oreil.ly/zHoNC*) in this shortest and final version of the function:

```
fn extract_chars(line: &str, char_pos: &[Range<usize>]) -> String {
    let chars: Vec<_> = line.chars().collect();
    char_pos
        .iter()
        .cloned()
        .flat_map(|range| range.filter_map(|i| chars.get(i)))
        .collect()
}
```

Selecting Bytes from a String

The selection of bytes is very similar, but I have to deal with the fact that `String::from_utf8_lossy` needs a slice of bytes, unlike the previous example where I could collect an iterator of references to characters into a `String`. As with extract_chars, the goal is to return a new string, but there is a potential problem if the byte selection breaks Unicode characters and so produces an invalid UTF-8 string:

```
fn extract_bytes(line: &str, byte_pos: &[Range<usize>]) -> String {
    let bytes = line.as_bytes(); ❶
    let selected: Vec<_> = byte_pos
        .iter()
        .cloned()
        .flat_map(|range| range.filter_map(|i| bytes.get(i)).copied()) ❷
        .collect();
    String::from_utf8_lossy(&selected).into_owned() ❸
}
```

❶ Break the line into a vector of bytes.

❷ Use Iterator::flat_map to select bytes at the wanted positions and copy the selected bytes.

❸ Use String::from_utf8_lossy (*https://oreil.ly/Bs4Zl*) to generate a possibly invalid UTF-8 string from the selected bytes. Use Cow::into_owned (*https:// oreil.ly/Jpdd0*) to clone the data, if needed.

In the preceding code, I'm using Iterator::get to select the bytes. This function returns a vector of byte references (&Vec<&u8>), but String::from_utf8_lossy expects a slice of bytes (&[u8]). To fix this, I use std::iter::Copied (*https://oreil.ly/ 5SvXY*) to create copies of the elements and avoid the following error:

```
error[E0308]: mismatched types
   --> src/main.rs:159:29
    |
159 |     String::from_utf8_lossy(&selected).into_owned()
    |     ---------------------- ^^^^^^^^^^ expected `&[u8]`, found `&Vec<&u8>`
    |     |
    |     arguments to this function are incorrect
    |
    = note: expected reference `&[u8]`
               found reference `&Vec<&u8>`
```

Finally, I would note the necessity of using Cow::into_owned at the end of the function. Without this, I get a compilation error that suggests an alternate solution to convert the Cow value to a String:

```
error[E0308]: mismatched types
   --> src/main.rs:159:5
    |
152 | fn extract_bytes(line: &str, byte_pos: &[Range<usize>]) -> String {
    |                                                            ------
    |                 expected `std::string::String` because of return type
...
```

```
159 |         String::from_utf8_lossy(&selected)
    |         ^^^^^^^^^^^^^^^^^^^^^^^^^^^^^^^^^^^- help: try using a conversion
    |         |                                  method: `.to_string()`
    |         |
    |         expected `String`, found `Cow<'_, str>`
    |
    = note: expected struct `std::string::String`
                 found enum `Cow<'_, str>`
```

While the Rust compiler is extremely strict, I appreciate how informative and helpful the error messages are.

Selecting Fields from a csv::StringRecord

Selecting the fields from a csv::StringRecord is almost identical to extracting characters from a line:

```
fn extract_fields(
    record: &StringRecord,
    field_pos: &[Range<usize>],
) -> Vec<String> {
    field_pos
        .iter()
        .cloned()
        .flat_map(|range| range.filter_map(|i| record.get(i))) ❶
        .map(String::from) ❷
        .collect()
}
```

❶ Use StringRecord::get (*https://oreil.ly/pIQuO*) to try to get the field for the index position.

❷ Use Iterator::map to turn &str values into String values.

There's another way to write this function so that it will return a Vec<&str>, which will be slightly more memory efficient as it will not make copies of the strings. The trade-off is that I must indicate the lifetimes. First, let me naively try to write it like so:

```
// This will not compile
fn extract_fields(
    record: &StringRecord,
    field_pos: &[Range<usize>],
) -> Vec<&str> {
    field_pos
        .iter()
        .cloned()
        .flat_map(|range| range.filter_map(|i| record.get(i)))
        .collect()
}
```

If I try to compile this, the Rust compiler will complain about lifetimes:

```
error[E0106]: missing lifetime specifier
  --> src/main.rs:165:10
   |
163 |      record: &StringRecord,
   |              -------------
164 |      field_pos: &[Range<usize>],
   |                 ---------------
165 | ) -> Vec<&str> {
   |          ^ expected named lifetime parameter
   |
   = help: this function's return type contains a borrowed value, but the
   signature does not say whether it is borrowed from `record` or `field_pos`
```

The error message continues with directions for how to amend the code to add lifetimes:

```
help: consider introducing a named lifetime parameter
   |
162 ~ fn extract_fields<'a>(
163 ~      record: &'a StringRecord,
164 ~      field_pos: &'a [Range<usize>],
165 ~ ) -> Vec<&'a str> {
```

The suggestion is actually overconstraining the lifetimes. The returned string slices refer to values owned by the StringRecord, so only record and the return value need to have the same lifetime. The following version with lifetimes works well:

```
fn extract_fields<'a>(
    record: &'a StringRecord,
    field_pos: &[Range<usize>],
) -> Vec<&'a str> {
    field_pos
        .iter()
        .cloned()
        .flat_map(|range| range.filter_map(|i| record.get(i)))
        .collect()
}
```

Both the version returning Vec<String> and the version returning Vec<&'a str> will pass the test_extract_fields unit test. The latter version is slightly more efficient and shorter but also has more cognitive overhead. Choose whichever version you feel you'll be able to understand six weeks from now.

Final Boss

For the following code, be sure to add the following imports:

```
use csv::{ReaderBuilder, StringRecord, WriterBuilder};
```

Here is my run function that passes all the tests for printing the desired ranges of characters, bytes, and records:

```rust
fn run(args: Args) -> Result<()> {
    let delim_bytes = args.delimiter.as_bytes();
    if delim_bytes.len() != 1 {
        bail!(r#"--delim "{}" must be a single byte"#, args.delimiter);
    }
    let delimiter: u8 = *delim_bytes.first().unwrap();

    let extract = if let Some(fields) =
        args.extract.fields.map(parse_pos).transpose()?
    {
        Extract::Fields(fields)
    } else if let Some(bytes) =
        args.extract.bytes.map(parse_pos).transpose()?
    {
        Extract::Bytes(bytes)
    } else if let Some(chars) =
        args.extract.chars.map(parse_pos).transpose()?
    {
        Extract::Chars(chars)
    } else {
        unreachable!("Must have --fields, --bytes, or --chars");
    };

    for filename in &args.files {
        match open(filename) {
            Err(err) => eprintln!("{filename}: {err}"),
            Ok(file) => match &extract {
                Extract::Fields(field_pos) => {
                    let mut reader = ReaderBuilder::new() ❶
                        .delimiter(delimiter)
                        .has_headers(false)
                        .from_reader(file);

                    let mut wtr = WriterBuilder::new() ❷
                        .delimiter(delimiter)
                        .from_writer(io::stdout());

                    for record in reader.records() { ❸
                        wtr.write_record(extract_fields( ❹
                            &record?, field_pos,
                        ))?;
                    }
                }
                Extract::Bytes(byte_pos) => {
                    for line in file.lines() { ❺
                        println!("{}", extract_bytes(&line?, byte_pos));
                    }
                }
                Extract::Chars(char_pos) => {
```

```
            for line in file.lines() { ❻
                println!("{}", extract_chars(&line?, char_pos));
            }
        }
    },
    }
}
Ok(())
}
```

❶ If the user has requested fields from a delimited file, use `csv::ReaderBuilder` to create a mutable reader using the given delimiter, and do not treat the first row as headers.

❷ Use `csv::WriterBuilder` to correctly escape delimiters in the output.

❸ Iterate through the records.

❹ Write the extracted fields to the output.

❺ Iterate the lines of text and print the extracted bytes.

❻ Iterate the lines of text and print the extracted characters.

The `csv::Reader` will attempt to parse the first row for the column names by default. For this program, I don't need to do anything special with these values, so I don't parse the first line as a header row. If I used the default behavior, I would have to handle the headers separately from the rest of the records.

Note that I'm using the `csv` crate to both parse the input and write the output, so this program will correctly handle delimited text files, which I feel is an improvement over the original `cut` programs. I'll use *tests/inputs/books.csv* again to demonstrate that `cutr` will correctly select a field containing the delimiter and will create output that properly escapes the delimiter and puts the columns in the requested order:

```
$ cargo run -- -d , -f 3,1 tests/inputs/books.csv
Title,Author
La Confession de Claude,Émile Zola
Waiting for Godot,Samuel Beckett
"20,000 Leagues Under the Sea",Jules Verne
```

This was a fairly complex program with a lot of options, but I found the strictness of the Rust compiler kept me focused on how to write a solution.

Going Further

I have several ideas for how you can expand this program. Alter the program to allow partial ranges like -3, meaning *1–3*, or 5- to mean *5 to the end*. Consider using `std::ops::RangeTo` (*https://oreil.ly/ZniC2*) to model -3 and `std::ops::RangeFrom` (*https://oreil.ly/azzZY*) for 5-. Be aware that `clap` will try to interpret the value -3 as an option when you run **cargo run -- -f -3 tests/inputs/books.tsv**, so use `-f=-3` instead.

The final version of the challenge program uses the `--delimiter` as the input and output delimiter. Add an option to specify the output delimiter, and have it default to the input delimiter.

The `-n` option that will prevent the splitting of multibyte characters seems like a fun challenge to implement, and I also quite like the `--complement` option from GNU cut that complements the set of selected bytes, characters, or fields so that the positions *not* indicated are shown. Finally, for more ideas on how to deal with delimited text records, check out the xsv crate (*https://oreil.ly/894fA*), a "fast CSV command line toolkit written in Rust" and csvchk (*https://crates.io/crates/csvchk*) to see a vertical view of delimited text records.

Summary

Gaze upon the knowledge you gained in this chapter:

- You learned how to dereference a variable that contains a reference using the `*` operator.
- Sometimes actions on iterators return other iterators. You saw how `Iterator::flatten` will remove the inner structures to flatten the result.
- You learned how the `Iterator::flat_map` method combines `Iterator::map` and `Iterator::flatten` into one operation for more concise code.
- You used a `get` function for selecting positions from a vector or fields from a `csv::StringRecord`. This action might fail, so you used `Iterator::filter_map` to return only those values that are successfully retrieved.
- You compared how to return a `String` versus a `&str` from a function, the latter of which required indicating lifetimes.
- You can now parse and create delimited text using the `csv` crate.

In the next chapter, you will learn more about regular expressions and chaining operations on iterators.

CHAPTER 9

Jack the Grepper

Please explain the expression on your face
— They Might Be Giants, "Unrelated Thing" (1994)

In this chapter, you will write a Rust version of `grep`, which will find lines of input that match a given regular expression.[1] By default the input comes from STDIN, but you can provide the names of one or more files or directories if you use a recursive option to find all the files in those directories. The normal output will be the lines that match the given pattern, but you can invert the match to find the lines that don't match. You can also instruct `grep` to print the number of matching lines instead of the lines of text. Pattern matching is normally case-sensitive, but you can use an option to perform case-insensitive matching. While the original program can do more, the challenge program will go only this far.

In writing this program, you'll learn about:

- Using a case-sensitive regular expression
- Variations of regular expression syntax
- Another syntax to indicate a trait bound
- Using Rust's bitwise exclusive-OR operator

---

1 The name `grep` comes from the `ed` command `g/re/p`, which means "global regular expression print," where `ed` is the standard text editor.

How grep Works

I'll start by showing the manual page for the BSD `grep` to give you a sense of the many options the command will accept:

```
GREP(1)                      BSD General Commands Manual                     GREP(1)

NAME
     grep, egrep, fgrep, zgrep, zegrep, zfgrep -- file pattern searcher

SYNOPSIS
     grep [-abcdDEFGHhIiJLlmnOopqRSsUVvwxZ] [-A num] [-B num] [-C[num]]
          [-e pattern] [-f file] [--binary-files=value] [--color[=when]]
          [--colour[=when]] [--context[=num]] [--label] [--line-buffered]
          [--null] [pattern] [file ...]

DESCRIPTION
     The grep utility searches any given input files, selecting lines that
     match one or more patterns.  By default, a pattern matches an input line
     if the regular expression (RE) in the pattern matches the input line
     without its trailing newline.  An empty expression matches every line.
     Each input line that matches at least one of the patterns is written to
     the standard output.

     grep is used for simple patterns and basic regular expressions (BREs);
     egrep can handle extended regular expressions (EREs).  See re_format(7)
     for more information on regular expressions.  fgrep is quicker than both
     grep and egrep, but can only handle fixed patterns (i.e. it does not
     interpret regular expressions).  Patterns may consist of one or more
     lines, allowing any of the pattern lines to match a portion of the input.
```

The GNU version is very similar:

```
GREP(1)                         General Commands Manual                      GREP(1)

NAME
     grep, egrep, fgrep - print lines matching a pattern

SYNOPSIS
        grep [OPTIONS] PATTERN [FILE...]
        grep [OPTIONS] [-e PATTERN | -f FILE] [FILE...]

DESCRIPTION
        grep searches the named input FILEs (or standard input if no files are
        named, or if a single hyphen-minus (-) is given as file name) for lines
        containing a match to the given PATTERN.  By default, grep prints the
        matching lines.
```

To demonstrate the features of `grep` that the challenge program is expected to implement, I'll use some files from the book's GitHub repository. If you want to follow along, change into the *09_grepr/tests/inputs* directory:

```
$ cd 09_grepr/tests/inputs
```

Here are the files that I've included:

- *empty.txt*: an empty file
- *fox.txt*: a file with a single line of text
- *bustle.txt*: a poem by Emily Dickinson with eight lines of text and one blank line
- *nobody.txt*: another poem by the Belle of Amherst with eight lines of text and one blank line

To start, verify for yourself that **grep fox empty.txt** will print nothing when using an empty file. As shown by the usage, grep accepts a regular expression as the first positional argument and optionally some input files for the rest. Note that an empty regular expression will match all lines of input, and here I'll use the input file *fox.txt*, which contains one line of text:

```
$ grep "" fox.txt
The quick brown fox jumps over the lazy dog.
```

In the following Emily Dickinson poem, notice that *Nobody* is always capitalized:

```
$ cat nobody.txt
I'm Nobody! Who are you?
Are you—Nobody—too?
Then there's a pair of us!
Don't tell! they'd advertise—you know!

How dreary—to be—Somebody!
How public—like a Frog—
To tell one's name—the livelong June—
To an admiring Bog!
```

If I search for *Nobody*, the two lines containing the string are printed:

```
$ grep Nobody nobody.txt
I'm Nobody! Who are you?
Are you—Nobody—too?
```

If I search for lowercase *nobody* with **grep nobody nobody.txt**, nothing is printed. I can, however, use -i|--ignore-case to find these lines:

```
$ grep -i nobody nobody.txt
I'm Nobody! Who are you?
Are you—Nobody—too?
```

I can use the -v|--invert-match option to find the lines that don't match the pattern:

```
$ grep -v Nobody nobody.txt
Then there's a pair of us!
Don't tell! they'd advertise—you know!
```

```
How dreary—to be—Somebody!
How public—like a Frog—
To tell one's name—the livelong June—
To an admiring Bog!
```

The -c|--count option will cause the output to be a summary of the number of times a match occurs:

```
$ grep -c Nobody nobody.txt
2
```

I can combine -v and -c to count the lines not matching:

```
$ grep -vc Nobody nobody.txt
7
```

When searching multiple input files, each line of output includes the source filename:

```
$ grep The *.txt
bustle.txt:The bustle in a house
bustle.txt:The morning after death
bustle.txt:The sweeping up the heart,
fox.txt:The quick brown fox jumps over the lazy dog.
nobody.txt:Then there's a pair of us!
```

The filename is also included for the counts:

```
$ grep -c The *.txt
bustle.txt:3
empty.txt:0
fox.txt:1
nobody.txt:1
```

Normally, the positional arguments are files, and the inclusion of a directory such as my *$HOME* directory will cause grep to print a warning:

```
$ grep The bustle.txt $HOME fox.txt
bustle.txt:The bustle in a house
bustle.txt:The morning after death
bustle.txt:The sweeping up the heart,
grep: /Users/kyclark: Is a directory
fox.txt:The quick brown fox jumps over the lazy dog.
```

Directory names are acceptable only when using the -r|--recursive option to find all the files in a directory that contain matching text. In this command, I'll use . to indicate the current working directory:

```
$ grep -r The .
./nobody.txt:Then there's a pair of us!
./bustle.txt:The bustle in a house
./bustle.txt:The morning after death
./bustle.txt:The sweeping up the heart,
./fox.txt:The quick brown fox jumps over the lazy dog.
```

The -r and -i short flags can be combined to perform a recursive, case-insensitive search of one or more directories:

```
$ grep -ri the .
./nobody.txt:Then there's a pair of us!
./nobody.txt:Don't tell! they'd advertise—you know!
./nobody.txt:To tell one's name—the livelong June—
./bustle.txt:The bustle in a house
./bustle.txt:The morning after death
./bustle.txt:The sweeping up the heart,
./fox.txt:The quick brown fox jumps over the lazy dog.
```

Without any positional arguments for inputs, grep will read STDIN:

```
$ cat * | grep -i the
The bustle in a house
The morning after death
The sweeping up the heart,
The quick brown fox jumps over the lazy dog.
Then there's a pair of us!
Don't tell! they'd advertise—you know!
To tell one's name—the livelong June—
```

This is as far as the challenge program is expected to go.

Getting Started

The name of the challenge program should be grepr (pronounced *grep-er*) for a Rust version of grep. Start with **cargo new grepr**, then copy the book's *09_grepr/tests* directory into your new project. Modify your *Cargo.toml* to include the following dependencies:

```
[dependencies]
anyhow = "1.0.79"
clap = { version = "4.5.0", features = ["derive"] }
regex = "1.10.3"
walkdir = "2.4.0"

[dev-dependencies]
assert_cmd = "2.0.13"
predicates = "3.0.4"
pretty_assertions = "1.4.0"
rand = "0.8.5"
sys-info = "0.9.1" ❶
```

❶ The tests use this crate to determine whether they are being run on Windows or not.

You can run **cargo test** to perform an initial build and run the tests, all of which should fail.

Defining the Arguments

To start, I'll update *src/main.rs* to define the Args struct for the program's arguments:

```
#[derive(Debug)]
struct Args {
    pattern: String, ❶
    files: Vec<String>, ❷
    insensitive: bool, ❸
    recursive: bool, ❹
    count: bool, ❺
    invert: bool, ❻
}
```

❶ The pattern is a required string.

❷ The files option is a vector of strings.

❸ The insensitive option is a Boolean for whether or not to match with case sensitivity.

❹ The recursive option is a Boolean for whether or not to recursively search directories.

❺ The count option is a Boolean for whether or not to display a count of the matches.

❻ The invert option is a Boolean for whether or not to find lines that do not match the pattern.

If you want to use the clap derive pattern, then annotate the preceding struct as needed. If you prefer the builder pattern, I suggest you start a get_args function like so:

```
fn get_args() -> Args {
    let matches = Command::new("grepr")
        .version("0.1.0")
        .author("Ken Youens-Clark <kyclark@gmail.com>")
        .about("Rust version of `grep`")
        // What goes here?
        .get_matches();

    Args {
        pattern: ...
        files: ...
        insensitive: ...
        recursive: ...
        count: ...
        invert: ...
```

```
    }
}
```

Update the `main` function to parse and pretty-print the arguments:

```
fn main() {
    let args = Args::parse();
    println!("{args:#?}");
}
```

Your program should produce the following usage:

```
$ cargo run -- -h
Rust version of `grep`

Usage: grepr [OPTIONS] <PATTERN> [FILE]...

Arguments:
  <PATTERN>  Search pattern ❶
  [FILE]...  Input file(s) [default: -] ❷

Options:
  -i, --insensitive   Case-insensitive
  -r, --recursive     Recursive search
  -c, --count         Count occurrences
  -v, --invert-match  Invert match
  -h, --help          Print help
  -V, --version       Print version
```

❶ The search pattern is a required argument.

❷ The input files are optional and default to a dash for STDIN.

Your program should be able to print the arguments like the following when provided a pattern and no input files:

```
$ cargo run -- dog
Args {
    pattern: "dog",
    files: [
        "-",
    ],
    insensitive: false,
    recursive: false,
    count: false,
    invert: false,
}
```

All the Boolean options default to `false`, so ensure they are properly set when the
flags are present:

```
$ cargo run -- dog -ricv tests/inputs/*.txt
Args {
```

```
        pattern: "dog",
        files: [
            "tests/inputs/bustle.txt",
            "tests/inputs/empty.txt",
            "tests/inputs/fox.txt",
            "tests/inputs/nobody.txt",
        ],
        insensitive: true,
        recursive: true,
        count: true,
        invert: true,
}
```

 Take a moment to get your program to this point. It should at least pass **cargo test dies_no_args**.

Following is how I wrote my get_args. Be sure to add use clap::{Arg, ArgAction, Command} for this code:

```
fn get_args() -> Args {
    let matches = Command::new("grepr")
        .version("0.1.0")
        .author("Ken Youens-Clark <kyclark@gmail.com>")
        .about("Rust version of `grep`")
        .arg(
            Arg::new("pattern") ❶
                .value_name("PATTERN")
                .help("Search pattern")
                .required(true),
        )
        .arg(
            Arg::new("files") ❷
                .value_name("FILE")
                .help("Input file(s)")
                .num_args(1..)
                .default_value("-"),
        )
        .arg(
            Arg::new("insensitive") ❸
                .short('i')
                .long("insensitive")
                .help("Case-insensitive")
                .action(ArgAction::SetTrue),
        )
        .arg(
            Arg::new("recursive") ❹
                .short('r')
                .long("recursive")
```

```
                .help("Recursive search")
                .action(ArgAction::SetTrue),
        )
        .arg(
            Arg::new("count") ⑤
                .short('c')
                .long("count")
                .help("Count occurrences")
                .action(ArgAction::SetTrue),
        )
        .arg(
            Arg::new("invert") ⑥
                .short('v')
                .long("invert-match")
                .help("Invert match")
                .action(ArgAction::SetTrue),
        )
        .get_matches();

    Args {
        pattern: matches.get_one("pattern").cloned().unwrap(),
        files: matches.get_many("files").unwrap().cloned().collect(),
        insensitive: matches.get_flag("insensitive"),
        recursive: matches.get_flag("recursive"),
        count: matches.get_flag("count"),
        invert: matches.get_flag("invert"),
    }
}
```

❶ The first positional argument is for the pattern.

❷ The rest of the positional arguments are for the inputs. The default is a dash.

❸ The insensitive flag will handle case-insensitive options.

❹ The recursive flag will handle searching for files in directories.

❺ The count flag will cause the program to print counts.

❻ The invert flag will search for lines not matching the pattern.

> Here, the order in which you declare the positional parameters is important, as the first one defined will be for the first positional argument. You may define the optional arguments before or after the positional parameters.

Following is how I wrote the derive pattern with use `clap::Parser`:

```
#[derive(Debug, Parser)]
#[command(author, version, about)]
/// Rust version of `grep`
struct Args {
    /// Search pattern
    #[arg()]
    pattern: String,

    /// Input file(s)
    #[arg(default_value = "-", value_name = "FILE")]
    files: Vec<String>,

    /// Case-insensitive
    #[arg(short, long)]
    insensitive: bool,

    /// Recursive search
    #[arg(short, long)]
    recursive: bool,

    /// Count occurrences
    #[arg(short, long)]
    count: bool,

    /// Invert match
    #[arg(short('v'), long("invert-match"))]
    invert: bool,
}
```

Next, it's time to have `main` call a `run` function as in previous programs.

```
fn main() {
    if let Err(e) = run(Args::parse()) {
        eprintln!("{e}");
        std::process::exit(1);
    }
}
```

In the run function, I use the arguments to create a regular expression that will incorporate the `insensitive` option. Be sure to use both `regex::RegexBuilder` and `anyhow::{anyhow, Result}` for the following code:

```
fn run(args: Args) -> Result<()> {
    let pattern = RegexBuilder::new(&args.pattern) ❶
        .case_insensitive(args.insensitive) ❷
        .build() ❸
        .map_err(|_| anyhow!(r#"Invalid pattern "{}""#, args.pattern))?; ❹
    println!(r#"pattern "{pattern}""#); ❺
    Ok(())
}
```

❶ The `RegexBuilder::new` method (*https://oreil.ly/Aw1Hk*) will create a new regular expression.

❷ The `RegexBuilder::case_insensitive` method (*https://oreil.ly/bvRkF*) will cause the regex to disregard case in comparisons when the `insensitive` flag is present.

❸ The `RegexBuilder::build` method (*https://oreil.ly/LbZh5*) will compile the regex.

❹ If `build` returns an error, use `Result::map_err` (*https://oreil.ly/4izCX*) to create an error message stating that the given pattern is invalid.

❺ Print the compiled regex.

Your program should reject an invalid regular expression. For instance, `*` signifies *zero or more* of the preceding pattern. By itself, this is incomplete and should cause an error message, which also means your program should also pass **cargo test dies_bad_pattern**:

```
$ cargo run -- \*
Invalid pattern "*"
```

Run the program with a pattern to ensure it prints something reasonable:

```
$ cargo run -- fox
pattern "fox"
```

 Printing a regular expression means calling the `Regex::as_str` method (*https://oreil.ly/SrNIX*). `RegexBuilder::build` (*https://oreil.ly/82KDm*) notes that this "will produce the pattern given to new verbatim. Notably, it will not incorporate any of the flags set on this builder," which includes the case-insensitive option.

`RegexBuilder::build` will reject any pattern that is not a valid regular expression, and this raises an interesting point. There are many syntaxes for writing regular expressions. If you look closely at the manual page for `grep`, you'll notice these options:

```
-E, --extended-regexp
        Interpret pattern as an extended regular expression (i.e. force
        grep to behave as egrep).

-e pattern, --regexp=pattern
        Specify a pattern used during the search of the input: an input
        line is selected if it matches any of the specified patterns.
        This option is most useful when multiple -e options are used to
```

specify multiple patterns, or when a pattern begins with a dash
('-').

The converse of these options is:

```
-G, --basic-regexp
        Interpret pattern as a basic regular expression (i.e. force grep
        to behave as traditional grep).
```

Regular expressions have been around since the 1950s when they were invented by the American mathematician Stephen Cole Kleene.[2] Since that time, the syntax has been modified and expanded by various groups, perhaps most notably by the Perl community, which created Perl Compatible Regular Expressions (PCRE). By default, grep will parse only basic regexes, but the preceding flags can allow it to use other varieties. For instance, I can use the pattern ee to search for any lines containing two adjacent *e*s. Note that I have added the bold style in the following output to help you see the pattern that was found:

```
$ grep 'ee' tests/inputs/*
tests/inputs/bustle.txt:The sw**ee**ping up the heart,
```

If I want to find any character that is repeated twice, the pattern is (.)\1, where the dot (.) represents any character, and the capturing parentheses allow me to use the backreference \1 to refer to the first capture group. This is an example of an extended expression and so requires the -E flag:

```
$ grep -E '(.)\1' tests/inputs/*
tests/inputs/bustle.txt:The sw**ee**ping up the heart,
tests/inputs/bustle.txt:And pu**tt**ing love away
tests/inputs/bustle.txt:We sha**ll** not want to use again
tests/inputs/nobody.txt:Are you—Nobody—**too**?
tests/inputs/nobody.txt:Don't te**ll**! they'd advertise—you know!
tests/inputs/nobody.txt:To te**ll** one's name—the livelong June—
```

The Rust regex crate's documentation (*https://oreil.ly/qCN0o*) notes that the "regex syntax supported by this crate is similar to other regex engines, but it lacks several features that are not known how to implement efficiently. This includes, but is not limited to, look-around and backreferences." (*Look-around* assertions allow the expression to assert that a pattern must be followed or preceded by another pattern, and *backreferences* allow the pattern to refer to previously captured values.) This means that the challenge program will work more like egrep in handling extended regular expressions by default. Sadly, this also means that the program will not be able to handle the preceding pattern because it requires backreferences. It will still be a wicked cool program to write, though, so let's keep going.

---

2 If you would like to learn more about regexes, I recommend *Mastering Regular Expressions*, 3rd ed., by Jeffrey E. F. Friedl (O'Reilly).

Finding the Files to Search

Next, I need to find all the files to search. Recall that the user might provide directory names with the --recursive option to search for all the files contained in each directory; otherwise, directory names should result in a warning printed to STDERR. I decided to write a function called find_files that will accept a vector of strings that may be file or directory names along with a Boolean for whether or not to recurse into directories. It returns a vector of Result values that will hold a string that is the name of a valid file or an error message. You can start your version with the following skeleton:

```
fn find_files(paths: &[String], recursive: bool) -> Vec<Result<String>> {
    unimplemented!();
}
```

To test this, I can add a tests module to *src/main.rs*. Note that this will use the rand crate that should be listed in the [dev-dependencies] section of your *Cargo.toml*, as noted earlier in the chapter:

```
#[cfg(test)]
mod tests {
    use super::find_files;
    use rand::{distributions::Alphanumeric, Rng};

    #[test]
    fn test_find_files() {
        // Verify that the function finds a file known to exist
        let files =
            find_files(&["./tests/inputs/fox.txt".to_string()], false);
        assert_eq!(files.len(), 1);
        assert_eq!(files[0].as_ref().unwrap(), "./tests/inputs/fox.txt");

        // The function should reject a directory without the recursive option
        let files = find_files(&["./tests/inputs".to_string()], false);
        assert_eq!(files.len(), 1);
        if let Err(e) = &files[0] {
            assert_eq!(e.to_string(), "./tests/inputs is a directory");
        }

        // Verify the function recurses to find four files in the directory
        let res = find_files(&["./tests/inputs".to_string()], true);
        let mut files: Vec<String> = res
            .iter()
            .map(|r| r.as_ref().unwrap().replace("\\", "/"))
            .collect();
        files.sort();
        assert_eq!(files.len(), 4);
        assert_eq!(
            files,
            vec![
                "./tests/inputs/bustle.txt",
```

```
            "./tests/inputs/empty.txt",
            "./tests/inputs/fox.txt",
            "./tests/inputs/nobody.txt",
        ]
    );

    // Generate a random string to represent a nonexistent file
    let bad: String = rand::thread_rng()
        .sample_iter(&Alphanumeric)
        .take(7)
        .map(char::from)
        .collect();

    // Verify that the function returns the bad file as an error
    let files = find_files(&[bad], false);
    assert_eq!(files.len(), 1);
    assert!(files[0].is_err());
    }
}
```

 Stop reading and write the code to pass **cargo test test_find_files**.

Here is how I can use find_files in my code:

```
fn run(args: Args) -> Result<()> {
    let pattern = RegexBuilder::new(&args.pattern)
        .case_insensitive(args.insensitive)
        .build()
        .map_err(|_| anyhow!(r#"Invalid pattern "{}""#, args.pattern))?;
    println!(r#"pattern "{pattern}""#);

    let entries = find_files(&args.files, args.recursive);
    for entry in entries {
        match entry {
            Err(e) => eprintln!("{e}"),
            Ok(filename) => println!(r#"file "{filename}""#),
        }
    }

    Ok(())
}
```

My solution uses WalkDir (*https://oreil.ly/oVQEG*), which I introduced in Chapter 7. See if you can get your program to reproduce the following output. To start, the default input should be a dash (-), to represent reading from STDIN:

```
$ cargo run -- fox
pattern "fox"
file "-"
```

Explicitly listing a dash as the input should produce the same output:

```
$ cargo run -- fox -
pattern "fox"
file "-"
```

The program should handle multiple input files:

```
$ cargo run -- fox tests/inputs/*
pattern "fox"
file "tests/inputs/bustle.txt"
file "tests/inputs/empty.txt"
file "tests/inputs/fox.txt"
file "tests/inputs/nobody.txt"
```

A directory name without the `--recursive` option should be rejected:

```
$ cargo run -- fox tests/inputs
pattern "fox"
tests/inputs is a directory
```

With the `--recursive` flag, it should find the directory's files:

```
$ cargo run -- -r fox tests/inputs
pattern "fox"
file "tests/inputs/empty.txt"
file "tests/inputs/nobody.txt"
file "tests/inputs/bustle.txt"
file "tests/inputs/fox.txt"
```

Invalid file arguments should be printed to STDERR in the course of handling each entry. In the following example, *blargh* represents a nonexistent file:

```
$ cargo run -- -r fox blargh tests/inputs/fox.txt
pattern "fox"
blargh: No such file or directory (os error 2)
file "tests/inputs/fox.txt"
```

Finding the Matching Lines of Input

Now it's time for your program to open the files and search for matching lines. I suggest you again use the open function and necessary imports from earlier chapters, which will open and read either an existing file or STDIN for a filename that equals a dash (-):

```
fn open(filename: &str) -> Result<Box<dyn BufRead>> {
    match filename {
        "-" => Ok(Box::new(BufReader::new(io::stdin()))),
        _ => Ok(Box::new(BufReader::new(File::open(filename)?))),
```

```
        }
    }
```

When reading the lines, be sure to preserve the line endings as one of the input files contains Windows-style CRLF endings. My solution uses a function called find_lines, which you can start with the following skeleton. Be sure to add use regex::Regex to your imports:

```
fn find_lines<T: BufRead>(
    mut file: T, ❶
    pattern: &Regex, ❷
    invert: bool, ❸
) -> Result<Vec<String>> {
    unimplemented!();
}
```

❶ The file option must implement the std::io::BufRead trait (*https://oreil.ly/c5fGP*).

❷ The pattern argument is a reference to a compiled regular expression.

❸ The invert argument is a Boolean for whether to reverse the match operation.

 In the wcr program from Chapter 5, I used impl BufRead to indicate a value that must implement the BufRead trait. In the preceding code, I'm using <T: BufRead> to indicate the trait bound for the type T. They both accomplish the same thing, but I wanted to show another common way to write this.

To test this function, I expanded my tests module by adding the following test_find_lines function, which again uses std::io::Cursor to create a fake filehandle that implements BufRead for testing:

```
#[cfg(test)]
mod test {
    use super::{find_files, find_lines};
    use rand::{distributions::Alphanumeric, Rng};
    use regex::{Regex, RegexBuilder};
    use std::io::Cursor;

    #[test]
    fn test_find_files() {} // Same as before

    #[test]
    fn test_find_lines() {
        let text = b"Lorem\nIpsum\r\nDOLOR";

        // The pattern _or_ should match the one line, "Lorem"
```

```rust
        let re1 = Regex::new("or").unwrap();
        let matches = find_lines(Cursor::new(&text), &re1, false);
        assert!(matches.is_ok());
        assert_eq!(matches.unwrap().len(), 1);

        // When inverted, the function should match the other two lines
        let matches = find_lines(Cursor::new(&text), &re1, true);
        assert!(matches.is_ok());
        assert_eq!(matches.unwrap().len(), 2);

        // This regex will be case-insensitive
        let re2 = RegexBuilder::new("or")
            .case_insensitive(true)
            .build()
            .unwrap();

        // The two lines "Lorem" and "DOLOR" should match
        let matches = find_lines(Cursor::new(&text), &re2, false);
        assert!(matches.is_ok());
        assert_eq!(matches.unwrap().len(), 2);

        // When inverted, the one remaining line should match
        let matches = find_lines(Cursor::new(&text), &re2, true);
        assert!(matches.is_ok());
        assert_eq!(matches.unwrap().len(), 1);
    }
}
```

 Stop reading and write the function that will pass **cargo test test_find_lines**.

Next, I suggest you incorporate these ideas into your run:

```rust
fn run(args: Args) -> Result<()> {
    let pattern = RegexBuilder::new(&args.pattern)
        .case_insensitive(args.insensitive)
        .build()
        .map_err(|_| anyhow!(r#"Invalid pattern "{}""#, args.pattern))?;

    let entries = find_files(&args.files, args.recursive); ❶
    for entry in entries {
        match entry {
            Err(e) => eprintln!("{e}"), ❷
            Ok(filename) => match open(&filename) { ❸
                Err(e) => eprintln!("{filename}: {e}"), ❹
                Ok(file) => {
                    let matches = find_lines(file, &pattern, args.invert); ❺
                    println!("Found {matches:?}");
```

```
                    }
                },
            }
        }

        Ok(())
    }
```

❶ Look for the input files.

❷ Handle the errors from finding input files.

❸ Try to open a valid filename.

❹ Handle errors opening a file.

❺ Use the open filehandle to find the lines matching (or not matching) the regex.

At this point, the program should show the following output:

```
$ cargo run -- -r fox tests/inputs/*
Found Ok([])
Found Ok([])
Found Ok(["The quick brown fox jumps over the lazy dog.\n"])
Found Ok([])
```

Modify this version to meet the criteria for the program. Start as simply as possible, perhaps by using an empty regular expression that should match all the lines from the input:

```
$ cargo run -- "" tests/inputs/fox.txt
The quick brown fox jumps over the lazy dog.
```

Be sure you are reading STDIN by default:

```
$ cargo run -- "" < tests/inputs/fox.txt
The quick brown fox jumps over the lazy dog.
```

Run with several input files and a case-sensitive pattern:

```
$ cargo run -- The tests/inputs/*
tests/inputs/bustle.txt:The bustle in a house
tests/inputs/bustle.txt:The morning after death
tests/inputs/bustle.txt:The sweeping up the heart,
tests/inputs/fox.txt:The quick brown fox jumps over the lazy dog.
tests/inputs/nobody.txt:Then there's a pair of us!
```

Then try to print the number of matches instead of the lines:

```
$ cargo run -- --count The tests/inputs/*
tests/inputs/bustle.txt:3
tests/inputs/empty.txt:0
tests/inputs/fox.txt:1
tests/inputs/nobody.txt:1
```

Incorporate the --insensitive option:

```
$ cargo run -- --count --insensitive The tests/inputs/*
tests/inputs/bustle.txt:3
tests/inputs/empty.txt:0
tests/inputs/fox.txt:1
tests/inputs/nobody.txt:3
```

Next, try to invert the matching:

```
$ cargo run -- --count --invert-match The tests/inputs/*
tests/inputs/bustle.txt:6
tests/inputs/empty.txt:0
tests/inputs/fox.txt:0
tests/inputs/nobody.txt:8
```

Be sure your --recursive option works:

```
$ cargo run -- -icr the tests/inputs
tests/inputs/empty.txt:0
tests/inputs/nobody.txt:3
tests/inputs/bustle.txt:3
tests/inputs/fox.txt:1
```

Handle errors such as the nonexistent file *blargh* while processing the files in order:

```
$ cargo run -- fox blargh tests/inputs/fox.txt
blargh: No such file or directory (os error 2)
tests/inputs/fox.txt:The quick brown fox jumps over the lazy dog.
```

Another potential problem you should gracefully handle is failure to open a file, perhaps due to insufficient permissions:

```
$ touch hammer && chmod 000 hammer
$ cargo run -- fox hammer tests/inputs/fox.txt
hammer: Permission denied (os error 13)
tests/inputs/fox.txt:The quick brown fox jumps over the lazy dog.
```

 It's go time. These challenges are getting harder, so it's OK to feel a bit overwhelmed by the requirements. Tackle each task in order, and keep running **cargo test** to see how many you're able to pass. When you get stuck, run grep with the arguments from the test and closely examine the output. Then run your program with the same arguments and try to find the differences.

Solution

I will always stress that your solution can be written however you like as long as it passes the provided test suite. In the following find_files function, I choose to use the imperative approach of manually pushing to a vector rather than collecting from an iterator. The function will either collect a single error for a bad path or flatten the iterable WalkDir to recursively get the files. Be sure you add use std::fs and use walkdir::WalkDir for this code:

```
fn find_files(paths: &[String], recursive: bool) -> Vec<Result<String>> {
    let mut results = vec![]; ❶

    for path in paths { ❷
        match path.as_str() {
            "-" => results.push(Ok(path.to_string())), ❸
            _ => match fs::metadata(path) { ❹
                Ok(metadata) => {
                    if metadata.is_dir() { ❺
                        if recursive { ❻
                            for entry in WalkDir::new(path) ❼
                                .into_iter()
                                .flatten() ❽
                                .filter(|e| e.file_type().is_file())
                            {
                                results.push(Ok(entry
                                    .path()
                                    .display()
                                    .to_string()));
                            }
                        } else {
                            results ❾
                                .push(Err(anyhow!("{path} is a directory")));
                        }
                    } else if metadata.is_file() { ❿
                        results.push(Ok(path.to_string()));
                    }
                }
                Err(e) => { ⓫
                    Err(e) => results.push(Err(anyhow!("{path}: {e}"))),
                }
            },
        }
    }

    results
}
```

❶ Initialize an empty vector to hold the results.

❷ Iterate over each of the given paths.

❸ First, accept a dash (-) as a path, for STDIN.

❹ Try to get the path's metadata.

❺ Check if the path is a directory.

❻ Check if the user wants to recursively search directories.

❼ Add all the files in the given directory to the results.

❽ Iterator::flatten (*https://oreil.ly/RzXDz*) will take the Ok or Some variants for Result and Option types and will ignore the Err and None variants, meaning it will ignore any errors with files found by recursing through directories.

❾ Note an error that the given entry is a directory.

❿ If the path is a file, add it to the results.

⓫ This arm will be triggered by nonexistent files.

Next, I will share my find_lines function. The following code requires that you add use std::mem to your imports. This borrows heavily from previous functions that read files line by line, so I won't comment on code I've used before:

```
fn find_lines<T: BufRead>(
    mut file: T,
    pattern: &Regex,
    invert: bool,
) -> Result<Vec<String>> {
    let mut matches = vec![];         ❶
    let mut line = String::new();

    loop {
        let bytes = file.read_line(&mut line)?;
        if bytes == 0 {
            break;
        }
        if pattern.is_match(&line) ^ invert {     ❷
            matches.push(mem::take(&mut line));   ❸
        }
        line.clear();
    }

    Ok(matches)
}
```

❶ Initialize a mutable vector to hold the matching lines.

❷ Use the `BitXor` *bit-wise exclusive OR* (*https://oreil.ly/fwIFt*) operator (^) to determine if the line should be included.

❸ Use `std::mem::take` (*https://oreil.ly/bKZz9*) to take ownership of the line. I could
have used `clone` (*https://oreil.ly/NkRmp*) to copy the string and add it to the
`matches`, but `take` avoids an unnecessary copy.

In the preceding function, the bitwise *XOR* comparison (^) could also be expressed
using a combination of the logical *AND* (&&) and *OR* operators (||) like so:

```
if (pattern.is_match(&line) && !invert) ❶
    || (!pattern.is_match(&line) && invert) ❷
{
    matches.push(line.clone());
}
```

❶ Verify that the line matches and the user does not want to invert the match.

❷ Alternatively, check if the line does not match and the user wants to invert the
match.

At the beginning of the `run` function, I decided to create a closure to handle the printing of the output with or without the filenames given the number of input files:

```
fn run(args: Args) -> Result<()> {
    let pattern = RegexBuilder::new(&args.pattern)
        .case_insensitive(args.insensitive)
        .build()
        .map_err(|_| anyhow!(r#"Invalid pattern "{}""#, args.pattern))?;

    let entries = find_files(&args.files, args.recursive); ❶
    let num_files = entries.len(); ❷
    let print = |fname: &str, val: &str| { ❸
        if num_files > 1 {
            print!("{fname}:{val}");
        } else {
            print!("{val}");
        }
    };
```

❶ Find all the inputs.

❷ Find the number of inputs.

❸ Create a `print` closure that uses the number of inputs to decide whether to print
the filenames in the output.

Continuing from there, the program attempts to find the matching lines from the
entries:

```
    for entry in entries {
        match entry {
            Err(e) => eprintln!("{e}"), ❶
            Ok(filename) => match open(&filename) { ❷
                Err(e) => eprintln!("{filename}: {e}"), ❸
                Ok(file) => match find_lines(file, &pattern, args.invert) { ❹
                    Err(e) => eprintln!("{e}"), ❺
                    Ok(matches) => {
                        if args.count { ❻
                            print(&filename, &format!("{}\n", matches.len()));
                        } else {
                            for line in &matches {
                                print(&filename, line);
                            }
                        }
                    }
                },
            },
        }
    }
    Ok(())
}
```

❶ Print errors like nonexistent files to STDERR.

❷ Attempt to open a file. This might fail due to permissions.

❸ Print an error to STDERR.

❹ Attempt to find the matching lines of text.

❺ Print errors to STDERR.

❻ Decide whether to print the number of matches or the matches themselves.

At this point, the program should pass all the tests.

Going Further

The Rust ripgrep tool (*https://oreil.ly/oqlzw*) implements many of the features of grep and is worthy of your study. You can install the program using the instructions provided and then execute rg. As shown in Figure 9-1, the matching text is highlighted in the output. Try to add that feature to your program using Regex::find (*https://oreil.ly/MzvvZ*) to find the start and stop positions of the matching pattern and something like termcolor (*https://oreil.ly/QRuAE*) to highlight the matches.

```
$ rg The tests/inputs
tests/inputs/nobody.txt
3:Then there's a pair of us!

tests/inputs/bustle.txt
1:The bustle in a house
2:The morning after death
6:The sweeping up the heart,

tests/inputs/fox.txt
1:The quick brown fox jumps over the lazy dog.
```

Figure 9-1. The ripgrep tool will highlight the matching text.

The author of ripgrep wrote an extensive blog post (*https://oreil.ly/JfnB8*) about design decisions that went into writing the program. In the section "Repeat After Me: Thou Shalt Not Search Line by Line," the author discusses the performance hit of searching over lines of text, the majority of which will not match.

Summary

This chapter challenged you to extend skills you learned in Chapter 7, such as recursively finding files in directories and using regular expressions. In this chapter, you combined those skills to find content inside files matching (or not matching) a given regex. In addition, you learned the following:

- How to use RegexBuilder to create more complicated regular expressions using, for instance, the case-insensitive option to match strings regardless of case.

- There are multiple syntaxes for writing regular expressions that different tools recognize, such as PCRE. Rust's regex engine does not implement some features of PCRE, such as look-around assertions or backreferences.

- You can indicate a trait bound like BufRead in function signatures using either impl BufRead or <T: BufRead>.

- Rust's bitwise *XOR* operator can replace more complex logical operations that combine *AND* and *OR* comparisons.

In the next chapter, you'll learn more about iterating the lines of a file, how to compare strings, and how to create a more complicated enum type.

CHAPTER 10

Boston Commons

Never looked at you before with / Common sense
— They Might Be Giants, "Circular Karate Chop" (2013)

In this chapter, you will write a Rust version of the comm (*common*) utility, which will read two files and report the lines of text that are common to both and the lines that are unique to each. These are set operations where the common lines are the *intersection* of the two files and the unique lines are the *difference*. If you are familiar with databases, you might also consider these as types of *join* operations.

You will learn how to:

- Manually iterate the lines of a filehandle using Iterator::next
- match on combinations of possibilities using a tuple
- Use std::cmp::Ordering when comparing strings

How comm Works

To show you what will be expected of your program, I'll start by reviewing part of the manual page for the BSD comm to see how the tool works:

```
COMM(1)                    BSD General Commands Manual                    COMM(1)

NAME
     comm -- select or reject lines common to two files

SYNOPSIS
     comm [-123i] file1 file2
```

DESCRIPTION
The comm utility reads file1 and file2, which should be sorted lexically, and produces three text columns as output: lines only in file1; lines only in file2; and lines in both files.

The filename ''-'' means the standard input.

The following options are available:

-1   Suppress printing of column 1.

-2   Suppress printing of column 2.

-3   Suppress printing of column 3.

-i   Case insensitive comparison of lines.

Each column will have a number of tab characters prepended to it equal to the number of lower numbered columns that are being printed. For example, if column number two is being suppressed, lines printed in column number one will not have any tabs preceding them, and lines printed in column number three will have one.

The comm utility assumes that the files are lexically sorted; all characters participate in line comparisons.

The GNU version has some additional options but lacks a case-insensitive option:

```
$ comm --help
Usage: comm [OPTION]... FILE1 FILE2
Compare sorted files FILE1 and FILE2 line by line.

When FILE1 or FILE2 (not both) is -, read standard input.

With no options, produce three-column output.  Column one contains
lines unique to FILE1, column two contains lines unique to FILE2,
and column three contains lines common to both files.

  -1              suppress column 1 (lines unique to FILE1)
  -2              suppress column 2 (lines unique to FILE2)
  -3              suppress column 3 (lines that appear in both files)

  --check-order    check that the input is correctly sorted, even
                     if all input lines are pairable
  --nocheck-order  do not check that the input is correctly sorted
  --output-delimiter=STR  separate columns with STR
  --total          output a summary
  -z, --zero-terminated   line delimiter is NUL, not newline
      --help       display this help and exit
      --version  output version information and exit

Note, comparisons honor the rules specified by 'LC_COLLATE'.
```

```
Examples:
  comm -12 file1 file2  Print only lines present in both file1 and file2.
  comm -3 file1 file2  Print lines in file1 not in file2, and vice versa.
```

At this point, you may be wondering exactly why you'd use this. Suppose you have a file containing a list of cities where your favorite band played on their last tour:

```
$ cd 10_commr/tests/inputs/
$ cat cities1.txt
Jackson
Denton
Cincinnati
Boston
Santa Fe
Tucson
```

Another file lists the cities on their current tour:

```
$ cat cities2.txt
San Francisco
Denver
Ypsilanti
Denton
Cincinnati
Boston
```

You can use comm to find which cities occur in both sets by suppressing columns 1 (the lines unique to the first file) and 2 (the lines unique to the second file) and only showing column 3 (the lines common to both files). This is like an *inner join* in SQL, where only data that occurs in both inputs is shown. Note that both files need to be sorted first:

```
$ comm -12 <(sort cities1.txt) <(sort cities2.txt)
Boston
Cincinnati
Denton
```

If you wanted the cities the band played only on the first tour, you could suppress columns 2 and 3:

```
$ comm -23 <(sort cities1.txt) <(sort cities2.txt)
Jackson
Santa Fe
Tucson
```

Finally, if you wanted the cities they played only on the second tour, you could suppress columns 1 and 3:

```
$ comm -13 <(sort cities1.txt) <(sort cities2.txt)
Denver
San Francisco
Ypsilanti
```

The first or second file can be STDIN, as denoted by a filename consisting of a dash (-):

```
$ sort cities2.txt | comm -12 <(sort cities1.txt) -
Boston
Cincinnati
Denton
```

As with the GNU comm, only one of the inputs may be a dash with the challenge program. Note that BSD comm can perform case-insensitive comparisons when the -i flag is present. For instance, I can put the first tour cities in lowercase:

```
$ cat cities1_lower.txt
jackson
denton
cincinnati
boston
santa fe
tucson
```

and the second tour cities in uppercase:

```
$ cat cities2_upper.txt
SAN FRANCISCO
DENVER
YPSILANTI
DENTON
CINCINNATI
BOSTON
```

Then I can use the -i flag to find the cities in common:

```
$ comm -i -12 <(sort cities1_lower.txt) <(sort cities2_upper.txt)
boston
cincinnati
denton
```

 I know the tour cities example is a trivial one, so I'll give you another example drawn from my experience in bioinformatics, which is the intersection of computer science and biology. Given a file of protein sequences, I can run an analysis that will group similar sequences into clusters. I can then use comm to compare the clustered proteins to the original list and find the proteins that failed to cluster. There may be something unique to these unclustered proteins that bears further analysis.

This is as much as the challenge program is expected to implement. One change from the BSD version is that I use the GNU version's optional output column delimiter that defaults to a tab character, which is the normal output from comm.

Getting Started

The program in this chapter will be called commr (pronounced *comm-er*, which is basically how the British pronounce the word *comma*) for a Rust version of comm. I suggest you use **cargo new commr** to start, then add the following dependencies to your *Cargo.toml* file:

```
[dependencies]
anyhow = "1.0.79"
clap = { version = "4.5.0", features = ["derive"] }

[dev-dependencies]
assert_cmd = "2.0.13"
predicates = "3.0.4"
pretty_assertions = "1.4.0"
rand = "0.8.5"
```

Copy my *10_commr/tests* directory into your project, and then run **cargo test** to run the tests, which should all fail.

Defining the Arguments

No surprises here, but I suggest you start by defining an Args struct:

```
#[derive(Debug)]
pub struct Args {
    file1: String,    ❶
    file2: String,    ❷
    show_col1: bool,  ❸
    show_col2: bool,  ❹
    show_col3: bool,  ❺
    insensitive: bool, ❻
    delimiter: String, ❼
}
```

❶ The first input filename is a String.

❷ The second input filename is a String.

❸ A Boolean for whether or not to show the first column of output.

❹ A Boolean for whether or not to show the second column of output.

❺ A Boolean for whether or not to show the third column of output.

❻ A Boolean for whether or not to perform case-insensitive comparisons.

❼ The output column delimiter, which will default to a tab.

Normally I give my Args fields the same names as the arguments, but I don't like the negative *suppress* verb, preferring instead the positive *show*. I feel this leads to more readable code, as I will demonstrate later.

Either annotate the preceding for the clap derive pattern or fill in the missing parts of the following code to begin your get_args function:

```
fn get_args() -> Args {
    let matches = Command::new("commr")
        .version("0.1.0")
        .author("Ken Youens-Clark <kyclark@gmail.com>")
        .about("Rust version of `comm`")
        // What goes here?
        .get_matches();

    Args {
        file1: ...
        file2: ...
        show_col1: ...
        show_col2: ...
        show_col3: ...
        insensitive: ...
        delimiter: ...
    }
}
```

Start your main function by pretty-printing the arguments:

```
fn main() {
    let args = get_args();
    println!("{:#?}", args);
}
```

Your program should be able to produce the following usage:

```
$ cargo run -- -h
Rust version of `comm`

Usage: commr [OPTIONS] <FILE1> <FILE2>

Arguments:
  <FILE1>  Input file 1
  <FILE2>  Input file 2

Options:
  -1                             Suppress printing of column 1
  -2                             Suppress printing of column 2
  -3                             Suppress printing of column 3
  -i                             Case-insensitive comparison of lines
  -d, --output-delimiter <DELIM>  Output delimiter [default: "\t"]
```

```
    -h, --help                      Print help
    -V, --version                   Print version
```

If you run your program with no arguments, it should fail with a message that the two file arguments are required:

```
$ cargo run
error: the following required arguments were not provided:
  <FILE1>
  <FILE2>

Usage: commr <FILE1> <FILE2>

For more information, try '--help'.
```

If you supply two positional arguments, you should get the following output:

```
$ cargo run -- tests/inputs/file1.txt tests/inputs/file2.txt
Args {
    file1: "tests/inputs/file1.txt", ❶
    file2: "tests/inputs/file2.txt",
    show_col1: true, ❷
    show_col2: true,
    show_col3: true,
    insensitive: false,
    delimiter: "\t",
}
```

❶ The two positional arguments are parsed into file1 and file2.

❷ All the rest of the values use defaults, which are true for the Booleans and the tab character for the output delimiter.

Verify that you can set all the other arguments as well:

```
$ cargo run -- tests/inputs/file1.txt tests/inputs/file2.txt -123 -d , -i
Args {
    file1: "tests/inputs/file1.txt",
    file2: "tests/inputs/file2.txt",
    show_col1: false, ❶
    show_col2: false,
    show_col3: false,
    insensitive: true, ❷
    delimiter: ",", ❸
}
```

❶ The -123 sets each of the *show* values to false.

❷ The -i sets insensitive to true.

❸ The -d option sets the output delimiter to a comma (,).

Stop reading and make your program match the preceding output.

Following is how I defined the arguments in my `get_args` and requires you add `use clap::{Arg, ArgAction, Command}`. I don't have much to comment on here since it's so similar to previous programs:

```
fn get_args() -> Args {
    let matches = Command::new("commr")
        .version("0.1.0")
        .author("Ken Youens-Clark <kyclark@gmail.com>")
        .about("Rust version of `comm`")
        .arg(
            Arg::new("file1")
                .value_name("FILE1")
                .help("Input file 1")
                .required(true),
        )
        .arg(
            Arg::new("file2")
                .value_name("FILE2")
                .help("Input file 2")
                .required(true),
        )
        .arg(
            Arg::new("suppress_col1")
                .short('1')
                .action(ArgAction::SetTrue)
                .help("Suppress printing of column 1"),
        )
        .arg(
            Arg::new("suppress_col2")
                .short('2')
                .action(ArgAction::SetTrue)
                .help("Suppress printing of column 2"),
        )
        .arg(
            Arg::new("suppress_col3")
                .short('3')
                .action(ArgAction::SetTrue)
                .help("Suppress printing of column 3"),
        )
        .arg(
            Arg::new("insensitive")
                .short('i')
                .action(ArgAction::SetTrue)
                .help("Case-insensitive comparison of lines"),
        )
        .arg(
```

```
        Arg::new("delimiter")
            .short('d')
            .long("output-delimiter")
            .value_name("DELIM")
            .help("Output delimiter")
            .default_value("\t"),
    )
    .get_matches();

Args {
    file1: matches.get_one("file1").cloned().unwrap(),
    file2: matches.get_one("file2").cloned().unwrap(),
    show_col1: !matches.get_flag("suppress_col1"),
    show_col2: !matches.get_flag("suppress_col2"),
    show_col3: !matches.get_flag("suppress_col3"),
    insensitive: matches.get_flag("insensitive"),
    delimiter: matches.get_one("delimiter").cloned().unwrap(),
}
}
```

For the derive pattern, add use clap::{ArgAction, Parser} and annotate the Args.
Note that I use ArgAction::SetFalse to invert the meaning of the flag from *suppress*
to *show* in the following code:

```
#[derive(Debug, Parser)]
#[command(author, version, about)]
/// Rust version of `comm`
struct Args {
    /// Input file 1
    #[arg()]
    file1: String,

    /// Input file 2
    #[arg()]
    file2: String,

    /// Suppress printing of column 1
    #[arg(short('1'), action(ArgAction::SetFalse))]
    show_col1: bool,

    /// Suppress printing of column 2
    #[arg(short('2'), action(ArgAction::SetFalse))]
    show_col2: bool,

    /// Suppress printing of column 3
    #[arg(short('3'), action(ArgAction::SetFalse))]
    show_col3: bool,

    /// Case-insensitive comparison of lines
    #[arg(short)]
    insensitive: bool,
```

```
/// Output delimiter
#[arg(short, long("output-delimiter"), default_value = "\t")]
delimiter: String,
}
```

Validating and Opening the Input Files

It's time to change the main function to call a run:

```
fn main() {
    if let Err(e) = run(Args::parse()) {
        eprintln!("{e}");
        std::process::exit(1);
    }
}
```

The next step is checking and opening the input files. I suggest a modification to the open function used in several previous chapters as follows:

```
fn open(filename: &str) -> Result<Box<dyn BufRead>> {
    match filename {
        "-" => Ok(Box::new(BufReader::new(io::stdin()))),
        _ => Ok(Box::new(BufReader::new(
            File::open(filename).map_err(|e| anyhow!("{filename}: {e}"))?,  ❶
        ))),
    }
}
```

❶ Incorporate the filename into the error message.

This will require you to expand your imports with the following:

```
use anyhow::{anyhow, Result};
use std::{
    fs::File,
    io::{self, BufRead, BufReader},
};
```

As noted earlier, only one of the inputs is allowed to be a dash, for STDIN. You can use the following code for your run that will check the filenames and then open the files. Be sure to add use anyhow::bail to your imports:

```
fn run(args: Args) -> Result<()> {
    let file1 = &args.file1;
    let file2 = &args.file2;

    if file1 == "-" && file2 == "-" {  ❶
        bail!(r#"Both input files cannot be STDIN ("-")"#);
    }

    let _fh1 = open(file1)?;  ❷
    let _fh2 = open(file2)?;
    println!(r#"Opened "{file1}" and "{file2}""#);  ❸
```

```
        Ok(())
    }
```

❶ Check that both of the filenames are not a dash (-).

❷ Attempt to open the two input files.

❸ Print a message so you know what happened.

Your program should reject two STDIN arguments:

```
$ cargo run -- - -
Both input files cannot be STDIN ("-")
```

It should be able to print the following for two good input files:

```
$ cargo run -- tests/inputs/file1.txt tests/inputs/file2.txt
Opened "tests/inputs/file1.txt" and "tests/inputs/file2.txt"
```

It should reject a bad file for either argument, such as the nonexistent *blargh*:

```
$ cargo run -- tests/inputs/file1.txt blargh
blargh: No such file or directory (os error 2)
```

At this point, your program should pass all the tests for **cargo test dies** that check for missing or bad input arguments:

```
running 4 tests
test dies_both_stdin ... ok
test dies_no_args ... ok
test dies_bad_file1 ... ok
test dies_bad_file2 ... ok
```

Processing the Files

Your program can now validate all the arguments and open the input files, either of which may be STDIN. Next, you need to iterate over the lines from each file to compare them. The files in *10_commr/tests/inputs* that are used in the tests are:

- *empty.txt*: an empty file
- *blank.txt*: a file with one blank line
- *file1.txt*: a file with four lines of text
- *file2.txt*: a file with two lines of text

You may use BufRead::lines (*https://oreil.ly/KhmCp*) to read files as it is not necessary to preserve line endings. Start simply, perhaps using the *empty.txt* file and *file1.txt*. Try to get your program to reproduce the following output from comm:

```
$ cd tests/inputs/
$ comm file1.txt empty.txt
a
b
c
d
```

Then reverse the argument order and ensure that you get the same output, but now in column 2, like this:

```
$ comm empty.txt file1.txt
        a
        b
        c
        d
```

Next, look at the output from the BSD version of comm using *file1.txt* and *file2.txt*. The order of the lines shown in the following command is the expected output for the challenge program:

```
$ comm file1.txt file2.txt
        B
a
b
                c
d
```

The GNU comm uses a different ordering for which lines to show first when they are not equal. Note that the line *B* is shown after *b*:

```
$ comm file1.txt file2.txt
a
b
        B
                c
d
```

Next, consider how you will handle the *blank.txt* file that contains a single blank line. In the following output, notice that the blank line is shown first, then the two lines from *file2.txt*:

```
$ comm tests/inputs/blank.txt tests/inputs/file2.txt

        B
        c
```

I suggest you start by trying to read a line from each file. The documentation for BufRead::lines notes that it will return a None when it reaches the end of the file. Start with the empty file as one of the arguments to force your code to deal with having an uneven number of lines, where you will have to advance one of the filehandles while the other stays the same. When you use two nonempty files, you'll have to consider how to read each of the files independently until you have matching lines.

Stop here and finish your program using the test suite to guide you. I'll see you on the flip side after you've written your solution.

Solution

As always, I'll stress that the only requirement for your code is to pass the test suite. I doubt you will have written the same code as I did, but that's what I find so fun and creative about coding. In my solution, I decided to create iterators to retrieve the lines from the filehandles. These iterators incorporate a closure to handle case-insensitive comparisons:

```
fn run(args: Args) -> Result<()> {
    let file1 = &args.file1;
    let file2 = &args.file2;

    if file1 == "-" && file2 == "-" {
        bail!(r#"Both input files cannot be STDIN ("-")"#);
    }

    let case = |line: String| { ❶
        if args.insensitive {
            line.to_lowercase()
        } else {
            line
        }
    };

    let mut lines1 = open(file1)?.lines().map_while(Result::ok).map(case); ❷
    let mut lines2 = open(file2)?.lines().map_while(Result::ok).map(case);

    let line1 = lines1.next(); ❸
    let line2 = lines2.next();
    println!("line1 = {:?}", line1); ❹
    println!("line2 = {:?}", line2);

    Ok(())
}
```

❶ Create a closure to lowercase each line of text when args.insensitive is true.

❷ Open the files, create iterators that remove errors, and then map the lines through the case closure.

❸ The Iterator::next method (*https://oreil.ly/7yJEJ*) advances an iterator and returns the next value. Here, it will retrieve the first line from a filehandle.

❹   Print the first line from each file.

In the preceding code, I used the function Result::ok rather than writing a closure |line| line.ok(). They both accomplish the same thing, but the first is shorter.

As I suggested, I'll start with one of the files being empty. Moving to the root directory of the chapter, I ran the program with the following input files:

```
$ cd ../..
$ cargo run -- tests/inputs/file1.txt tests/inputs/empty.txt
line1 = Some("a")
line2 = None
```

That led me to think about how I can move through the lines of each iterator based on the four different combinations of Some(line) and None that I can get from two iterators. In the following code, I place the possibilities inside a tuple (*https://oreil.ly/ Cmywl*), which is a finite heterogeneous sequence surrounded by parentheses:

```
let mut line1 = lines1.next(); ❶
let mut line2 = lines2.next();

while line1.is_some() || line2.is_some() { ❷
    match (&line1, &line2) { ❸
        (Some(_), Some(_)) => { ❹
            line1 = lines1.next();
            line2 = lines2.next();
        }
        (Some(_), None) => { ❺
            line1 = lines1.next();
        }
        (None, Some(_)) => { ❻
            line2 = lines2.next();
        }
        _ => (), ❼
    };
}
```

❶   Make the line variables mutable.

❷   Execute the loop as long as one of the filehandles produces a line.

❸   Compare all possible combinations of the two line variables for two variants.

❹   When both are Some values, use Iterator::next to retrieve the next line from both filehandles.

❺ When there is only the first value, ask for the next line from the first filehandle.

❻ Do the same for the second filehandle.

❼ Do nothing for any other condition.

When I have only one value from the first or second file, I should print the value in the first or second column, respectively. When I have two values from the files and they are the same, I should print a value in column 3. When I have two values and the first value is less than the second, I should print the first value in column 1; otherwise, I should print the second value in column 2. To understand this last point, consider the following two input files, which I'll place side by side so you can imagine how the code will read the lines:

```
$ cat tests/inputs/file1.txt          $ cat tests/inputs/file2.txt
a                                      B
b                                      C
c
d
```

To help you see the output from BSD comm, I will pipe the output into sed (*stream editor*) to replace each tab character (\t) with the string ---> to make it clear which columns are being printed:

```
$ comm tests/inputs/file1.txt tests/inputs/file2.txt | sed "s/\t/--->/g"  ❶
--->B
a
b
--->--->C
d
```

❶ The sed command s// will *substitute* values, replacing the string between the first pair of slashes with the string between the second pair. The final g is the *global* flag to substitute every occurrence.

Now imagine your code reads the first line from each input and has *a* from *file1.txt* and B from *file2.txt*. They are not equal, so the question is which to print. The goal is to mimic BSD comm, so I know that the B should come first and be printed in the second column. When I compare *a* and B, I find that B is less than *a* when they are ordered by their *code point*, or numerical value. To help you see this, I've included a program in *util/ascii* that will show you a range of the ASCII table starting at the first printable character. Note that B has a value of 66 while *a* is 97:

```
33: !    52: 4    71: G    90: Z    109: m
34: "    53: 5    72: H    91: [    110: n
35: #    54: 6    73: I    92: \    111: o
36: $    55: 7    74: J    93: ]    112: p
37: %    56: 8    75: K    94: ^    113: q
```

```
38: &    57: 9    76: L    95: _    114: r
39: '    58: :    77: M    96: `    115: s
40: (    59: ;    78: N    97: a    116: t
41: )    60: <    79: 0    98: b    117: u
42: *    61: =    80: P    99: c    118: v
43: +    62: >    81: Q    100: d   119: w
44: ,    63: ?    82: R    101: e   120: x
45: -    64: @    83: S    102: f   121: y
46: .    65: A    84: T    103: g   122: z
47: /    66: B    85: U    104: h   123: {
48: 0    67: C    86: V    105: i   124: |
49: 1    68: D    87: W    106: j   125: }
50: 2    69: E    88: X    107: k   126: ~
51: 3    70: F    89: Y    108: l   127: DEL
```

To mimic BSD comm, I should print the *lower* value (B) first and draw another value from that file for the next iteration; the GNU version does the opposite. In the following code, I'm concerned only with the ordering, and I'll handle the indentation in a moment. Note that you should add use `std::cmp::Ordering::*` to your imports for this code:

```
let mut line1 = lines1.next();
let mut line2 = lines2.next();

while line1.is_some() || line2.is_some() {
    match (&line1, &line2) {
        (Some(val1), Some(val2)) => match val1.cmp(val2) { ❶
            Equal => { ❷
                println!("{val1}");
                line1 = lines1.next();
                line2 = lines2.next();
            }
            Less => { ❸
                println!("{val1}");
                line1 = lines1.next();
            }
            Greater => { ❹
                println!("{val2}");
                line2 = lines2.next();
            }
        },
        (Some(val1), None) => {
            println!("{val1}"); ❺
            line1 = lines1.next();
        }
        (None, Some(val2)) => {
            println!("{val2}"); ❻
            line2 = lines2.next();
        }
        _ => (),
    }
}
```

❶ Use `Ord::cmp` (*https://oreil.ly/cTw3P*) to compare the first value to the second. This will return an `enum` variant of `std::cmp::Ordering` (*https://oreil.ly/ytvJ9*).

❷ When the two values are equal, print the first and get values from each of the files.

❸ When the value from the first file is less than the value from the second file, print the first and request the next value from the first file.

❹ When the first value is greater than the second, print the value from the second file and request the next value from the second file.

❺ When there is a value only from the first file, print it and continue requesting values from the first file.

❻ When there is a value only from the second file, print it and continue requesting values from the second file.

If I run this code using a nonempty file and an empty file, it works:

```
$ cargo run -- tests/inputs/file1.txt tests/inputs/empty.txt
a
b
c
d
```

If I use *file1.txt* and *file2.txt*, it's not far from the expected output:

```
$ cargo run -- tests/inputs/file1.txt tests/inputs/file2.txt
B
a
b
c
d
```

I decided to create an `enum` called `Column` to represent the column where the value should be printed. Each variant holds a `&str`, which requires a lifetime annotation. You can place the following at the top of *src/main.rs*, near your `Args` declaration. Be sure to add `use crate::Column::*` to your import so you can reference `Col1` instead of `Column::Col1`:

```
enum Column<'a> {
    Col1(&'a str),
    Col2(&'a str),
    Col3(&'a str),
}
```

Next, I created a closure called `print` to handle the printing of the output. The following code belongs in the `run` function:

```
let print = |col: Column| {
    let mut columns = vec![];  ❶
    match col {
        Col1(val) => {
            if args.show_col1 {  ❷
                columns.push(val);
            }
        }
        Col2(val) => {
            if args.show_col2 {  ❸
                if args.show_col1 {
                    columns.push("");
                }
                columns.push(val);
            }
        }
        Col3(val) => {
            if args.show_col3 {  ❹
                if args.show_col1 {
                    columns.push("");
                }
                if args.show_col2 {
                    columns.push("");
                }
                columns.push(val);
            }
        }
    };

    if !columns.is_empty() {  ❺
        println!("{}", columns.join(&args.delimiter));
    }
};
```

❶ Create a mutable vector to hold the output columns.

❷ Given text for column 1, add the value only if the column is shown.

❸ Given text for column 2, add the values for the two columns only if they are shown.

❹ Given text for column 3, add the values for the three columns only if they are shown.

❺ If there are columns to print, join them on the output delimiter.

Originally I used the field `suppress_col1`, which had me writing `if !args.suppress_col1`, a double negative that is much harder to comprehend. In general, I would recommend using positive names like *do_something* rather than *dont_do_something*.

Here is how I incorporate the `print` closure:

```
let mut line1 = lines1.next(); ❶
let mut line2 = lines2.next();

while line1.is_some() || line2.is_some() {
    match (&line1, &line2) {
        (Some(val1), Some(val2)) => match val1.cmp(val2) {
            Equal => {
                print(Col3(val1)); ❷
                line1 = lines1.next();
                line2 = lines2.next();
            }
            Less => {
                print(Col1(val1)); ❸
                line1 = lines1.next();
            }
            Greater => {
                print(Col2(val2)); ❹
                line2 = lines2.next();
            }
        },
        (Some(val1), None) => {
            print(Col1(val1)); ❺
            line1 = lines1.next();
        }
        (None, Some(val2)) => {
            print(Col2(val2)); ❻
            line2 = lines2.next();
        }
        _ => (),
    }
}
```

❶ Draw the initial values from the two input files.

❷ When the values are the same, print one of them in column 3.

❸ When the first value is less than the second, print the first value in column 1.

❹ When the first value is greater than the second, print the second value in column 2.

❺ When there is a value only from the first file, print it in column 1.

❻ When there is a value only from the second file, print it in column 2.

I like having the option to change the output delimiter from a tab to something more visible:

```
$ cargo run -- -d="--->" tests/inputs/file1.txt tests/inputs/file2.txt
--->B
a
b
--->--->C
d
```

With these changes, all the tests pass.

Going Further

The version I presented mimics the BSD version of comm. Alter the program to match the GNU output, and also add the additional options from that version. Be sure you update the test suite and test files to verify that your program works exactly like the GNU version.

Change the column suppression flags to selection flags, so -12 would mean *show the first two columns only*. Without any column selections, all the columns should be shown. This is similar to how the wcr program works, where the default is to show all the columns for lines, words, and characters, and the selection of any of those columns suppresses those not selected. Update the tests to verify that your program works correctly.

As I noted in the chapter introduction, comm performs basic join operations on two files, which is similar to the join program. Run **man join** to read the manual page for that program, and use your experience from writing commr to write a Rust version. I would suggest the ingenious name joinr. Generate input files, and then use join to create the output files you can use to verify that your version maintains fidelity to the original tool.

Summary

Until I wrote this version of comm, I had to look at the manual page every time to remember what the flags meant. I also imagined it to be a very complicated program, but I find the solution quite simple and elegant. Consider what you learned:

- You can choose when to advance any iterator by using Iterator::next. For instance, when used with a filehandle, you can manually select the next line.
- You can use match on combinations of possibilities by grouping them into a tuple.

- You can use the `cmp` method of the `Ord` trait to compare one value to another. The result is a variant of `std::cmp::Ordering`.

- You can create an `enum` called `Column` where the variants can hold a `&str` value as long as you include lifetime annotations.

In the next chapter, you'll learn how to move to a line or byte position in a file.

CHAPTER 11

Tailor Swyfte

From the embryonic whale to the monkey with no tail
— They Might Be Giants, "Mammal" (1992)

The challenge in this chapter will be to write a version of tail, which is the converse of head from Chapter 4. The program will show you the last bytes or lines of one or more files or STDIN, usually defaulting to the last 10 lines. Again the program will have to deal with bad input and will possibly mangle Unicode characters. The challenge program will read only regular files, so we won't bother with STDIN.

In this chapter, you will learn how to do the following:

- Initialize a static, global, computed value
- Seek to a line or byte position in a filehandle
- Indicate multiple trait bounds on a type using the where clause
- Build a release binary with Cargo
- Benchmark programs to compare runtime performance

How tail Works

To demonstrate how the challenge program should work, I'll first show you a portion of the manual page for the BSD tail. Note that the challenge program will only implement some of these features:

```
TAIL(1)                   BSD General Commands Manual                   TAIL(1)

NAME
     tail -- display the last part of a file
```

```
     tail [-F | -f | -r] [-q] [-b number | -c number | -n number] [file ...]
```

DESCRIPTION
```
     The tail utility displays the contents of file or, by default, its stan-
     dard input, to the standard output.

     The display begins at a byte, line or 512-byte block location in the
     input.  Numbers having a leading plus ('+') sign are relative to the
     beginning of the input, for example, ''-c +2'' starts the display at the
     second byte of the input.  Numbers having a leading minus ('-') sign or
     no explicit sign are relative to the end of the input, for example,
     ''-n2'' displays the last two lines of the input.  The default starting
     location is ''-n 10'', or the last 10 lines of the input.
```

The BSD version has many options, but these are the only ones relevant to the challenge program:

```
     -c number
             The location is number bytes.

     -n number
             The location is number lines.

     -q      Suppresses printing of headers when multiple files are being
             examined.

     If more than a single file is specified, each file is preceded by a
     header consisting of the string ''==> XXX <=='' where XXX is the name of
     the file unless -q flag is specified.
```

Here's part of the manual page for GNU `tail`, which includes long option names:

```
TAIL(1)                          User Commands                          TAIL(1)

NAME
     tail - output the last part of files

SYNOPSIS
     tail [OPTION]... [FILE]...

DESCRIPTION
     Print the last  10  lines of each FILE to standard output.  With more
     than one FILE, precede each with a header giving the file  name.   With
     no FILE, or when FILE is -, read standard input.

     Mandatory  arguments  to  long  options are mandatory for short options
     too.

     -c, --bytes=K
             output the last K bytes; or use -c +K to output  bytes  starting
             with the Kth of each file
```

```
-n, --lines=K
        output the last K lines, instead of the last 10; or use -n +K to
        output starting with the Kth
```

I'll use files in the book's *11_tailr/tests/inputs* directory to demonstrate the features of tail that the challenge will implement. As in previous chapters, there are examples with Windows line endings that must be preserved in the output. The files I'll use are:

- *empty.txt*: an empty file
- *one.txt*: a file with one line of UTF-8 Unicode text
- *two.txt*: a file with two lines of ASCII text
- *three.txt*: a file with three lines of ASCII text and CRLF line terminators
- *twelve.txt*: a file with 12 lines of ASCII text

Change into the chapter's directory:

```
$ cd 11_tailr
```

By default, tail will show the last 10 lines of a file, which you can see with *tests/inputs/twelve.txt*:

```
$ tail tests/inputs/twelve.txt
three
four
five
six
seven
eight
nine
ten
eleven
twelve
```

Run it with -n 4 to see the last four lines:

```
$ tail -n 4 tests/inputs/twelve.txt
nine
ten
eleven
twelve
```

Use -c 10 to select the last ten bytes of the file. In the following output, there are eight byte-sized characters and two byte-sized newline characters, for a total of ten bytes. Pipe the output to cat -e to display the dollar sign ($) to indicate the newlines:

```
$ tail -c 10 tests/inputs/twelve.txt | cat -e
en$
twelve$
```

With multiple input files, `tail` will print separators between each file. Any errors opening files (such as for nonexistent or unreadable files) will be noted to STDERR without any file headers. For instance, *blargh* represents a nonexistent file in the following command:

```
$ tail -n 1 tests/inputs/one.txt blargh tests/inputs/three.txt
==> tests/inputs/one.txt <==
One line, four words.
tail: blargh: No such file or directory

==> tests/inputs/three.txt <==
four words.
```

The -q flag will suppress the file headers:

```
$ tail -q -n 1 tests/inputs/*.txt
One line, four words.
ten
four words.
Four words.
```

Requesting more lines or bytes than a file contains is not an error and will cause `tail` to print the entire file:

```
$ tail -n 1000 tests/inputs/one.txt
One line, four words.
$ tail -c 1000 tests/inputs/one.txt
One line, four words.
```

As noted in the manual pages, -n or -c values may begin with a plus sign to indicate a line or byte position from the *beginning* of the file rather than the end. A start position beyond the end of the file is not an error, and `tail` will print nothing, which you can see if you run **tail -n +1000 tests/inputs/one.txt**. In the following command, I use -n +8 to start printing from line 8:

```
$ tail -n +8 tests/inputs/twelve.txt
eight
nine
ten
eleven
twelve
```

It's possible to split multibyte characters with byte selection. For example, the *tests /inputs/one.txt* file starts with the Unicode character Ö, which is two bytes long. In the following command, I use -c +2 to start printing from the second byte, which will split the multibyte character, resulting in the unknown character:

```
$ tail -c +2 tests/inputs/one.txt
◆ne line, four words.
```

To start printing from the second *character*, I must use `-c +3` to start printing from the third *byte*:

```
$ tail -c +3 tests/inputs/one.txt
ne line, four words.
```

The end of *tests/inputs/one.txt* has a funky Unicode *ś* thrown in for good measure, which is a multibyte Unicode character. If you request the last four bytes of the file, two will be for *ś*, one for the period, and one for the final newline:

```
$ tail -c 4 tests/inputs/one.txt
ś.
```

If you ask for only three, the *ś* will be split, and you should see the Unicode *unknown* character:

```
$ tail -c 3 tests/inputs/one.txt
◆.
```

Both the BSD and GNU versions will accept `0` and `-0` for `-n` or `-c`. The GNU version will show no output at all, while the BSD version will show no output when run with a single file but will still show the file headers when there are multiple input files. The following behavior of BSD is expected of the challenge program:

```
$ tail -n 0 tests/inputs/*
==> tests/inputs/empty.txt <==

==> tests/inputs/one.txt <==

==> tests/inputs/three.txt <==

==> tests/inputs/twelve.txt <==

==> tests/inputs/two.txt <==
```

Both versions interpret the value `+0` as starting at the zeroth line or byte, so the whole file will be shown:

```
$ tail -n +0 tests/inputs/one.txt
Öne line, four words.
$ tail -c +0 tests/inputs/one.txt
Öne line, four words.
```

Both versions will reject any value for `-n` or `-c` that cannot be parsed as an integer:

```
$ tail -c foo tests/inputs/one.txt
tail: illegal offset -- foo
```

While `tail` has several more features, this is as much as your program needs to implement.

Getting Started

The challenge program will be called `tailr` (pronounced *tay-ler*). I recommend you begin with `cargo new tailr` and then add the following dependencies to *Cargo.toml*:

```
[dependencies]
anyhow = "1.0.79"
clap = { version = "4.5.0", features = ["derive"] }
num = "0.4.1"
once_cell = "1.19.0" ❶
regex = "1.10.3"

[dev-dependencies]
assert_cmd = "2.0.13"
predicates = "3.0.4"
pretty_assertions = "1.4.0"
rand = "0.8.5"
```

❶ The `once_cell` crate (*https://oreil.ly/DXeXE*) will be used to create a computed static value.

Copy the book's *11_tailr/tests* directory into your project, and then run `cargo test` to download the needed crates, build your program, and ensure that you fail all the tests.

Defining the Arguments

I'll start by defining the `Args` struct in *src/main.rs* as in previous chapters:

```
#[derive(Debug)]
struct Args {
    files: Vec<String>,    ❶
    lines: String,         ❷
    bytes: Option<String>, ❸
    quiet: bool,           ❹
}
```

❶ `files` is a vector of strings.

❷ `lines` should default to "10" to indicate the last 10 lines.

❸ `bytes` is an optional number of bytes to select.

❹ The `quiet` flag is a Boolean for whether or not to suppress the headers between multiple files.

Either annotate the `Args` for the `clap` derive pattern, or use the following as a skeleton for `get_args`:

```
fn get_args() -> Args {
    let matches = Command::new("tailr")
        .version("0.1.0")
        .author("Ken Youens-Clark <kyclark@gmail.com>")
        .about("Rust version of `tail`")
        // What goes here?
        .get_matches();

    Args {
        files: ...
        lines: ...
        bytes: ...
        quiet: ...
    }
}
```

I suggest you start your `main` function by printing the arguments:

```
fn main() {
    let args = get_args();
    println!("{args:#?}");
}
```

First, get your program to print the following usage:

```
$ cargo run -- -h
Rust version of `tail`

Usage: tailr [OPTIONS] <FILE>...

Arguments:
  <FILE>...  Input file(s)

Options:
  -n, --lines <LINES>  Number of lines [default: 10]
  -c, --bytes <BYTES>  Number of bytes
  -q, --quiet          Suppress headers
  -h, --help           Print help
  -V, --version        Print version
```

If you run the program with no arguments, it should fail with an error that at least one file argument is required because this program will not read STDIN by default:

```
$ cargo run
error: the following required arguments were not provided:
  <FILE>...

Usage: tailr <FILE>...
```

The `--bytes` and `--lines` options should be mutually exclusive:

```
$ cargo run -- tests/inputs/empty.txt --bytes 1 --lines 1
error: the argument '--bytes <BYTES>' cannot be used with '--lines <LINES>'

Usage: tailr --bytes <BYTES> <FILES>...
```

Run the program with a file argument and see if you can get this output:

```
$ cargo run -- tests/inputs/one.txt
Args {
    files: [
        "tests/inputs/one.txt", ❶
    ],
    lines: "10", ❷
    bytes: None, ❸
    quiet: false, ❹
}
```

❶ The positional argument goes into files.

❷ The lines argument should default to "10" to take the last 10 lines.

❸ The bytes argument should default to None.

❹ The quiet option should default to false.

Run the program with multiple file arguments and the -c option to ensure you get the following output:

```
$ cargo run -- -q -c 4 tests/inputs/*.txt
Args {
    files: [
        "tests/inputs/empty.txt", ❶
        "tests/inputs/one.txt",
        "tests/inputs/three.txt",
        "tests/inputs/twelve.txt",
        "tests/inputs/two.txt",
    ],
    lines: "10", ❷
    bytes: Some( ❸
        "4",
    ),
    quiet: true, ❹
}
```

❶ The positional arguments are parsed as files.

❷ The lines argument is still set to the default.

❸ Now bytes is set to Some("4") to indicate the last four bytes should be taken.

❹ The -q flag causes the quiet option to be true.

 Pause here and get your program output to match the preceding examples. Your program should also pass two of the tests included with **cargo test dies**.

Parsing and Validating the Command-Line Arguments

I'll show you how I wrote my get_args function. Be sure to add use clap::{Arg, ArgAction, Command} for the following:

```
fn get_args() -> Args {
    let matches = Command::new("tailr")
        .version("0.1.0")
        .author("Ken Youens-Clark <kyclark@gmail.com>")
        .about("Rust version of `tail`")
        .arg(
            Arg::new("files") ❶
                .value_name("FILE")
                .help("Input file(s)")
                .required(true)
                .num_args(1..),
        )
        .arg(
            Arg::new("lines") ❷
                .short('n')
                .long("lines")
                .value_name("LINES")
                .help("Number of lines")
                .default_value("10"),
        )
        .arg(
            Arg::new("bytes") ❸
                .short('c')
                .long("bytes")
                .value_name("BYTES")
                .conflicts_with("lines")
                .help("Number of bytes"),
        )
        .arg(
            Arg::new("quiet") ❹
                .short('q')
                .long("quiet")
                .action(ArgAction::SetTrue)
                .help("Suppress headers"),
        )
        .get_matches();
```

```
Args {
    files: matches.get_many("files").unwrap().cloned().collect(),
    lines: matches.get_one("lines").cloned().unwrap(),
    bytes: matches.get_one("bytes").cloned(),
    quiet: matches.get_flag("quiet"),
    }
}
```

❶ The `files` argument is positional and requires at least one value.

❷ The `lines` argument has a default value of `10`.

❸ The `bytes` argument is optional and conflicts with `lines`.

❹ The `quiet` flag is optional.

 Because the `--lines` and `--bytes` are mutually exclusive, you might prefer to put them into an `ArgGroup` as in Chapter 8.

For the derive pattern, add `use clap::Parser` and the following annotations to the `Args` struct;

```
#[derive(Debug, Parser)]
#[command(author, version, about)]
/// Rust version of `tail`
struct Args {
    /// Input file(s)
    #[arg(required = true)]
    files: Vec<String>,

    /// Number of lines
    #[arg(value_name = "LINES", short('n'), long, default_value = "10")]
    lines: String,

    /// Number of bytes
    #[arg(value_name = "BYTES", short('c'), long, conflicts_with("lines"))]
    bytes: Option<String>,

    /// Suppress headers
    #[arg(short, long)]
    quiet: bool,
}
```

Next, I'll restructure my code to call a `run` function as in previous chapters. Add `use anyhow::Result` for the following code:

```
fn main() {
    if let Err(e) = run(Args::parse()) {
        eprintln!("{e}");
        std::process::exit(1);
    }
}

fn run(_args: Args) -> Result<()> {
    Ok(())
}
```

My next challenge is to validate the `lines` and `bytes` arguments.

Parsing Positive and Negative Numeric Arguments

The challenge program has similar options as `headr`, but this program must handle both positive and negative values for the number of lines or bytes. In `headr`, I used an *unsigned* integer that can represent only positive values. In this program, I will use `i64` (*https://oreil.ly/7grA6*), the 64-bit signed integer type, to also store negative numbers. Additionally, I need some way to differentiate between 0, which means *nothing* should be selected, and +0, which means *everything* should be selected. I decided to create an `enum` called `TakeValue` to represent this, but you may choose a different way:

```
#[derive(Debug, PartialEq)] ❶
enum TakeValue {
    PlusZero, ❷
    TakeNum(i64), ❸
}
```

❶ The `PartialEq` is needed by the tests to compare values.

❷ This variant represents an argument of +0.

❸ This variant represents a valid integer value.

To refer to the `enum` values without the `TakeValue` prefix, add the following to your imports:

```
use crate::TakeValue::*;
```

Following is the start of the function `parse_num` I'd like you to write that will accept a string and will return a `TakeValue` or an error:

```
fn parse_num(val: String) -> Result<TakeValue> {
    unimplemented!();
}
```

Add the following unit test to a `tests` module in your *src/main.rs*:

```
#[cfg(test)]
mod tests {
    use super::{parse_num, TakeValue::*};

    #[test]
    fn test_parse_num() {
        // All integers should be interpreted as negative numbers
        let res = parse_num("3".to_string());
        assert!(res.is_ok());
        assert_eq!(res.unwrap(), TakeNum(-3));

        // A leading "+" should result in a positive number
        let res = parse_num("+3".to_string());
        assert!(res.is_ok());
        assert_eq!(res.unwrap(), TakeNum(3));

        // An explicit "-" value should result in a negative number
        let res = parse_num("-3".to_string());
        assert!(res.is_ok());
        assert_eq!(res.unwrap(), TakeNum(-3));

        // Zero is zero
        let res = parse_num("0".to_string());
        assert!(res.is_ok());
        assert_eq!(res.unwrap(), TakeNum(0));

        // Plus zero is special
        let res = parse_num("+0".to_string());
        assert!(res.is_ok());
        assert_eq!(res.unwrap(), PlusZero);

        // Test boundaries
        let res = parse_num(i64::MAX.to_string());
        assert!(res.is_ok());
        assert_eq!(res.unwrap(), TakeNum(i64::MIN + 1));

        let res = parse_num((i64::MIN + 1).to_string());
        assert!(res.is_ok());
        assert_eq!(res.unwrap(), TakeNum(i64::MIN + 1));

        let res = parse_num(format!("+{}", i64::MAX));
        assert!(res.is_ok());
        assert_eq!(res.unwrap(), TakeNum(i64::MAX));

        let res = parse_num(i64::MIN.to_string());
        assert!(res.is_ok());
        assert_eq!(res.unwrap(), TakeNum(i64::MIN));

        // A floating-point value is invalid
        let res = parse_num("3.14".to_string());
```

```
        assert!(res.is_err());
        assert_eq!(res.unwrap_err().to_string(), "3.14");

        // Any non-integer string is invalid
        let res = parse_num("foo".to_string());
        assert!(res.is_err());
        assert_eq!(res.unwrap_err().to_string(), "foo");
    }
}
```

 I suggest that you stop reading and take some time to write this function. Do not proceed until it passes **cargo test test_parse_num**. In the next section, I'll share my solution.

Once you have a working function, use it in your run to parse the lines and bytes. For the following code, be sure to add use anyhow::anyhow to your imports:

```
fn run(args: Args) -> Result<()> {
    let lines = parse_num(args.lines)
        .map_err(|e| anyhow!("illegal line count -- {e}"))?;

    let bytes = args
        .bytes
        .map(parse_num)
        .transpose()
        .map_err(|e| anyhow!("illegal byte count -- {e}"))?;

    println!("lines = {lines:?}");
    println!("bytes = {bytes:?}");
    Ok(())
}
```

When run with the default values, the output should look like the following:

```
$ cargo run -- tests/inputs/empty.txt
lines = TakeNum(-10)
bytes = None
```

Run your program with a value for the bytes to ensure it is parsed correctly:

```
$ cargo run -- -c 4 tests/inputs/empty.txt
lines = TakeNum(-10)
bytes = Some(TakeNum(-4))
```

You probably noticed that the value 4 was parsed as a negative number even though it was provided as a positive value. The numeric values for lines and bytes should be negative to indicate that the program will take values from the *end* of the file. A plus sign is required to indicate that the starting position is from the *beginning* of the file:

```
$ cargo run -- -n +5 tests/inputs/twelve.txt ❶
lines = TakeNum(5) ❷
bytes = None
```

❶ The +5 argument indicates the program should start printing on the fifth line.

❷ The value is interpreted as a positive integer.

Both -n and -c are allowed to have a value of 0, which will mean that no lines or bytes will be shown:

```
$ cargo run -- tests/inputs/empty.txt -c 0
lines = TakeNum(-10)
bytes = Some(TakeNum(0))
```

As with the original versions, the value +0 indicates that the starting point is the beginning of the file, so all the content will be shown:

```
$ cargo run -- tests/inputs/empty.txt -n +0
lines = PlusZero ❶
bytes = None
```

❶ The PlusZero variant represents +0.

Any noninteger value for -n and -c should be rejected:

```
$ cargo run -- tests/inputs/empty.txt -n foo
illegal line count -- foo
$ cargo run -- tests/inputs/empty.txt -c bar
illegal byte count -- bar
```

Stop here and implement this much of the program. If you need some guidance on validating the numeric arguments for bytes and lines, I'll discuss that in the next section.

Using a Regular Expression to Match an Integer with an Optional Sign

Following is one version of the parse_num function that passes the tests. Here I chose to use a regular expression to see if the input value matches an expected pattern of text. If you want to include this version in your program, be sure to add use regex::Regex:

```
fn parse_num(val: String) -> Result<TakeValue> {
    let num_re = Regex::new(r"^([+-])?(\d+)$").unwrap(); ❶

    match num_re.captures(&val) {
        Some(caps) => {
            let sign = caps.get(1).map_or("-", |m| m.as_str()); ❷
            let signed_num =
```

```
            format!("{sign}{}", caps.get(2).unwrap().as_str()); ❸

        if let Ok(num) = signed_num.parse() { ❹
            if sign == "+" && num == 0 { ❺
                Ok(PlusZero) ❻
            } else {
                Ok(TakeNum(num)) ❼
            }
        } else {
            bail!(val) ❽
        }
    }
    _ => bail!(val), ❾
    }
}
```

❶ Create a regex to find an optional leading + or - sign followed by one or more numbers.

❷ If the regex matches, the optional sign will be the first capture. Assume the minus sign if there is no match.

❸ The digits of the number will be in the second capture. Format the sign and digits into a string.

❹ Attempt to parse the number as an i64, which Rust infers from the function's return type.

❺ Check if the sign is a plus and the parsed value is 0.

❻ If so, return the PlusZero variant.

❼ Otherwise, return the parsed value as the TakeNum variant.

❽ Return the unparsable number as an error.

❾ Return an invalid argument as an error.

Regular expression syntax can be daunting to the uninitiated. Figure 11-1 shows each element of the pattern used in the preceding function.

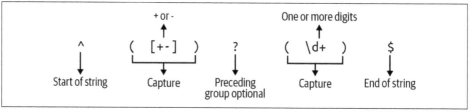

Figure 11-1. This is a regular expression that will match a positive or negative integer.

You've seen much of this syntax in previous programs. Here's a review of all the parts of this regex:

- The ^ indicates the beginning of a string. Without this, the pattern could match anywhere inside the string.
- Parentheses group and capture values, making them available through Regex::captures (*https://oreil.ly/O6frw*).
- Square brackets ([]) create a *character class* that will match any of the contained values. A dash (-) inside a character class can be used to denote a range, such as [0-9] to indicate all the characters from 0 to 9.[1] To indicate a literal dash, it should occur last.
- A ? makes the preceding pattern optional.
- The \d is shorthand for the character class [0-9] and so matches any digit. The + suffix indicates *one or more* of the preceding pattern.
- The $ indicates the end of the string. Without this, the regular expression would match even when additional characters follow a successful match.

I'd like to make one small change. The first line of the preceding function creates a regular expression by parsing the pattern *each time* the function is called:

```
fn parse_num(val: String) -> Result<TakeValue> {
    let num_re = Regex::new(r"^([+-])?(\d+)$").unwrap();
    ...
}
```

I'd like my program to do the work of compiling the regex just once. You've seen in earlier tests how I've used const to create a constant value. It's common to use

---

1 The *range* here means all the characters between those two code points. Refer to the output from the ascii program in Chapter 10 to see that the contiguous values from 0 to 9 are all numbers. Contrast this with the values from *A* to *z* where various punctuation characters fall in the middle, which is why you will often see the range [A-Za-z] to select ASCII alphabet characters.

ALL_CAPS to name global constants and to place them near the top of the crate, like so:

```
// This will not compile
const NUM_RE: Regex = Regex::new(r"^([+-])?(\d+)$").unwrap();
```

If I try to run the test again, I get the following error telling me that I cannot use a computed value for a constant:

```
error[E0015]: cannot call non-const fn `regex::Regex::new` in constants
 --> src/main.rs:7:23
  |
7 | const NUM_RE: Regex = Regex::new(r"^([+-])?(\d+)$").unwrap();
  |                       ^^^^^^^^^^^^^^^^^^^^^^^^^^^^^^
  |
  = note: calls in constants are limited to constant functions, tuple structs
    and tuple variants
```

Enter once_cell, which provides a mechanism for creating lazily evaluated statics. To use this, you must first add the dependency to *Cargo.toml*, which I included at the start of this chapter. To create a lazily evaluated regular expression just one time in my program, I add the following to the top of *src/main.rs*:

```
use once_cell::sync::OnceCell;

static NUM_RE: OnceCell<Regex> = OnceCell::new();
```

The only change to the parse_num function is to initialize NUM_RE the first time the function is called:

```
fn parse_num(val: String) -> Result<TakeValue> {
    let num_re =
        NUM_RE.get_or_init(|| Regex::new(r"^([+-])?(\d+)$").unwrap());
    // Same as before
}
```

It is not a requirement that you use a regular expression to parse the numeric arguments. Here's a method that relies only on Rust's internal parsing capabilities:

```
fn parse_num(val: String) -> Result<TakeValue> {
    let signs: &[char] = &['+', '-']; ❶
    let res = val
        .starts_with(signs) ❷
        .then(|| val.parse())
        .unwrap_or_else(|| val.parse().map(i64::wrapping_neg)); ❸

    match res {
        Ok(num) => {
            if num == 0 && val.starts_with('+') { ❹
                Ok(PlusZero)
            } else {
                Ok(TakeNum(num))
            }
        }
```

```
            }
            _ => bail!(val),  ❺
        }
    }
}
```

❶ The type annotation is required because Rust infers the type &[char; 2], which is a reference to an array, but I want to coerce the value to a slice.

❷ If the given value starts with a plus or minus sign, use str::parse, which will use the sign to create a positive or negative number, respectively.

❸ Otherwise, parse the number and use i64::wrapping_neg (*https://oreil.ly/ H2gWn*) to compute the negative value; that is, a positive value will be returned as negative, while a negative value will remain negative.

❹ If the result is a successfully parsed i64, check whether to return PlusZero when the number is 0 and the given value starts with a plus sign; otherwise, return the parsed value.

❺ Return the unparsable value as an error.

You may have found another way to figure this out, and that's the point with functions and testing. It doesn't much matter *how* a function is written as long as it passes the tests. A function is a black box where something goes in and something comes out, and we write enough tests to convince ourselves that the function works correctly.

Processing the Files

Expand your run function to iterate the given files and attempt to open them. Since the challenge does not include reading STDIN, you only need to add use std::fs::File for the following code:

```
fn run(args: Args) -> Result<()> {
    // Same as before

    for filename in args.files {
        match File::open(&filename) {
            Err(err) => eprintln!("{filename}: {err}"),
            Ok(_) => println!("Opened {filename}"),
        }
    }

    Ok(())
}
```

Run your program with both good and bad filenames to verify this works. Additionally, your program should now pass **cargo test skips_bad_file**. In the following command, *blargh* represents a nonexistent file:

```
$ cargo run -- tests/inputs/one.txt blargh
Opened tests/inputs/one.txt
blargh: No such file or directory (os error 2)
```

Counting the Total Lines and Bytes in a File

Next, it's time to figure out how to read a file from a given byte or line location. For instance, the default case is to print the last 10 lines of a file, so I need to know how many lines are in the file to figure out which is the tenth from the end. The same is true for bytes. I also need to determine if the user has requested more lines or bytes than the file contains. When this value is negative—meaning the user wants to start beyond the beginning of the file—the program should print the entire file. When this value is positive—meaning the user wants to start beyond the end of the file—the program should print nothing.

I decided to create a function called count_lines_bytes that takes a filename and returns a tuple containing the total number of lines and bytes in the file. Here is the function's signature:

```
fn count_lines_bytes(filename: &str) -> Result<(i64, i64)> {
    unimplemented!()
}
```

If you want to create this function, modify your **tests** module to add the following unit test:

```
#[cfg(test)]
mod tests {
    use super::{count_lines_bytes, parse_num, TakeValue::*};

    #[test]
    fn test_parse_num() {} // Same as before

    #[test]
    fn test_count_lines_bytes() {
        let res = count_lines_bytes("tests/inputs/one.txt");
        assert!(res.is_ok());
        let (lines, bytes) = res.unwrap();
        assert_eq!(lines, 1);
        assert_eq!(bytes, 24);

        let res = count_lines_bytes("tests/inputs/twelve.txt");
        assert!(res.is_ok());
        let (lines, bytes) = res.unwrap();
        assert_eq!(lines, 12);
        assert_eq!(bytes, 63);
```

```
        }
    }
```

 Pause here and write the code that passes **cargo test test_count_lines_bytes**.

You can expand your run to temporarily print the count of lines and bytes in input files:

```
fn run(args: Args) -> Result<()> {
    // Same as before

    for filename in args.files {
        match File::open(&filename) {
            Err(err) => eprintln!("{filename}: {err}"),
            Ok(_) => {
                let (total_lines, total_bytes) =
                    count_lines_bytes(&filename)?;
                println!(
                    "{filename} has {total_lines} lines, {total_bytes} bytes"
                );
            }
        }
    }
    Ok(())
}
```

 I decided to pass the filename to the count_lines_bytes function instead of the filehandle that is returned by File::open because the filehandle will be consumed by the function, making it unavailable for use in selecting the bytes or lines.

Verify that it looks OK:

```
$ cargo run tests/inputs/one.txt tests/inputs/twelve.txt
tests/inputs/one.txt has 1 lines, 24 bytes
tests/inputs/twelve.txt has 12 lines, 63 bytes
```

Finding the Starting Line to Print

My next step was to write a function to print the lines of a given file. Following is the signature of my print_lines function. Be sure to add use std::io::BufRead for this:

```
fn print_lines(
    mut file: impl BufRead, ❶
    num_lines: &TakeValue, ❷
    total_lines: i64, ❸
) -> Result<()> {
    unimplemented!();
}
```

❶ The file argument should implement the BufRead trait.

❷ The num_lines argument is a TakeValue describing the number of lines to print.

❸ The total_lines argument is the total number of lines in this file.

 There is no unit test because this function prints to the command line. If I had chosen to return a vector of lines, I risk reading an entire file into memory, which may exceed the available memory. We will rely on the integration tests for the program's output to ensure this works correctly.

I can find the starting line's index using the number of lines the user wants to print and the total number of lines in the file. Since I will also need this logic to find the starting byte position, I decided to write a function called get_start_index that will return Some<u64> when there is a valid starting position or None when there is not. A valid starting position must be a positive number, so I decided to return a u64. Additionally, the functions where I will use the returned index also require this type:

```
fn get_start_index(take_val: &TakeValue, total: i64) -> Option<u64> {
    unimplemented!();
}
```

Following is a unit test you can add to the tests module that might help you see all the possibilities more clearly. For instance, the function returns None when the given file is empty or when trying to read from a position beyond the end of the file. Be sure to add get_start_index to the list of super imports:

```
#[test]
fn test_get_start_index() {
    // +0 from an empty file (0 lines/bytes) returns None
    assert_eq!(get_start_index(&PlusZero, 0), None);

    // +0 from a nonempty file returns an index that
    // is one less than the number of lines/bytes
    assert_eq!(get_start_index(&PlusZero, 1), Some(0));

    // Taking 0 lines/bytes returns None
    assert_eq!(get_start_index(&TakeNum(0), 1), None);
```

```
        // Taking any lines/bytes from an empty file returns None
        assert_eq!(get_start_index(&TakeNum(1), 0), None);

        // Taking more lines/bytes than is available returns None
        assert_eq!(get_start_index(&TakeNum(2), 1), None);

        // When starting line/byte is less than total lines/bytes,
        // return one less than starting number
        assert_eq!(get_start_index(&TakeNum(1), 10), Some(0));
        assert_eq!(get_start_index(&TakeNum(2), 10), Some(1));
        assert_eq!(get_start_index(&TakeNum(3), 10), Some(2));

        // When starting line/byte is negative and less than total,
        // return total - start
        assert_eq!(get_start_index(&TakeNum(-1), 10), Some(9));
        assert_eq!(get_start_index(&TakeNum(-2), 10), Some(8));
        assert_eq!(get_start_index(&TakeNum(-3), 10), Some(7));

        // When starting line/byte is negative and more than total,
        // return 0 to print the whole file
        assert_eq!(get_start_index(&TakeNum(-20), 10), Some(0));
    }
```

Once you figure out the line index to start printing, use this information in the
print_lines function to iterate the lines of the input file and print all the lines after
the starting index, if there is one.

Finding the Starting Byte to Print

I also wrote a function called print_bytes that works very similarly to print_lines.
The function's signature indicates that the file argument must implement the traits
Read (*https://oreil.ly/wDxvY*) and Seek (*https://oreil.ly/vJD1W*), the latter of which is a
word used in many programming languages for moving what's called a *cursor* or *read
head* to a particular position in a stream. For the following code, you will need to
expand your imports to include std::io::{BufRead, Read, Seek}:

```
fn print_bytes<T: Read + Seek>( ❶
    mut file: T, ❷
    num_bytes: &TakeValue, ❸
    total_bytes: i64, ❹
) -> Result<()> {
    unimplemented!();
}
```

❶ The generic type T has the trait bounds Read and Seek.

❷ The file argument must implement the indicated traits.

❸ The num_bytes argument is a TakeValue describing the byte selection.

---

❹ The `total_bytes` argument is the file size in bytes.

I can also write the generic types and bounds using a `where` clause (*https://oreil.ly/aM1vI*), which you might find more readable:

```
fn print_bytes<T>(
    mut file: T,
    num_bytes: &TakeValue,
    total_bytes: i64,
) -> Result<()>
where
    T: Read + Seek,
{
    unimplemented!();
}
```

You can use the `get_start_index` function to find the starting byte position from the beginning of the file, and then move the cursor to that position. Remember that the selected byte string may contain invalid UTF-8, so my solution uses `String::from_utf8_lossy` (*https://oreil.ly/Bs4ZI*) when printing the selected bytes.

Testing the Program with Large Input Files

I have included a program in the *util/biggie* directory of my repository that will generate large input text files that you can use to stress test your program. For instance, you can use it to create a file with a million lines of random text to use when selecting various ranges of lines and bytes. Here is the usage for the `biggie` program:

```
Make big text files

Usage: biggie [OPTIONS]

Options:
  -o, --outfile <FILE>   Output filename [default: out.txt]
  -l, --lines <LINES>    Number of lines [default: 100000]
  -h, --help             Print help
  -V, --version          Print version
```

This should be enough hints for you to write a solution. There's no hurry to finish the program. Sometimes you need to step away from a difficult problem for a day or more while your subconscious mind works. Come back when your solution passes **cargo test**.

Solution

I'll walk you through how I arrived at a solution, which will incorporate several dependencies as follows:

```
use crate::TakeValue::*;
use anyhow::{anyhow, bail, Result};
use clap::Parser;
use once_cell::sync::OnceCell;
use regex::Regex;
use std::{
    fs::File,
    io::{BufRead, BufReader, Read, Seek, SeekFrom},
};
```

I suggested writing several intermediate functions in the first part of this chapter, so next I'll show my versions that pass the unit tests I provided.

Counting All the Lines and Bytes in a File

I will start by showing my count_lines_bytes function to count all the lines and bytes in a file. In previous programs, I have used BufRead::read_line (*https:// oreil.ly/aJFkc*), which writes into a String. In the following function, I use Buf Read::read_until (*https://oreil.ly/7BJaH*) to read raw bytes to avoid the cost of creating strings, which I don't need:

```
fn count_lines_bytes(filename: &str) -> Result<(i64, i64)> {
    let mut file = BufReader::new(File::open(filename)?); ❶
    let mut num_lines = 0; ❷
    let mut num_bytes = 0;
    let mut buf = Vec::new();
    loop {
        let bytes_read = file.read_until(b'\n', &mut buf)?; ❸
        if bytes_read == 0 { ❹
            break;
        }
        num_lines += 1; ❺
        num_bytes += bytes_read as i64; ❻
        buf.clear(); ❼
    }
    Ok((num_lines, num_bytes)) ❽
}
```

❶ Create a mutable filehandle to read the given filename.

❷ Initialize counters for the number of lines and bytes as well as a buffer for reading the lines.

❸ Use BufRead::read_until to read bytes until a newline byte. This function returns the number of bytes that were read from the filehandle.

❹ When no bytes were read, exit the loop.

❺ Increment the line count.

❻ Increment the byte count. Note that BufRead::read_until returns a usize that must be cast to i64 to add the value to the num_bytes tally.

❼ Clear the buffer before reading the next line.

❽ Return a tuple containing the number of lines and bytes in the file.

Finding the Start Index

To find the starting line or byte position, my program relies on a get_start_index function that uses the desired location and the total number of lines or bytes in the file:

```
fn get_start_index(take_val: &TakeValue, total: i64) -> Option<u64> {
    match take_val {
        PlusZero => {
            if total > 0 { ❶
                Some(0)
            } else {
                None
            }
        }
        TakeNum(num) => {
            if num == &0 || total == 0 || num > &total { ❷
                None
            } else {
                let start = if num < &0 { total + num } else { num - 1 }; ❸
                Some(if start < 0 { 0 } else { start as u64 }) ❹
            }
        }
    }
}
```

❶ When the user wants to start at index 0, return 0 if the file is not empty; otherwise, return None.

❷ Return None if the user wants to select nothing, the file is empty, or the user wants to select more data than is available in the file.

❸   If the desired number of lines or bytes is negative, add it to the total; otherwise, subtract one from the desired number to get the zero-based offset.

❹   If the starting index is less than 0, return 0; otherwise, return the starting index as a u64.

Printing the Lines

The following is my `print_lines` function, much of which is similar to `count_lines_bytes`:

```
fn print_lines(
    mut file: impl BufRead,
    num_lines: &TakeValue,
    total_lines: i64,
) -> Result<()> {
    if let Some(start) = get_start_index(num_lines, total_lines) { ❶
        let mut line_num = 0; ❷
        let mut buf = Vec::new();
        loop {
            let bytes_read = file.read_until(b'\n', &mut buf)?;
            if bytes_read == 0 {
                break;
            }
            if line_num >= start { ❸
                print!("{}", String::from_utf8_lossy(&buf)); ❹
            }
            line_num += 1;
            buf.clear();
        }
    }

    Ok(())
}
```

❶   Check if there is a valid starting position when trying to read the given number of lines from the total number of lines available.

❷   Initialize variables for counting and reading lines from the file.

❸   Check if the given line is at or beyond the starting point.

❹   If so, convert the bytes to a string and print.

Here is how I can integrate this into my run function:

```
fn run(args: Args) -> Result<()> {
    let lines = parse_num(args.lines)
        .map_err(|e| anyhow!("illegal line count -- {e}"))?;
```

```
let _bytes = args
    .bytes
    .map(parse_num)
    .transpose()
    .map_err(|e| anyhow!("illegal byte count -- {e}"))?;

for filename in args.files {
    match File::open(&filename) {
        Err(err) => eprintln!("{filename}: {err}"),
        Ok(file) => {
            let (total_lines, _total_bytes) =
                count_lines_bytes(&filename)?; ❶
            let file = BufReader::new(file); ❷
            print_lines(file, &lines, total_lines)?; ❸
        }
    }
}

Ok(())
}
```

❶ Count the total lines and bytes in the current file.

❷ Create a `BufReader` with the opened filehandle.

❸ Print the requested number of lines.

A quick check shows this will select, for instance, the last five lines:

```
$ cargo run -- -n 5 tests/inputs/twelve.txt
eight
nine
ten
eleven
twelve
```

I can get the same output by starting on the eighth line:

```
$ cargo run -- -n +8 tests/inputs/twelve.txt
eight
nine
ten
eleven
twelve
```

If I run **cargo test** at this point, I pass more than two-thirds of the tests.

Printing the Bytes

Next, I will show my `print_bytes` function:

```
fn print_bytes<T: Read + Seek>(
    mut file: T,
    num_bytes: &TakeValue,
    total_bytes: i64,
) -> Result<()> {
    if let Some(start) = get_start_index(num_bytes, total_bytes) { ❶
        file.seek(SeekFrom::Start(start))?; ❷
        let mut buffer = Vec::new(); ❸
        file.read_to_end(&mut buffer)?; ❹
        if !buffer.is_empty() {
            print!("{}", String::from_utf8_lossy(&buffer)); ❺
        }
    }

    Ok(())
}
```

❶ See if there is a valid starting byte position.

❷ Use `Seek::seek` (*https://oreil.ly/ki8DT*) to move to the desired byte position as defined by `SeekFrom::Start` (*https://oreil.ly/Bi8Bp*).

❸ Create a mutable buffer for reading the bytes.

❹ Read from the byte position to the end of the file and place the results into the buffer.

❺ If the buffer is not empty, convert the selected bytes to a `String` and print.

Here's how I integrated this into the run function:

```
fn run(args: Args) -> Result<()> {
    let lines = parse_num(args.lines)
        .map_err(|e| anyhow!("illegal line count -- {e}"))?;

    let bytes = args
        .bytes
        .map(parse_num)
        .transpose()
        .map_err(|e| anyhow!("illegal byte count -- {e}"))?;

    for filename in args.files {
        match File::open(&filename) {
            Err(err) => eprintln!("{filename}: {err}"),
            Ok(file) => {
                let (total_lines, total_bytes) =
                    count_lines_bytes(&filename)?;
```

```
            let file = BufReader::new(file);
            if let Some(num_bytes) = &&bytes { ❶
                print_bytes(file, &num_bytes, total_bytes)?; ❷
            } else {
                print_lines(file, &lines, total_lines)?; ❸
            }
        }
    }
}
Ok(())
}
```

❶ Check if the user has requested a byte selection.

❷ If so, print the selected bytes.

❸ Otherwise, print the line selection.

A quick check with **cargo test** shows I'm inching ever closer to passing all my tests. All the failing tests start with *multiple*, and they are failing because my program is not printing the headers separating the output from each file. I'll modify the code from Chapter 4 for this where we did something similar. Here is my final run function that will pass all the tests:

```
fn run(args: Args) -> Result<()> {
    let lines = parse_num(args.lines)
        .map_err(|e| anyhow!("illegal line count -- {e}"))?;

    let bytes = args
        .bytes
        .map(parse_num)
        .transpose()
        .map_err(|e| anyhow!("illegal byte count -- {e}"))?;

    let num_files = args.files.len(); ❶
    for (file_num, filename) in args.files.iter().enumerate() { ❷
        match File::open(filename) {
            Err(err) => eprintln!("{filename}: {err}"),
            Ok(file) => {
                if !args.quiet && num_files > 1 { ❸
                    println!(
                        "{}==> {filename} <==",
                        if file_num > 0 { "\n" } else { "" },
                    );
                }

                let (total_lines, total_bytes) = count_lines_bytes(filename)?;
                let file = BufReader::new(file);
                if let Some(num_bytes) = &bytes {
                    print_bytes(file, num_bytes, total_bytes)?;
                } else {
```

```
                        print_lines(file, &lines, total_lines)?;
                    }
                }
            }
        }

        Ok(())
    }
```

❶ Find the number of files.

❷ Use `Iterator::enumerate` to iterate through the index positions and filenames.

❸ If the `quiet` option is `false` and there are multiple files, print the header.

Benchmarking the Solution

How does the `tailr` program compare to `tail` for the subset of features it shares? I suggested earlier that you could use the `biggie` program to create large input files to test your program. I created a file called *1M.txt* that has one million lines of randomly generated text to use in testing my program. I can use the `time` command to see how long it takes for `tail` to find the last 10 lines of the *1M.txt* file:[2]

```
$ time tail 1M.txt > /dev/null  ❶

real    0m0.022s  ❷
user    0m0.006s  ❸
sys     0m0.015s  ❹
```

❶ I don't want to see the output from the command, so I redirect it to `/dev/null`, a special system device that ignores its input.

❷ The `real` time is *wall clock time*, measuring how long the process took from start to finish.

❸ The `user` time is how long the CPU spent in *user* mode outside the kernel.

❹ The `sys` time is how long the CPU spent working inside the kernel.

I want to build the fastest version of `tailr` possible to compare to `tail`, so I'll use **cargo build --release** to create a release build (*https://oreil.ly/A9BMw*). The binary will be created at *target/release/tailr*. This build of the program appears to be much slower than `tail`:

---

2 I used macOS 14.2.1 running on a MacBook Pro M1 with 8 cores and 8 GB RAM for all the benchmarking tests.

```
$ time target/release/tailr 1M.txt > /dev/null

real    0m0.505s
user    0m0.072s
sys     0m0.024s
```

This is the start of a process called *benchmarking*, where I try to compare how well different programs work. Running one iteration and eyeballing the output is not very scientific or effective. Luckily, there is a Rust crate called hyperfine (*https://oreil.ly/ICXBY*) that can do this much better. After installing it with **cargo install hyperfine**, I can run benchmarks and find that my Rust program is much slower than the system tail when printing the last 10 lines from the *1M.txt* file:

```
$ hyperfine -i -L prg tail,target/release/tailr '{prg} 1M.txt > /dev/null'
Benchmark 1: tail 1M.txt > /dev/null
  Time (mean ± σ):      4.3 ms ±   6.6 ms    [User: 1.7 ms, System: 3.2 ms]
  Range (min … max):    2.6 ms …  49.9 ms    50 runs

Benchmark 2: target/release/tailr 1M.txt > /dev/null
  Time (mean ± σ):     86.9 ms ±   3.2 ms    [User: 70.2 ms, System: 16.5 ms]
  Range (min … max):   84.8 ms … 100.5 ms    27 runs

Summary
  tail 1M.txt > /dev/null ran
   20.32 ± 31.44 times faster than target/release/tailr 1M.txt > /dev/null
```

If I request the last 100K lines, however, the Rust version fares better:

```
$ hyperfine -i -L prg tail,target/release/tailr '{prg} -n 100000 1M.txt
  > /dev/null'
Benchmark 1: tail -n 100000 1M.txt > /dev/null
  Time (mean ± σ):     26.8 ms ±   0.5 ms    [User: 19.8 ms, System: 5.4 ms]
  Range (min … max):   25.9 ms …  28.9 ms    82 runs

Benchmark 2: target/release/tailr -n 100000 1M.txt > /dev/null
  Time (mean ± σ):    154.7 ms ±   1.4 ms    [User: 108.1 ms, System: 43.8 ms]
  Range (min … max):  153.4 ms … 158.1 ms    18 runs

Summary
  tail -n 100000 1M.txt > /dev/null ran
    5.78 ± 0.12 times faster than target/release/tailr -n 100000 1M.txt
    > /dev/null
```

If I change the command to {prg} -c 100 1M.txt to print the last 100 bytes, the Rust version is still slower:

```
Summary
  tail -c 100 1M.txt ran
    14.98 ± 2.51 times faster than target/release/tailr -c 100 1M.txt
```

If I request the last million bytes, however, the Rust version is a little faster:

```
Summary
  target/release/tailr -c 1000000 1M.txt ran
    1.34 ± 0.04 times faster than tail -c 1000000 1M.txt
```

To improve the performance, the next step would probably be profiling the code to find where Rust is using most of the time and memory. Program optimization is a fascinating and deep topic well beyond the scope of this book.

Going Further

See how many of the BSD and GNU options you can implement, including the size suffixes and reading STDIN. One of the more challenging options is to *follow* the files. When I'm developing web applications, I often use tail -f to watch the access and error logs of a web server to see requests and responses as they happen. I suggest you search *crates.io* for "tail" (*https://oreil.ly/Lo6rG*) to see how others have implemented these ideas.

Summary

Reflect upon your progress in this chapter:

- You learned how to create a regular expression as a static, global variable using the once_cell crate.
- You learned how to seek a line or byte position in a filehandle.
- You saw how to indicate multiple trait bounds like <T: Read + Seek> and also how to write this using where.
- You learned how to make Cargo build a release binary.
- You used hyperfine to benchmark programs.

In the next chapter, you will learn how to use and control pseudorandom number generators to make random selections.

CHAPTER 12

Fortunate Son

Now I laugh and make a fortune / Off the same ones that I tortured

— They Might Be Giants, "Kiss Me, Son of God" (1988)

In this chapter, you will create a Rust version of the `fortune` program that will print a randomly selected aphorism or bit of trivia or interesting ASCII art[1] from a database of text files. The program gets its name from a fortune cookie, a crisp cookie that contains a small piece of paper printed with a short bit of text that might be a fortune like "You will take a trip soon" or maybe a short joke or saying. When I was first learning to use a Unix terminal in my undergraduate days,[2] a successful login would often include the output from `fortune`.

You will learn how to do the following:

- Use the `Path` and `PathBuf` structs to represent system paths
- Parse records of text spanning multiple lines from a file
- Use randomness and control it with seeds
- Use the `OsStr` and `OsString` types to represent filenames

---

1 *ASCII art* is a term for graphics that use only ASCII text values.

2 This was in the 1990s, which I believe the kids nowadays refer to as "the late 1900s."

How fortune Works

I will start by describing how `fortune` works so you will have an idea of what your
version will need to do. You may first need to install the program,[3] as it is not often
present by default on most systems. Here's a bit of the manual page, which you can
read with **man fortune**:

```
NAME
        fortune - print a random, hopefully interesting, adage

SYNOPSIS
        fortune [-acefilosuw] [-n length] [ -m pattern] [[n%] file/dir/all]

DESCRIPTION
        When  fortune  is run with no arguments it prints out a random epigram.
        Epigrams are divided into several categories, where  each  category  is
        sub-divided  into those which are potentially offensive and those which
        are not.
```

The original program has many options, but the challenge program will be concerned
only with the following:

```
-m pattern
        Print out all fortunes which match the basic regular  expression
        pattern.   The  syntax  of these expressions depends on how your
        system defines re_comp(3) or regcomp(3), but it should neverthe-
        less be similar to the syntax used in grep(1).

        The  fortunes  are output to standard output, while the names of
        the file from which each fortune comes are printed  to  standard
        error.   Either or both can be redirected; if standard output is
        redirected to a file, the result is a  valid  fortunes  database
        file.   If  standard  error is also redirected to this file, the
        result is still valid, but there  will  be  ''bogus''  fortunes,
        i.e. the filenames themselves, in parentheses.  This can be use-
        ful if you wish to remove the gathered matches from their origi-
        nal  files,  since each filename-record will precede the records
        from the file it names.

-i      Ignore case for -m patterns.
```

When the `fortune` program is run with no arguments, it will randomly choose and
print some text:

```
$ fortune
Laughter is the closest distance between two people.
                -- Victor Borge
```

---

3 On Ubuntu, sudo apt install fortune-mod; on macOS, brew install fortune.

Whence does this text originate? The manual page notes that you can supply one or more files or directories of the text sources. If no files are given, then the program will read from some default location. On my laptop, this is what the manual page says:

```
FILES
        Note: these are the defaults as defined at compile time.

        /opt/homebrew/Cellar/fortune/9708/share/games/fortunes
                Directory for inoffensive fortunes.
        /opt/homebrew/Cellar/fortune/9708/share/games/fortunes/off
                Directory for offensive fortunes.
```

I created a few representative files in the *12_fortuner/tests/inputs* directory for testing purposes, along with an empty directory:

```
$ cd 12_fortuner
$ ls tests/inputs/
ascii-art   empty/     jokes       literature  quotes
```

Use head to look at the structure of a file. A fortune record can span multiple lines and is terminated with a percent sign (%) on a line by itself:

```
$ head -n 9 tests/inputs/jokes
Q. What do you call a head of lettuce in a shirt and tie?
A. Collared greens.
%
Q: Why did the gardener quit his job?
A: His celery wasn't high enough.
%
Q. Why did the honeydew couple get married in a church?
A. Their parents told them they cantaloupe.
%
```

You can tell fortune to read a particular file like *tests/inputs/ascii-art*, but first you will need to use the program strfile (*https://oreil.ly/jYa5O*) to create index files for randomly selecting the text records. I have provided a bash script called *mk-dat.sh* in the *12_fortuner* directory that will index the files in the *tests/inputs* directory. After running this program, each input file should have a companion file ending in *.dat*:

```
$ ls -1 tests/inputs/
ascii-art
ascii-art.dat
empty/
jokes
jokes.dat
literature
literature.dat
quotes
quotes.dat
```

Now you should be able to run the following command to, for instance, randomly select a bit of ASCII art. You may or may not see a cute frog:

```
$ fortune tests/inputs/ascii-art
```

You can also supply the *tests/inputs* directory to tell `fortune` to select a record from any of the files therein:

```
$ fortune tests/inputs
A classic is something that everyone wants to have read
and nobody wants to read.
                -- Mark Twain, "The Disappearance of Literature"
```

If a provided path does not exist, `fortune` will immediately halt with an error. Here I'll use *blargh* for a nonexistent file:

```
$ fortune tests/inputs/jokes blargh tests/inputs/ascii-art
blargh: No such file or directory
```

Oddly, if the input source exists but is not readable, one version of `fortune` will complain that the file does not exist and produces no further output:

```
$ touch hammer && chmod 000 hammer
$ fortune hammer
hammer: No such file or directory
```

Another version explains that the file is not readable and informs the user that no fortunes were available for choosing:

```
$ fortune hammer
/home/u20/kyclark/hammer: Permission denied
No fortunes found
```

Using the `-m` option, I can search for all the text records matching a given string. The output will include a header printed to STDERR listing the filename that contains the records followed by the records printed to STDOUT. For instance, here are all the quotes by Yogi Berra:

```
$ fortune -m 'Yogi Berra' tests/inputs/
(quotes)
%
It's like deja vu all over again.
-- Yogi Berra
%
You can observe a lot just by watching.
-- Yogi Berra
%
```

If I search for *Mark Twain* and redirect both STDERR and STDOUT to files, I find that quotes of his are found in the *literature* and *quotes* files. Note that the headers printed to STDERR include only the basename of the file, like *literature*, and not the full path, like *tests/inputs/literature*:

```
$ fortune -m 'Mark Twain' tests/inputs/ 1>out 2>err
$ cat err
(literature)
%
(quotes)
%
```

Searching is case-sensitive by default, so searching for lowercase *yogi berra* will return no results. I must use the -i flag to perform case-insensitive matching:

```
$ fortune -i -m 'yogi berra' tests/inputs/
(quotes)
%
It's like deja vu all over again.
-- Yogi Berra
%
You can observe a lot just by watching.
-- Yogi Berra
%
```

While fortune can do a few more things, this is as much as the challenge program will re-create.

Getting Started

The challenge program for this chapter will be called fortuner (pronounced *for-chu-ner*) for a Rust version of fortune. You should begin with **cargo new fortuner**, and then add the following dependencies to your *Cargo.toml*:

```
[dependencies]
anyhow = "1.0.79"
clap = { version = "4.5.0", features = ["derive"] }
rand = "0.8.5"
regex = "1.10.3"
walkdir = "2.4.0"
```

```
[dev-dependencies]
assert_cmd = "2.0.13"
predicates = "3.0.4"
pretty_assertions = "1.4.0"
```

Copy the book's *12_fortuner/tests* directory into your project. Run **cargo test** to build the program and run the tests, all of which should fail.

Defining the Arguments

Update your *src/main.rs* to the following to define the program's arguments:

```
#[derive(Debug)]
pub struct Args {
    sources: Vec<String>,    ❶
    pattern: Option<String>, ❷
    insensitive: bool,       ❸
    seed: Option<u64>,       ❹
}
```

❶ The sources argument is a list of files or directories.

❷ The pattern is an optional string to filter fortunes.

❸ insensitive is a Boolean option for whether or not to search with case-sensitivity.

❹ The seed is an optional u64 value to control random selections.

Either annotate the Args for the clap derive pattern or start the builder pattern with the following skeleton for a get_args function:

```
fn get_args() -> Args {
    let matches = Command::new("fortuner")
        .version("0.1.0")
        .author("Ken Youens-Clark <kyclark@gmail.com>")
        .about("Rust version of `fortune`")
        // What goes here?
        .get_matches();

    Args {
        sources: ...
        seed: ...
        pattern: ...
        insensitive: ...
    }
}
```

Have the main pretty-print the arguments to start:

```
fn main() {
    let args = get_args();
    println!("{args:#?}");
}
```

Your program should be able to print a usage statement like the following:

```
$ cargo run -- -h
Rust version of `fortune`

Usage: fortuner [OPTIONS] <FILE>...

Arguments:
  <FILE>...  Input files or directories

Options:
  -m, --pattern <PATTERN>  Pattern
  -i, --insensitive        Case-insensitive pattern matching
  -s, --seed <SEED>        Random seed
  -h, --help               Print help
  -V, --version            Print version
```

Unlike the original `fortune`, the challenge program will require one or more input files or directories. When run with no arguments, it should halt and print the usage:

```
$ cargo run
error: the following required arguments were not provided:
  <FILE>...

Usage: fortuner <FILE>...

For more information, try '--help'.
```

Verify that the arguments are parsed correctly:

```
$ cargo run -- ./tests/inputs -m 'Yogi Berra' -s 1
Args {
    sources: [
        "./tests/inputs", ❶
    ],
    pattern: Some( ❷
        "Yogi Berra",
    ),
    insensitive: false, ❸
    seed: Some( ❹
        1,
    ),
}
```

❶ Positional arguments should be interpreted as `sources`.

❷ The `-m` option should be the value for the `pattern`.

❸ The insensitive flag defaults to false.

❹ The -s option should be parsed as a u64, if present.

Any value for the --seed that cannot be parsed as a u64 should also be rejected:

```
$ cargo run -- ./tests/inputs -s blargh
error: invalid value 'blargh' for '--seed <SEED>':
invalid digit found in string
```

 Stop reading and get your program to match the preceding output. It should also pass the tests *dies_not_enough_args* and *dies_bad_seed*.

Seeding Random Number Generators

The challenge program will randomly choose some text to show, but computers don't usually make completely random choices. As Robert R. Coveyou stated, "Random number generation is too important to be left to chance."[4] The challenge program will use a *pseudorandom number generator* (PRNG) that will always make the same selection following from some starting value, often called a *seed*. That is, for any given seed, the same "random" choices will follow. This makes it possible to test pseudo-random programs because we can use a known seed to verify that it produces some expected output. I'll be using the rand crate (*https://oreil.ly/aKH3G*) to create a PRNG, optionally using the args.seed value when present. When no seed is present, then the program will make a different pseudorandom choice based on some other random input and so will appear to actually be random. For more information, consult "The Rust Rand Book" (*https://oreil.ly/J7gRz*).

Here is how I define the arguments in my get_args. I won't comment on this as it's similar to many previous programs. Be sure to add use clap::{Arg, ArgAction, Command} for the following code:

```
fn get_args() -> Args {
    let matches = Command::new("fortuner")
        .version("0.1.0")
        .author("Ken Youens-Clark <kyclark@gmail.com>")
        .about("Rust version of `fortune`")
        .arg(
            Arg::new("sources")
```

---

4 Robert R. Coveyou, "Random Number Generation Is Too Important to Be Left to Chance," *Studies in Applied Mathematics* 3(1969): 70–111.

```
                    .value_name("FILE")
                    .num_args(1..)
                    .required(true)
                    .help("Input files or directories"),
            )
            .arg(
                Arg::new("pattern")
                    .value_name("PATTERN")
                    .short('m')
                    .long("pattern")
                    .help("Pattern"),
            )
            .arg(
                Arg::new("insensitive")
                    .short('i')
                    .long("insensitive")
                    .help("Case-insensitive pattern matching")
                    .action(ArgAction::SetTrue),
            )
            .arg(
                Arg::new("seed")
                    .value_name("SEED")
                    .short('s')
                    .long("seed")
                    .value_parser(clap::value_parser!(u64))
                    .help("Random seed"),
            )
            .get_matches();

    Args {
        sources: matches.get_many("sources").unwrap().cloned().collect(),
        seed: matches.get_one("seed").cloned(),
        pattern: matches.get_one("pattern").cloned(),
        insensitive: matches.get_flag("insensitive"),
    }
}
```

For the derive pattern, I include use clap::Parser and the following:

```
#[derive(Debug, Parser)]
#[command(author, version, about)]
/// Rust version of `fortune`
struct Args {
    /// Input files or directories
    #[arg(required(true), value_name = "FILE")]
    sources: Vec<String>,

    /// Pattern
    #[arg(short('m'), long)]
    pattern: Option<String>,

    /// Case-insensitive pattern matching
    #[arg(short, long)]
```

```
    insensitive: bool,

    /// Random seed
    #[arg(short, long, value_parser(clap::value_parser!(u64)))]
    seed: Option<u64>,
}
```

Next, I will have main call a run function.

```
fn main() {
    if let Err(e) = run(Args::parse()) {
        eprintln!("{e}");
        std::process::exit(1);
    }
}
```

Inside my run, I want to use the --insensitive flag with regex::RegexBuilder (*https://oreil.ly/oXA6X*) to create a regular expression that might be case-insensitive. This is similar to what we did in Chapter 9, except that the args.pattern here is an optional string that I want to turn into an optional regex. Be sure to use regex::RegexBuilder and anyhow::{anyhow, Result} for the following:

```
fn run(args: Args) -> Result<()> {
    let pattern = args
        .pattern ❶
        .map(|val: String| { ❷
            RegexBuilder::new(val.as_str()) ❸
                .case_insensitive(args.insensitive) ❹
                .build() ❺
                .map_err(|_| anyhow!(r#"Invalid --pattern "{val}""#)) ❻
        })
        .transpose()?; ❼

    println!("{pattern:?}");
    Ok(())
}
```

❶ args.pattern is an Option<String>.

❷ Use Option::map (*https://oreil.ly/JaDYG*) to handle Some(val).

❸ Call RegexBuilder::new with the given value.

❹ The RegexBuilder::case_insensitive method (*https://oreil.ly/rRTXv*) will cause the regex to disregard case in comparisons when the insensitive flag is present.

❺ The RegexBuilder::build method (*https://oreil.ly/wrXyO*) will compile the regex.

```
```

❻   If build returns an error, use Result::map_err (*https://oreil.ly/4izCX*) to create an error message stating that the given pattern is invalid.

❼   The result of Option::map will be an Option<Result>, and Option::transpose (*https://oreil.ly/QCi0s*) will turn this into a Result<Option>. Use ? to fail on an invalid regex.

An invalid regular expression should be rejected at this point, and your program should pass **cargo test dies_bad_pattern**. As noted in Chapter 9, for instance, a lone asterisk is not a valid regex:

```
$ cargo run -- ./tests/inputs -m "*"
Invalid --pattern "*"
```

Your program should now be able to print a debug representation of the regex pattern:

```
$ cargo run -- -m Yogi tests/inputs/
Some(Regex("Yogi"))
```

Finding the Input Sources

You are free to write your solution however you see fit so long as it passes the integration tests. This is a rather complicated program, so I'm going to break it into many small, testable functions to help you arrive at a solution.[5] If you want to follow my lead, then the next order of business is finding the input files from the given sources, which might be filenames or directories. When a source is a directory, all the files in the directory will be used. To read the fortune files, the fortune program requires the *.dat files created by strfile. These are binary files that contain data for randomly accessing the records. The challenge program will not use these and so should skip them, if present. If you ran the *mk-dat.sh* program, you can either remove the *.dat* files from *tests/inputs* or include logic in your program to skip them.

I decided to write a function to find all the files in a list of paths provided by the user. While I could return the files as strings, I want to introduce you to a couple of useful structs Rust has for representing paths. The first is Path (*https://oreil.ly/H9eW4*), which, according to the documentation, "supports a number of operations for inspecting a path, including breaking the path into its components (separated by / on Unix and by either / or \ on Windows), extracting the file name, determining whether the path is absolute, and so on." That sounds useful, so you might think my function should return the results as Path objects, but the documentation notes:

---

5   "The art in engineering is not so much to make something very complicated. The art is to make a complicated problem simpler." Niklaus Wirth, quoted in Ken Takara, "Programming Philosophy: Interviews with Donald Knuth and Niklaus Wirth," *Computer Language* 2, no. 5 (May 1985): 25-35.

"This is an *unsized* type, meaning that it must always be used behind a pointer like &
or Box. For an owned version of this type, see PathBuf."

This leads us to PathBuf (*https://oreil.ly/Mth0r*), the second useful module for representing paths. Just as String is an owned, modifiable version of &str, PathBuf is an
owned, modifiable version of Path. Returning a Path from my function would lead to
compiler errors, as my code would be trying to reference dropped values, but there
will be no such problem returning a PathBuf. You are not required to use either of
these structs, but they will make your program portable across operating systems and
will save you a lot of work that's been done to parse paths correctly. Following is the
signature of my find_files function, which you are welcome to use. Be sure to add
use std::path::PathBuf to your imports:

```
fn find_files(paths: &[String]) -> Result<Vec<PathBuf>> {
    unimplemented!();
}
```

Add the following unit test to *src/main.rs*:

```
#[cfg(test)]
mod tests {
    use super::find_files; ❶

    #[test]
    fn test_find_files() {
        // Verify that the function finds a file known to exist
        let res = find_files(&["./tests/inputs/jokes".to_string()]);
        assert!(res.is_ok());

        let files = res.unwrap();
        assert_eq!(files.len(), 1);
        assert_eq!(
            files.get(0).unwrap().to_string_lossy(),
            "./tests/inputs/jokes"
        );

        // Fails to find a bad file
        let res = find_files(&["/path/does/not/exist".to_string()]);
        assert!(res.is_err());

        // Finds all the input files, excludes ".dat"
        let res = find_files(&["./tests/inputs".to_string()]);
        assert!(res.is_ok());

        // Check number and order of files
        let files = res.unwrap();
        assert_eq!(files.len(), 5); ❷
        let first = files.get(0).unwrap().display().to_string();
        assert!(first.contains("ascii-art"));
        let last = files.last().unwrap().display().to_string();
        assert!(last.contains("quotes"));
```

```
        // Test for multiple sources, path must be unique and sorted
        let res = find_files(&[
            "./tests/inputs/jokes".to_string(),
            "./tests/inputs/ascii-art".to_string(),
            "./tests/inputs/jokes".to_string(),
        ]);
        assert!(res.is_ok());
        let files = res.unwrap();
        assert_eq!(files.len(), 2);
        if let Some(filename) = files.first().unwrap().file_name() {
            assert_eq!(filename.to_string_lossy(), "ascii-art".to_string())
        }
        if let Some(filename) = files.last().unwrap().file_name() {
            assert_eq!(filename.to_string_lossy(), "jokes".to_string())
        }
    }
}
```

❶ Import find_files.

❷ The *tests/inputs/empty* directory contains the empty, hidden file *.gitkeep* so that
Git will track this directory. If you choose to ignore empty files, you can change
the expected number of files from five to four.

Note that the find_files function must return the paths in sorted order. Different
operating systems will return the files in different orders, which will lead to the fortunes being in different orders, leading to difficulties in testing. You will nip the problem in the bud if you return the files in a consistent, sorted order. Furthermore, the
returned paths should be unique, and you can use a combination of Vec::sort
(*https://oreil.ly/ua40G*) and Vec::dedup (*https://oreil.ly/7FvsZ*) for this.

Stop reading and write the function that will satisfy **cargo test
find_files**.

Next, update your run function to print the found files:

```
fn run(args: Args) -> Result<()> {
    let _pattern = // Sames as before
    let files = find_files(&args.sources)?;
    println!("{files:#?}");
    Ok(())
}
```

When given a list of existing, readable files, it should print them in order:

```
$ cargo run tests/inputs/jokes tests/inputs/ascii-art
[
    "tests/inputs/ascii-art",
    "tests/inputs/jokes",
]
```

Test your program to see if it will find the files (that don't end with *.dat*) in the *tests /inputs* directory:

```
$ cargo run tests/inputs/
[
    "tests/inputs/ascii-art",
    "tests/inputs/empty/.gitkeep",
    "tests/inputs/jokes",
    "tests/inputs/literature",
    "tests/inputs/quotes",
]
```

Previous challenge programs in this book would note unreadable or nonexistent files and move on, but fortune dies immediately when given even one file it can't use. Be sure your program does the same if you provide an invalid file, such as the nonexistent *blargh*:

```
$ cargo run tests/inputs/jokes blargh tests/inputs/ascii-art
blargh: No such file or directory (os error 2)
```

Note that my version of find_files tries only to *find* files and does not try to open them, which means an unreadable file does not trigger a failure at this point:

```
$ touch hammer && chmod 000 hammer
$ cargo run -- hammer
[
    "hammer",
]
```

Reading the Fortune Files

Once you have found the input files, the next step is to read the records of text from them. I wrote a function that accepts the list of found files and possibly returns a list of the contained fortunes. When the program is run with the -m option to find all the matching fortunes for a given pattern, I will need both the fortune text and the source filename, so I decided to create a struct called Fortune to contain these. If you want to use this idea, add the following struct perhaps just after the Args:

```
#[derive(Debug)]
struct Fortune {
    source: String,  ❶
    text: String,  ❷
}
```

❶ The source is the filename containing the record.

❷ The text is the contents of the record up to but not including the terminating percent sign (%).

My read_fortunes function accepts a list of input paths and possibly returns a vector of Fortune structs. In the event of a problem such as an unreadable file, the function will return an error. If you would like to write this function, here is the signature you can use:

```
fn read_fortunes(paths: &[PathBuf]) -> Result<Vec<Fortune>> {
    unimplemented!();
}
```

Following is a test_read_fortunes unit test you can add to the tests module:

```
#[cfg(test)]
mod tests {
    use super::{find_files, read_fortunes, Fortune}; ❶
    use std::path::PathBuf;

    #[test]
    fn test_find_files() {} // Same as before

    #[test]
    fn test_read_fortunes() {
        // One input file
        let res = read_fortunes(&[PathBuf::from("./tests/inputs/jokes")]);
        assert!(res.is_ok());

        if let Ok(fortunes) = res {
            // Correct number and sorting
            assert_eq!(fortunes.len(), 6); ❷
            assert_eq!(
                fortunes.first().unwrap().text,
                "Q. What do you call a head of lettuce in a shirt and tie?\n\
                A. Collared greens."
            );
            assert_eq!(
                fortunes.last().unwrap().text,
                "Q: What do you call a deer wearing an eye patch?\n\
                A: A bad idea (bad-eye deer)."
            );
        }

        // Multiple input files
        let res = read_fortunes(&[
            PathBuf::from("./tests/inputs/jokes"),
            PathBuf::from("./tests/inputs/quotes"),
        ]);
        assert!(res.is_ok());
```

```
        assert_eq!(res.unwrap().len(), 11);
    }
}
```

❶ Import `read_fortunes`, `Fortune`, and `PathBuf` for testing.

❷ The *tests/inputs/jokes* file contains an empty fortune that is expected to be removed.

 Stop here and implement a version of the function that passes `cargo test read_fortunes`.

Update `run` to print, for instance, one of the found records:

```
fn run(args: Args) -> Result<()> {
    let _pattern = // Same as before
    let files = find_files(&args.sources)?;
    let fortunes = read_fortunes(&files)?;
    println!("{:#?}", fortunes.last());
    Ok(())
}
```

When passed good input sources, the program should print a fortune like so:

```
$ cargo run tests/inputs
Some(
    Fortune {
        source: "quotes",
        text: "You can observe a lot just by watching.\n-- Yogi Berra",
    },
)
```

When provided an unreadable file, such as the previously created *hammer* file, the program should die with a useful error message:

```
$ cargo run hammer
hammer: Permission denied (os error 13)
```

Randomly Selecting a Fortune

The program will have two possible outputs. When the user supplies a `pattern`, the program should print all the fortunes matching the pattern; otherwise, the program should randomly select one fortune to print. For the latter option, I wrote a `pick_fortune` function that takes some fortunes and an optional seed and returns an optional string:

```
fn pick_fortune(fortunes: &[Fortune], seed: Option<u64>) -> Option<String> {
    unimplemented!();
}
```

My function uses the rand crate to select the fortune using a *random number genera-tor* (RNG), as described earlier in the chapter. When there is no seed value, I use rand::thread_rng (*https://oreil.ly/V2gh5*) to create an RNG that is seeded by the sys-tem. When there is a seed value, I use rand::rngs::StdRng::seed_from_u64 (*https:// oreil.ly/hcrzg*). Finally, I use Slice Random::choose (*https://oreil.ly/hBg3S*) with the RNG to select a fortune.

Following is how you can expand your tests module to include the test_read _fortunes unit test:

```
#[cfg(test)]
mod tests {
    use super::{find_files, pick_fortune, read_fortunes, Fortune}; ❶
    use std::path::PathBuf;

    #[test]
    fn test_find_files() {} // Same as before

    #[test]
    fn test_read_fortunes() {} // Same as before

    #[test]
    fn test_pick_fortune() {
        // Create a slice of fortunes
        let fortunes = &[
            Fortune {
                source: "fortunes".to_string(),
                text: "You cannot achieve the impossible without \
                    attempting the absurd."
                    .to_string(),
            },
            Fortune {
                source: "fortunes".to_string(),
                text: "Assumption is the mother of all screw-ups."
                    .to_string(),
            },
            Fortune {
                source: "fortunes".to_string(),
                text: "Neckties strangle clear thinking.".to_string(),
            },
        ];

        // Pick a fortune with a seed
        assert_eq!(
            pick_fortune(fortunes, Some(1)).unwrap(), ❷
            "Neckties strangle clear thinking.".to_string()
        );
```

```
        }
    }
```

❶ Import the pick_fortune function for testing.

❷ Supply a seed to verify that the pseudorandom selection is reproducible.

 Stop reading and write the function that will pass **cargo test pick_fortune**.

You can integrate this function into your run like so:

```
fn run(args: Args) -> Result<()> {
    let _pattern = // Same as before
    let files = find_files(&args.sources)?;
    let fortunes = read_fortunes(&files)?;
    println!("{:#?}", pick_fortune(&fortunes, args.seed));
    Ok(())
}
```

Run your program with no seed and revel in the ensuing chaos of randomness:

```
$ cargo run tests/inputs/
Some(
    "Q: Why did the gardener quit his job?\nA: His celery wasn't high enough.",
)
```

When provided a seed, the program should always select the same fortune:

```
$ cargo run tests/inputs/ -s 1
Some(
    "You can observe a lot just by watching.\n-- Yogi Berra",
)
```

 The tests I wrote are predicated on the fortunes being in a particular order. I wrote find_files to return the files in sorted order, which means the list of fortunes passed to pick_fortune are ordered first by their source filename and then by their order inside the file. If you use a different data structure to represent the fortunes or parse them in a different order, then you'll need to change the tests to reflect your decisions. The key is to find a way to make your pseudorandom choices predictable and testable.

Printing Records Matching a Pattern

You now have all the pieces for finishing the program. The last step is to decide whether to print all the fortunes that match a given regular expression or to randomly select one fortune. You can expand your run function like so:

```
fn run(args: Args) -> Result<()> {
    // Same as before

    match pattern {
        Some(pattern) => {
            for fortune in fortunes {
                // Print all the fortunes matching the pattern
            }
        }
        _ => {
            // Select and print one fortune
        }
    }

    Ok(())
}
```

Remember that the program should let the user know when there are no fortunes, such as when using the *tests/inputs/empty* directory:

```
$ cargo run tests/inputs/empty
No fortunes found
```

That should be enough information for you to finish this program using the provided tests. This is a tough problem, but don't give up.

Solution

For my solution, you will need to include the following imports:

```
use anyhow::{anyhow, bail, Result};
use rand::prelude::SliceRandom;
use rand::{rngs::StdRng, RngCore, SeedableRng};
use regex::RegexBuilder;
use std::{
    ffi::OsStr,
    fs::{self, File},
    io::{BufRead, BufReader},
    path::PathBuf,
};
use walkdir::WalkDir;
```

I'll show you how I wrote each of the functions I described in the previous section, starting with the find_files function. You will notice that it filters out files that have the extension .*dat* using the type OsStr (*https://oreil.ly/CAeUi*), which is a Rust type for an operating system's preferred representation of a string that might not be a valid UTF-8 string. The type OsStr is borrowed, and the owned version is OsString (*https://oreil.ly/J3nFa*). These are similar to the Path and PathBuf distinctions. Both versions encapsulate the complexities of dealing with filenames on both Windows and Unix platforms. In the following code, you'll see that I use Path::extension (*https://oreil.ly/aOffl*), which returns Option<&OsStr>:

```
fn find_files(paths: &[String]) -> Result<Vec<PathBuf>> {
    let dat = OsStr::new("dat"); ❶
    let mut files = vec![]; ❷

    for path in paths {
        match fs::metadata(path) {
            Err(e) => bail!("{path}: {e}"), ❸
            Ok(_) => files.extend( ❹
                WalkDir::new(path) ❺
                    .into_iter()
                    .filter_map(Result::ok) ❻
                    .filter(|e| {
                        e.file_type().is_file() ❼
                            && e.path().extension() != Some(dat)
                    })
                    .map(|e| e.path().into()), ❽
            ),
        }
    }

    files.sort(); ❾
    files.dedup(); ❿
    Ok(files) ⓫
}
```

❶ Create an OsStr value for the string *dat*.

❷ Create a mutable vector for the results.

❸ If fs::metadata (*https://oreil.ly/VsRxb*) fails, return a useful error message.

❹ Use Vec::extend (*https://oreil.ly/nWMcd*) to add the results from WalkDir to the results.

❺ Use walkdir::WalkDir (*https://oreil.ly/o6mZn*) to find all the entries from the starting path.

❻ This will ignore any errors for unreadable files or directories, which is the behavior of the original program.

❼ Take only regular files that do not have the *.dat* extension.

❽ The `walkdir::DirEntry::path` function (*https://oreil.ly/1dWxe*) returns a `Path`, so convert it into a `PathBuf`.

❾ Use `Vec::sort` (*https://oreil.ly/ua40G*) to sort the entries in place.

❿ Use `Vec::dedup` (*https://oreil.ly/7FvsZ*) to remove consecutive repeated values.

⓫ Return the sorted, unique files.

The files found by the preceding function are the inputs to the `read_fortunes` function:

```
fn read_fortunes(paths: &[PathBuf]) -> Result<Vec<Fortune>> {
    let mut fortunes = vec![]; ❶
    let mut buffer = vec![];

    for path in paths { ❷
        let basename = ❸
            path.file_name().unwrap().to_string_lossy().into_owned();
        let file = File::open(path)
            .map_err(|e| anyhow!("{}: {e}", path.to_string_lossy()))?; ❹

        for line in BufReader::new(file).lines().map_while(Result::ok) { ❺
            if line == "%" { ❻
                if !buffer.is_empty() { ❼
                    fortunes.push(Fortune {
                        source: basename.clone(),
                        text: buffer.join("\n"),
                    });
                    buffer.clear();
                }
            } else {
                buffer.push(line.to_string()); ❽
            }
        }
    }

    Ok(fortunes)
}
```

❶ Create mutable vectors for the fortunes and a record buffer.

❷ Iterate through the given filenames.

❸ Convert `Path::file_name` (*https://oreil.ly/PVqKf*) from `OsStr` to `String`, using the *lossy* version in case this is not valid UTF-8. The result is a *clone-on-write* smart pointer, so use `Cow::into_owned` (*https://oreil.ly/Jpdd0*) to clone the data if it is not already owned.

❹ Open the file or return an error message.

❺ Iterate through the lines of the file.

❻ A sole percent sign (%) indicates the end of a record.

❼ If the buffer is not empty, set the `text` to the buffer lines joined on newlines and then clear the buffer.

❽ Otherwise, add the current line to the `buffer`.

Writing the `pick_fortune` function was a journey. I first tried to write it as follows:

```
// This will not compile
fn pick_fortune(fortunes: &[Fortune], seed: Option<u64>) -> Option<String> {
    let mut rng = match seed {
        Some(val) => StdRng::seed_from_u64(val),
        _ => rand::thread_rng(),
    };

    fortunes.choose(&mut rng).map(|f| f.text.to_string())
}
```

The compiler rejected this because one arm of the `match` returns the type `StdRng` and the other a `ThreadRng`:

```
error[E0308]: `match` arms have incompatible types
  --> src/main.rs:150:14
   |
148 |         let mut rng = match seed {
   |                       _____-
149 | |             Some(val) => StdRng::seed_from_u64(val),
   | |                          -------------------------- this is found to be
   | |                                                     of type `StdRng`
150 | |             _ => rand::thread_rng(),
   | |                  ^^^^^^^^^^^^^^^^^^^ expected `StdRng`, found `ThreadRng`
151 | |         };
   | |_____- `match` arms have incompatible types
```

So I thought I might place them into a Box as follows:

```
// This will still not compile
fn pick_fortune(fortunes: &[Fortune], seed: Option<u64>) -> Option<String> {
    let mut rng = match seed {
        Some(val) => Box::new(StdRng::seed_from_u64(val)),
        _ => Box::new(rand::thread_rng()),
    };

    fortunes.choose(&mut rng).map(|f| f.text.to_string())
}
```

That still creates incompatible types because one arm returns Box<StdRng> and the other Box<ThreadRng>. The key to solving this error was to see that the Slice::choose function requires an argument that implements the trait rand::RngCore (*https://oreil.ly/DLh4z*), which I use as the type annotation for the contents of the Box:

```
fn pick_fortune(fortunes: &[Fortune], seed: Option<u64>) -> Option<String> {
    let mut rng: Box<dyn RngCore> = match seed {
        Some(val) => Box::new(StdRng::seed_from_u64(val)), ❶
        _ => Box::new(rand::thread_rng()), ❷
    };

    fortunes.choose(&mut rng).map(|f| f.text.to_string()) ❸
}
```

❶ Create a PRNG using the provided seed.

❷ Otherwise, use a PRNG seeded by the system.

❸ Use the PRNG to select one of the fortunes.

I can bring all these ideas together in my run like so:

```
fn run(args: Args) -> Result<()> {
    let pattern = args
        .pattern
        .map(|val: String| {
            RegexBuilder::new(val.as_str())
                .case_insensitive(args.insensitive)
                .build()
                .map_err(|_| anyhow!(r#"Invalid --pattern "{val}""#))
        })
        .transpose()?;

    let files = find_files(&args.sources)?;
    let fortunes = read_fortunes(&files)?;
    match pattern {
        Some(pattern) => { ❶
            let mut prev_source = None; ❷
```

```
                for fortune in fortunes ❸
                    .iter()
                    .filter(|fortune| pattern.is_match(&fortune.text))
                {
                    if prev_source.as_ref().map_or(true, |s| s != &fortune.source)
                    {
                        eprintln!("({})\n%", fortune.source); ❹
                        prev_source = Some(fortune.source.clone()); ❺
                    }
                    println!("{}\n%", fortune.text); ❻
                }
            }
            _ => {
                println!( ❼
                    "{}",
                    pick_fortune(&fortunes, args.seed)
                        .or_else(|| Some("No fortunes found".to_string()))
                        .unwrap()
                );
            }
        }
        Ok(())
}
```

❶ Check if the user has provided a `pattern` option.

❷ Initialize a mutable variable to remember the last fortune source.

❸ Iterate over the found fortunes and filter for those matching the provided regular expression.

❹ Print the source header if the current source is not the same as the previous one seen.

❺ Store the current fortune source.

❻ Print the text of the fortune.

❼ Print a random fortune or a message that states that there are no fortunes to be found.

> The fortunes are stored with embedded newlines that may cause the regular expression matching to fail if the sought-after phrase spans multiple lines. This mimics how the original `fortune` works but may not match the expectations of the user.

At this point, the program passes all the provided tests. I provided more guidance on this challenge because of the many steps involved in finding and reading files and then printing all the matching records or using a PRNG to randomly select one. I hope you enjoyed that as much as I did.

Going Further

Read the `fortune` manual page to learn about other options your program can implement. For instance, you could add the `-n length` option to restrict fortunes to those less than the given length. Knowing the lengths of the fortunes would be handy for implementing the `-s` option, which picks only *short* fortunes. As noted in the final solution, the regular expression matching may fail because of the embedded newlines in the fortunes. Can you find a way around this limitation?

Randomness is integral to many games that you could try to write. Perhaps start with a game where the user must guess a randomly selected number in a range; then you could move on to a more difficult game like "Wheel of Fortune," where the user guesses letters in a randomly selected word or phrase. Many systems have the file */usr/share/dict/words* that contains many thousands of English words; you could use that as a source, or you could create your own input file of words and phrases.

Summary

Programs that incorporate randomness are some of my favorites. In my salad days of programming, I wrote a Perl script to stub out new Perl scripts that would include a random quote from one of my favorite poets.[6] Random events are useful for creating games as well as machine learning programs, so it's important to understand how to control and test randomness. Here's some of what you learned in this chapter:

- The fortune records span multiple lines and use a lone percent sign to indicate the end of the record. You learned to read the lines into a buffer and dump the buffer when the record or file terminator is found.

- You can use the `rand` crate to make pseudorandom choices that can be controlled using a seed value.

- The `Path` (borrowed) and `PathBuf` (owned) types are useful abstractions for dealing with system paths on both Windows and Unix. They are similar to the `&str` and `String` types for dealing with borrowed and owned strings.

- The names of files and directories may be invalid UTF-8, so Rust uses the types `OsStr` (borrowed) and `OsString` (owned) to represent these strings.

---

6 See, Mom, an English lit degree is actually useful.

- Using abstractions like `Path` and `OsStr` makes your Rust code more portable across operating systems.

In the next chapter, you'll learn to manipulate dates as you create a terminal-based calendar program.

CHAPTER 13

Rascalry

Time is flying like an arrow
And the clock hands go so fast, they make the wind blow
And it makes the pages of the calendar go flying out the window, one by one

— They Might Be Giants, "Hovering Sombrero" (2001)

In this chapter, you will create a clone of `cal`, which will show you a text calendar in the terminal. I often don't know what the date is (or even the day of the week), so I use this (along with `date`) to see vaguely where I am in the space-time continuum. As is commonly the case, what appears to be a simple app becomes much more complicated as you get into the specifics of implementation.

You will learn how to do the following:

- Find today's date and do basic date manipulations
- Use `Vec::chunks` to create groupings of items
- Combine elements from multiple iterators
- Produce highlighted text in the terminal

How cal Works

I'll start by showing you the manual page for BSD `cal` to consider what's required. It's rather long, so I'll just include some parts relevant to the challenge program:

```
CAL(1)                    BSD General Commands Manual                    CAL(1)

NAME
     cal, ncal — displays a calendar and the date of Easter
```

```
SYNOPSIS
     cal [-31jy] [-A number] [-B number] [-d yyyy-mm] [[month] year]
     cal [-31j] [-A number] [-B number] [-d yyyy-mm] -m month [year]
     ncal [-C] [-31jy] [-A number] [-B number] [-d yyyy-mm] [[month] year]
     ncal [-C] [-31j] [-A number] [-B number] [-d yyyy-mm] -m month [year]
     ncal [-31bhjJpwySM] [-A number] [-B number] [-H yyyy-mm-dd] [-d yyyy-mm]
          [-s country_code] [[month] year]
     ncal [-31bhJeoSM] [-A number] [-B number] [-d yyyy-mm] [year]

DESCRIPTION
     The cal utility displays a simple calendar in traditional format and ncal
     offers an alternative layout, more options and the date of Easter.  The
     new format is a little cramped but it makes a year fit on a 25x80 termi-
     nal.  If arguments are not specified, the current month is displayed.

     ...

     A single parameter specifies the year (1-9999) to be displayed; note the
     year must be fully specified: ``cal 89'' will not display a calendar for
     1989.  Two parameters denote the month and year; the month is either a
     number between 1 and 12, or a full or abbreviated name as specified by
     the current locale.  Month and year default to those of the current sys-
     tem clock and time zone (so ``cal -m 8'' will display a calendar for the
     month of August in the current year).
```

GNU cal responds to --help and has both short and long option names. Note that this version also allows the week to start on either Sunday or Monday, but the challenge program will start it on Sunday:

```
$ cal --help

Usage:
 cal [options] [[[day] month] year]

Options:
 -1, --one       show only current month (default)
 -3, --three     show previous, current and next month
 -s, --sunday    Sunday as first day of week
 -m, --monday    Monday as first day of week
 -j, --julian    output Julian dates
 -y, --year      show whole current year
 -V, --version   display version information and exit
 -h, --help      display this help text and exit
```

Given no arguments, cal will print the current month and will highlight the current day by reversing foreground and background colors in your terminal. I can't show this in print, so I'll show today's date (March 3) in bold, and you can pretend this is what you see when you run the command in your terminal:

```
$ cal
      March 2024
Su Mo Tu We Th Fr Sa
                1  2
 3  4  5  6  7  8  9
10 11 12 13 14 15 16
17 18 19 20 21 22 23
24 25 26 27 28 29 30
31
```

A single positional argument will be interpreted as the year. If this value is a valid integer in the range of 1–9999, cal will show the calendar for that year. For example, the following is a calendar for the year 1066. Note that the year is shown centered on the first line in the following output:

```
$ cal 1066
                             1066
        January                February                March
Su Mo Tu We Th Fr Sa    Su Mo Tu We Th Fr Sa    Su Mo Tu We Th Fr Sa
 1  2  3  4  5  6  7              1  2  3  4              1  2  3  4
 8  9 10 11 12 13 14     5  6  7  8  9 10 11     5  6  7  8  9 10 11
15 16 17 18 19 20 21    12 13 14 15 16 17 18    12 13 14 15 16 17 18
22 23 24 25 26 27 28    19 20 21 22 23 24 25    19 20 21 22 23 24 25
29 30 31                26 27 28                26 27 28 29 30 31


         April                   May                    June
Su Mo Tu We Th Fr Sa    Su Mo Tu We Th Fr Sa    Su Mo Tu We Th Fr Sa
                   1        1  2  3  4  5  6                 1  2  3
 2  3  4  5  6  7  8     7  8  9 10 11 12 13     4  5  6  7  8  9 10
 9 10 11 12 13 14 15    14 15 16 17 18 19 20    11 12 13 14 15 16 17
16 17 18 19 20 21 22    21 22 23 24 25 26 27    18 19 20 21 22 23 24
23 24 25 26 27 28 29    28 29 30 31             25 26 27 28 29 30
30


          July                  August                September
Su Mo Tu We Th Fr Sa    Su Mo Tu We Th Fr Sa    Su Mo Tu We Th Fr Sa
                   1        1  2  3  4  5                    1  2
 2  3  4  5  6  7  8     6  7  8  9 10 11 12     3  4  5  6  7  8  9
 9 10 11 12 13 14 15    13 14 15 16 17 18 19    10 11 12 13 14 15 16
16 17 18 19 20 21 22    20 21 22 23 24 25 26    17 18 19 20 21 22 23
23 24 25 26 27 28 29    27 28 29 30 31          24 25 26 27 28 29 30
30 31


        October                November               December
Su Mo Tu We Th Fr Sa    Su Mo Tu We Th Fr Sa    Su Mo Tu We Th Fr Sa
 1  2  3  4  5  6  7              1  2  3  4                    1  2
 8  9 10 11 12 13 14     5  6  7  8  9 10 11     3  4  5  6  7  8  9
15 16 17 18 19 20 21    12 13 14 15 16 17 18    10 11 12 13 14 15 16
22 23 24 25 26 27 28    19 20 21 22 23 24 25    17 18 19 20 21 22 23
29 30 31                26 27 28 29 30          24 25 26 27 28 29 30
                                                31
```

Both the BSD and GNU versions show similar error messages if the year is not in the acceptable range:

```
$ cal 0
cal: year `0' not in range 1..9999
$ cal 10000
cal: year `10000' not in range 1..9999
```

Both versions will interpret two integer values as the ordinal value of the month and year, respectively. For example, in the incantation **cal 3 1066**, the 3 will be interpreted as the third month, which is March. Note that when showing a single month, the year is included with the month name:

```
$ cal 3 1066
     March 1066
Su Mo Tu We Th Fr Sa
          1  2  3  4
 5  6  7  8  9 10 11
12 13 14 15 16 17 18
19 20 21 22 23 24 25
26 27 28 29 30 31
```

Use the -y|--year flag to show the whole current year, which I find useful because I often forget what year it is too. If both -y|--year and the positional year are present, cal will use the positional year argument, but the challenge program should consider this an error. Oddly, GNU cal will not complain if you combine -y with both a month and a year, but BSD cal will error out. This is as much as the challenge program will implement.

Getting Started

The program in this chapter should be called calr (pronounced *cal-ar*) for a Rust calendar. Use **cargo new calr** to get started, then add the following dependencies to *Cargo.toml*:

```
[dependencies]
ansi_term = "0.12.1" ❶
anyhow = "1.0.79"
chrono = "0.4.34" ❷
clap = { version = "4.5.0", features = ["derive"] }
itertools = "0.12.1" ❸

[dev-dependencies]
assert_cmd = "2.0.13"
predicates = "3.0.4"
pretty_assertions = "1.4.0"
```

❶ The ansi_term crate will be used to highlight today's date.

❷ The chrono crate (*https://oreil.ly/_JDTq*) will provide access to date and time functions.

❸ The itertools (*https://oreil.ly/wcg_8*) crate will be used to join lines of text.

Copy the book's *13_calr/tests* directory into your project, and run **cargo test** to build and test your program, which should fail most ignominiously.

Defining and Validating the Arguments

I suggest you update *src/main.rs* to the to add the following struct for the program's arguments:

```
#[derive(Debug)]
struct Args {
    year: Option<i32>, ❶
    month: Option<String>, ❷
    show_current_year: bool, ❸
}
```

❶ The year is an optional i32 value.

❷ The month is an optional string as the user may provide a month name or number.

❸ show_current_year is a Boolean for whether or not to show the entire year.

 Because our program will only allow positive year values like the original cal, you might expect the year field to be a u32; however, the chrono crate I'll use for handling dates uses i32 to allow both positive (CE or *common era*) and negative (BCE or *before common era*) values.

Either annotate Args for the clap derive pattern or use the following skeleton for your get_args function:

```
fn get_args() -> Args {
    let matches = Command::new("calr")
        .version("0.1.0")
        .author("Ken Youens-Clark <kyclark@gmail.com>")
        .about("Rust version of `cal`")
        // What goes here?
        .get_matches();

    Args {
        year: ...
        month: ...
```

```
            show_current_year: ...
        }
    }
```

Start in `main` by printing the arguments:

```
fn main() {
    let args = get_args();
    println!("{args:?}");
}
```

Your program should be able to produce the following usage:

```
$ cargo run -- -h
Rust version of `cal`

Usage: calr [OPTIONS] [YEAR]

Arguments:
  [YEAR]  Year (1-9999)

Options:
  -m <MONTH>       Month name or number (1-12)
  -y, --year       Show whole current year
  -h, --help       Print help
  -V, --version    Print version
```

All the arguments are optional, so the program should show the following defaults:

```
$ cargo run
Args { year: None, month: None, show_current_year: false }
```

A single integer positional argument should be interpreted as the year:

```
$ cargo run -- 1000
Args { year: Some(1000), month: None, show_current_year: false }
```

Any year outside the range 1–9999 should be rejected:

```
$ cargo run -- 0
error: invalid value '0' for '[YEAR]': 0 is not in 1..=9999
$ cargo run -- 10000
error: invalid value '10000' for '[YEAR]': 10000 is not in 1..=9999
```

The `-y|--year` flag should cause `show_current_year` to be `true`:

```
$ cargo run -- -y
Args { year: None, month: None, show_current_year: true }
```

The `-y|--year` flag cannot be used with the month:

```
$ cargo run -- -m 1 -y
error: the argument '-m <MONTH>' cannot be used with '--year'

Usage: calr -m <MONTH> [YEAR]
```

Nor can -y|--year flag be combined with the year positional argument:

```
$ cargo run -- -y 1972
error: the argument '--year' cannot be used with '[YEAR]'

Usage: calr --year [YEAR]
```

 Pause here to get your program working to this point. Your program should also pass several tests under **cargo test dies**.

Following is how I wrote my `get_args` to parse and validate the command-line arguments and choose the defaults. Be sure add use `clap::{Arg, ArgAction, Command}`:

```
fn get_args() -> Args {
    let matches = Command::new("calr")
        .version("0.1.0")
        .author("Ken Youens-Clark <kyclark@gmail.com>")
        .about("Rust version of `cal`")
        .arg(
            Arg::new("year")
                .value_name("YEAR")
                .value_parser(clap::value_parser!(i32).range(1..=9999)) ❶
                .help("Year (1-9999)"),
        )
        .arg(
            Arg::new("month")
                .value_name("MONTH")
                .short('m')
                .help("Month name or number (1-12)"), ❷
        )
        .arg(
            Arg::new("show_current_year")
                .value_name("SHOW_YEAR")
                .short('y')
                .long("year")
                .help("Show whole current year")
                .conflicts_with_all(["month", "year"]) ❸
                .action(ArgAction::SetTrue),
        )
        .get_matches();

    Args {
        year: matches.get_one("year").cloned(),
        month: matches.get_one("month").cloned(),
        show_current_year: matches.get_flag("show_current_year"),
    }
}
```

❶ The year must parsed to an i32 in the range 1-9999.

❷ The month can be a string or a number, which I will validate later.

❸ Ensure this flag is not used with the other arguments.

For the derive pattern, I add use clap::Parser and the following code:

```
#[derive(Debug, Parser)]
#[command(author, version, about)]
/// Rust version of `cal`
struct Args {
    /// Year (1-9999)
    #[arg(value_parser(clap::value_parser!(i32).range(1..=9999)))]
    year: Option<i32>,

    /// Month name or number (1-12)
    #[arg(short)]
    month: Option<String>,

    /// Show the whole current year
    #[arg(short('y'), long("year"), conflicts_with_all(["month", "year"]))]
    show_current_year: bool,
}
```

I'll restructure my main to call a run function as in previous chapters:

```
fn main() {
    if let Err(e) = run(Args::parse()) {
        eprintln!("{e}");
        std::process::exit(1);
    }
}
```

I have some more work to validate the arguments, which I'll tackle in a run function. Be sure to add use anyhow::Result for the following:

```
fn run(_args: Args) -> Result<()> {
    Ok(())
}
```

First, I want to validate the month argument, so I'll create a parse_month function that possibly returns an integer if the given string can be parsed as an integer in the range 1-12 or matched to a known month name:

```
fn parse_month(month: String) -> Result<u32> {
    unimplemented!();
}
```

Since the month will only be in the range 1–12, a u32 may seem excessively large, but this is the type that chrono crate uses for months.

Add the following unit test to check the function using the bounds 1 and 12 and a sample case-insensitive month like *jan* (for *January*) and an unknown month name.

```
#[cfg(test)]
mod tests {
    use super::parse_month;

    #[test]
    fn test_parse_month() {
        let res = parse_month("1".to_string());
        assert!(res.is_ok());
        assert_eq!(res.unwrap(), 1u32);

        let res = parse_month("12".to_string());
        assert!(res.is_ok());
        assert_eq!(res.unwrap(), 12u32);

        let res = parse_month("jan".to_string());
        assert!(res.is_ok());
        assert_eq!(res.unwrap(), 1u32);

        let res = parse_month("0".to_string());
        assert!(res.is_err());
        assert_eq!(
            res.unwrap_err().to_string(),
            r#"month "0" not in the range 1 through 12"#
        );

        let res = parse_month("13".to_string());
        assert!(res.is_err());
        assert_eq!(
            res.unwrap_err().to_string(),
            r#"month "13" not in the range 1 through 12"#
        );

        let res = parse_month("foo".to_string());
        assert!(res.is_err());
        assert_eq!(res.unwrap_err().to_string(), r#"Invalid month "foo""#);
    }
}
```

Stop reading here and write the function that passes **cargo test** **test_parse_month**.

My `parse_month` function needs a list of valid month names, so I declare a constant value at the top of my *src/main.rs*:

```
const MONTH_NAMES: [&str; 12] = [
    "January",
    "February",
    "March",
    "April",
    "May",
    "June",
    "July",
    "August",
    "September",
    "October",
    "November",
    "December",
];
```

Following is how I use the month names to help figure out the given month. Be sure to add use `anyhow::bail` to your imports:

```
fn parse_month(month: String) -> Result<u32> {
    match month.parse() {  ❶
        Ok(num) => {
            if (1..=12).contains(&num) {  ❷
                Ok(num)
            } else {
                bail!(r#"month "{month}" not in the range 1 through 12"#)  ❸
            }
        }
        _ => {
            let lower = &month.to_lowercase();  ❹
            let matches: Vec<_> = MONTH_NAMES
                .iter()
                .enumerate()  ❺
                .filter_map(|(i, name)| {
                    if name.to_lowercase().starts_with(lower) {  ❻
                        Some(i + 1)  ❼
                    } else {
                        None
                    }
                })
                .collect();  ❽

            if matches.len() == 1 {  ❾
                Ok(matches[0] as u32)
```

```
            } else {
                bail!(r#"Invalid month "{month}""#)
            }
        }
    }
}
```

❶ Attempt to parse a numeric argument.

❷ If the parsed number is in the range 1–12, return the value.

❸ Otherwise, create an informative error message.

❹ If the month didn't parse as an integer, compare the lowercased value to the month names.

❺ Enumerate the month names to get the index and value.

❻ See if the given value is the start of a month name.

❼ If so, return the zero-based index position corrected to one-based counting.

❽ Collect all the possible month values.

❾ If there was exactly one possible month, return it as a u32 value; otherwise, return an informative error message.

I can use this to validate the month in my run function:

```
fn run(args: Args) -> Result<()> {
    let month = args.month.map(parse_month).transpose()?;
    println!("month = {month:?}");
    println!("year  = {:?}", args.year);
    Ok(())
}
```

Your program should accept valid integer values for the month and year:

```
$ cargo run -- -m 7 1776
month = Some(7)
year  = Some(1776)
```

Any month number outside the range 1–12 should be rejected:

```
$ cargo run -- -m 0
month "0" not in the range 1 through 12
$ cargo run -- -m 13
month "13" not in the range 1 through 12
```

Any unknown month name should be rejected:

```
$ cargo run -- -m Fortinbras
Invalid month "Fortinbras"
```

Months may be provided as any distinguishing starting substring, so *Jul* or *July* should work:

```
$ cargo run -- -m Jul
month = Some(7)
year  = None
```

The string *Ju* is not enough to disambiguate *June* and *July*:

```
$ cargo run -- -m Ju
Invalid month "Ju"
```

Month names should also be case-insensitive, so *s* is enough to distinguish *September*:

```
$ cargo run -- -m s 1999
month = Some(9)
year  = Some(1999)
```

When no arguments are given, the program should default to the current month and year, which was March 2024 when I was writing this. To figure out the default values for year and month, I recommend that you use the chrono crate. The chrono::Local::now (*https://oreil.ly/V2xTo*) function returns a DateTime struct (*https://oreil.ly/yEGzP*) set to your local time zone. You can then use methods like Datelike::month (*https://oreil.ly/jw2t-*) and Datelike::year (*https://oreil.ly/o4-d4*) to get integer values representing the current month and year. If the -y|--year flag is present, then show the entire current year and set the month to None. For the following code, add use chrono::{Datelike, Local} to your imports:

```
fn run(args: Args) -> Result<()> {
    let today = Local::now().date_naive(); ❶
    let mut month = args.month.map(parse_month).transpose()?; ❷
    let mut year = args.year;

    if args.show_current_year { ❸
        month = None;
        year = Some(today.year());
    } else if month.is_none() && year.is_none() { ❹
        month = Some(today.month());
        year = Some(today.year());
    }
    let year = year.unwrap_or(today.year()); ❺

    println!("month = {month:?}");
    println!("year  = {year:?}");
    Ok(())
}
```

❶ Get the current date as a `NaiveDate` (*https://oreil.ly/ktLQU*), which is an ISO 8601 calendar date without a time zone that can represent dates from January 1, 262145 BCE to December 31, 262143 CE. Naive dates are fine for this application as it does not require time zones.

❷ Make the `month` and `year` variables mutable.

❸ If `args.show_current_year` is `true`, set the year to the current year and the month to `None`.

❹ If there are no values for `month` or `year`, use the values from `today`.

❺ The `year` variable must have `Some` value, it's safe to call `Option::unwrap`.

> The `chrono` crate also has `chrono::Utc` (*https://oreil.ly/dT_t0*) to get the current time based on Coordinated Universal Time (UTC), which is the successor to Greenwich Mean Time (GMT) and is the time standard used for regulating the world's clocks. You may be asking, "Why isn't it abbreviated as CUT?" Apparently, it's because the International Telecommunication Union and the International Astronomical Union wanted to have one universal acronym. The English speakers proposed CUT (for *coordinated universal time*), while the French speakers wanted TUC (for *temps universel coordonné*). Using the wisdom of Solomon, they compromised with UTC, which doesn't mean anything in particular but conforms to the abbreviation convention for universal time.

Ensure that the program will use the current month and year when given no arguments:

```
$ cargo run
month = Some(3)
year  = 2024
```

With just the `-y|--year` flag, the current year is selected:

```
$ cargo run -- -y
month = None
year  = 2024
```

When only the month is indicated, select the current year:

```
$ cargo run -- -m July
month = Some(7)
year  = 2024
```

At this point, your program should pass **cargo test dies**:

```
running 8 tests
test dies_year_10000 ... ok
test dies_y_and_month ... ok
test dies_y_and_year ... ok
test dies_year_0 ... ok
test dies_month_0 ... ok
test dies_invalid_month ... ok
test dies_month_13 ... ok
test dies_invalid_year ... ok
```

Writing the Program

Now that you have good input, it's time to write the rest of the program. First, consider how to print just one month, like April 2016, which I will place beside the same month from 2017. I'll pipe the output from cal into cat -e, which will show the dollar sign ($) for the ends of the lines. The following shows that each month has eight lines: one for the name of the month, one for the day headers, and six for the weeks of the month. Additionally, each line must be 22 columns wide:

```
$ cal -m 4 2016 | cat -e          $ cal -m 4 2017 | cat -e
      April 2016        $               April 2017        $
Su Mo Tu We Th Fr Sa  $         Su Mo Tu We Th Fr Sa  $
                1  2  $                             1  $
 3  4  5  6  7  8  9  $          2  3  4  5  6  7  8  $
10 11 12 13 14 15 16  $          9 10 11 12 13 14 15  $
17 18 19 20 21 22 23  $         16 17 18 19 20 21 22  $
24 25 26 27 28 29 30  $         23 24 25 26 27 28 29  $
                      $         30                    $
```

I decided to create a function called format_month to create the output for one month. Be sure to add chrono::NaiveDate to your imports for the following code:

```
fn format_month(
    year: i32, ❶
    month: u32, ❷
    print_year: bool, ❸
    today: NaiveDate, ❹
) -> Vec<String> { ❺
    unimplemented!();
}
```

❶ The year of the month.

❷ The month number to format.

❸ Whether or not to include the year in the month's header.

❹ Today's date, used to highlight today.

❺ The function returns a Vec<String>, which is the eight lines of text.

You can expand your **tests** module to include the following unit test:

```
#[cfg(test)]
mod tests {
    use super::{format_month, parse_month}; ❶
    use chrono::NaiveDate;

    #[test]
    fn test_parse_month() {} // Same as before

    #[test]
    fn test_format_month() {
        let today = NaiveDate::from_ymd_opt(0, 1, 1).unwrap();
        let leap_february = vec![
            "    February 2020      ",
            "Su Mo Tu We Th Fr Sa  ",
            "                   1  ",
            " 2  3  4  5  6  7  8  ",
            " 9 10 11 12 13 14 15  ",
            "16 17 18 19 20 21 22  ",
            "23 24 25 26 27 28 29  ",
            "                      ",
        ];
        assert_eq!(format_month(2020, 2, true, today), leap_february); ❷

        let may = vec![
            "        May           ",
            "Su Mo Tu We Th Fr Sa  ",
            "                1  2  ",
            " 3  4  5  6  7  8  9  ",
            "10 11 12 13 14 15 16  ",
            "17 18 19 20 21 22 23  ",
            "24 25 26 27 28 29 30  ",
            "31                    ",
        ];
        assert_eq!(format_month(2020, 5, false, today), may); ❸

        let april_hl = vec![
            "     April 2021       ",
            "Su Mo Tu We Th Fr Sa  ",
            "             1  2  3  ",
            " 4  5  6 \u{1b}[7m 7\u{1b}[0m  8  9 10  ", ❹
            "11 12 13 14 15 16 17  ",
            "18 19 20 21 22 23 24  ",
            "25 26 27 28 29 30     ",
            "                      ",
        ];
        let today = NaiveDate::from_ymd_opt(2021, 4, 7).unwrap();
        assert_eq!(format_month(2021, 4, true, today), april_hl); ❺
```

```
        }
    }
```

❶ Import the `format_month` function and the `chrono::NaiveDate` struct.

❷ This February month should include a blank line at the end and have 29 days because this is a leap year.

❸ This May month should span the same number of lines as April.

❹ `ansi_term::Style::reverse` (*https://oreil.ly/F3TpC*) is used to create the highlighting of April 7 in this output.

❺ Create a `today` that falls in the given month and verify the output highlights the date.

 The escape sequences that `Style::reverse` creates are not exactly the same as BSD `cal`, but the effect is equivalent. You can choose any method of highlighting the current date you like, but be sure to update the test accordingly.

You might start your `format_month` function by numbering all the days in a month from one to the last day of the month. It's not as trivial as the "thirty days hath September" mnemonic because February can have a different number of days depending on whether it's a leap year. I wrote a function called `last_day_in_month` that will return a `NaiveDate` representing the last day of any month:

```
fn last_day_in_month(year: i32, month: u32) -> NaiveDate {
    unimplemented!();
}
```

Following is a unit test you can add, which you might notice includes a leap year check. Be sure to add `last_day_in_month` to the imports at the top of the `tests` module:

```
#[test]
fn test_last_day_in_month() {
    assert_eq!(
        last_day_in_month(2020, 1),
        NaiveDate::from_ymd(2020, 1, 31)
    );
    assert_eq!(
        last_day_in_month(2020, 2),
        NaiveDate::from_ymd(2020, 2, 29)
    );
    assert_eq!(
        last_day_in_month(2020, 4),
```

```
        NaiveDate::from_ymd(2020, 4, 30)
    );
}
```

 Stop reading and write the code to pass **cargo test test_format _month**.

At this point, you should have all the pieces to finish the program. The challenge program will only ever print a single month or all 12 months, so start by getting your program to print the current month with the current day highlighted. Next, have it print all the months for a year, one month after the other. Then consider how you could create four rows that group three months side by side to mimic the output of cal. Because each month is a vector of lines, you need to combine all the first lines of each row, and then all the second lines, and so forth. This operation is often called a *zip*, and Rust iterators have a zip method (*https://oreil.ly/2zGKh*) you might find useful. Keep going until you pass all of **cargo test**. When you're done, check out my solution.

Solution

I'll walk you through how I built up my version of the program. Following are all the imports you'll need besides clap:

```
use ansi_term::Style;
use anyhow::{bail, Result};
use chrono::{Datelike, Local, NaiveDate};
use itertools::izip;
```

I also added another constant for the width of the lines:

```
const LINE_WIDTH: usize = 22;
```

I'll start with my last_day_in_month function, which figures out the first day of the *next* month and then finds its predecessor:

```
fn last_day_in_month(year: i32, month: u32) -> NaiveDate {
    // The first day of the next month...
    let (y, m) = if month == 12 { ❶
        (year + 1, 1)
    } else {
        (year, month + 1) ❷
    };

    // ...is preceded by the last day of the original month
    NaiveDate::from_ymd_opt(y, m, 1) ❸
        .unwrap()
```

```
        .pred_opt()
        .unwrap()
}
```

❶ If this is December, then advance the year by one and set the month to January.

❷ Otherwise, increment the month by one.

❸ Use `NaiveDate::from_ymd_opt` (*https://oreil.ly/RS5jG*) to create a `NaiveDate`, and then call `NaiveDate::pred_opt` (*https://oreil.ly/l_1dS*) to get the previous calendar date.

 You might be tempted to roll your own solution rather than using the `chrono` crate, but the calculation of leap years could prove onerous. For instance, a leap year must be evenly divisible by 4—except for end-of-century years, which must be divisible by 400. This means that the year 2000 was a leap year but 1900 was not, and 2100 won't be, either. It's more advisable to stick with a library that has a good reputation and is well-tested.

Next, I'll break down my `format_month` function to format a given month:

```
fn format_month(
    year: i32,
    month: u32,
    print_year: bool,
    today: NaiveDate,
) -> Vec<String> {
    let first = NaiveDate::from_ymd_opt(year, month, 1).unwrap(); ❶
    let mut days: Vec<String> = (1..first.weekday().number_from_sunday()) ❷
        .map(|_| "  ".to_string()) // two spaces
        .collect();
```

❶ Construct a `NaiveDate` for the start of the given month.

❷ Initialize a mutable `Vec<String>` with a buffer of the days from Sunday until the start of the month.

The initialization of `days` handles, for instance, the fact that April 2020 starts on a Wednesday. In this case, I want to fill up the days of the first week with two spaces for each day from Sunday through Tuesday. Continuing from there:

```
    let is_today = |day: u32| { ❶
        year == today.year() && month == today.month() && day == today.day()
    };

    let last = last_day_in_month(year, month); ❷
    days.extend((first.day()..=last.day()).map(|num| { ❸
```

```
        let fmt = format!("{num:>2}"); ❹
        if is_today(num) { ❺
            Style::new().reverse().paint(fmt).to_string()
        } else {
            fmt
        }
    }));
```

❶ Create a closure to determine if a given day of the month is today.

❷ Find the last day of this month.

❸ Extend days by iterating through each chrono::Datelike::day (*https://oreil.ly/7pMJ1*) from the first to the last of the month.

❹ Format the day right-justified in two columns.

❺ If the given day is today, use Style::reverse (*https://oreil.ly/F3TpC*) to highlight the text; otherwise, use the text as is.

Here is the last part of this function:

```
    let month_name = MONTH_NAMES[month as usize - 1]; ❶
    let mut lines = Vec::with_capacity(8); ❷
    lines.push(format!( ❸
        "{:^20}  ", // two trailing spaces
        if print_year {
            format!("{month_name} {year}")
        } else {
            month_name.to_string()
        }
    ));

    lines.push("Su Mo Tu We Th Fr Sa  ".to_string()); // two trailing spaces ❹

    for week in days.chunks(7) { ❺
        lines.push(format!( ❻
            "{:width$}  ", // two trailing spaces
            week.join(" "),
            width = LINE_WIDTH - 2
        ));
    }

    while lines.len() < 8 { ❼
        lines.push(" ".repeat(LINE_WIDTH)); ❽
    }

    lines ❾
}
```

❶ Get the current month's display name, which requires casting `month` as a `usize` and correcting for zero-offset counting.

❷ Initialize an empty, mutable vector that can hold eight lines of text.

❸ The month header may or may not have the year. Format the header centered in a space 20 characters wide followed by 2 spaces.

❹ Add the days of the week.

❺ Use `Vec::chunks` (*https://oreil.ly/wBfGb*) to get seven weekdays at a time. This will start on Sunday because of the earlier buffer.

❻ Join the days on a space and format the result into the correct width.

❼ Pad with as many lines as needed to bring the total to eight.

❽ Use `str::repeat` (*https://oreil.ly/cXKMU*) to create a new `String` by repeating a single space to the width of the line.

❾ Return the lines.

Finally, here is how I bring everything together in my run:

```
pub fn run(config: Config) -> MyResult<()> {
    let today = Local::now().date_naive();
    let mut month = args.month.map(parse_month).transpose()?;
    let mut year = args.year;

    if args.show_current_year {
        month = None;
        year = Some(today.year());
    } else if month.is_none() && year.is_none() {
        month = Some(today.month());
        year = Some(today.year());
    }
    let year = year.unwrap_or(today.year());

    match month {
        Some(month) => { ❶
            let lines = format_month(year, month, true, today); ❷
            println!("{}", lines.join("\n")); ❸
        }
        None => { ❹
            println!("{year:>32}"); ❺
            let months: Vec<_> = (1..=12) ❻
                .map(|month| format_month(year, month, false, today))
                .collect();
```

```
        for (i, chunk) in months.chunks(3).enumerate() { ❼
            if let [m1, m2, m3] = chunk { ❽
                for lines in izip!(m1, m2, m3) { ❾
                    println!("{}{}{}", lines.0, lines.1, lines.2); ❿
                }
                if i < 3 { ⓫
                    println!();
                }
            }
        }
    }

    Ok(())
}
```

❶ Handle the case of a single month.

❷ Format the one month with the year in the header.

❸ Print the lines joined on newlines.

❹ When there is no month, then print the whole year.

❺ When printing all the months, first print the year as the first header.

❻ Format all the months, leaving out the year from the headers.

❼ Use Vec::chunks to group into slices of three, and use Iterator::enumerate to track the grouping numbers.

❽ Use the pattern match [m1, m2, m3] to destructure the slice into the three months.

❾ Use itertools::izip (*https://oreil.ly/t00b3*) to create an iterator that combines the lines from the three months.

❿ Print the lines from each of the three months.

⓫ If not on the last set of months, print a newline to separate the groupings.

Rust iterators have a `zip` function (*https://oreil.ly/2zGKh*) that, according to the documentation, "returns a new iterator that will iterate over two other iterators, returning a tuple where the first element comes from the first iterator, and the second element comes from the second iterator." Unfortunately, it only works with two iterators. If you look closely, you'll notice that the call to `izip!` is a macro. The documentation says, "The result of this macro is in the general case an iterator composed of repeated `.zip()` and a `.map()`."

With that, all the tests pass, and you can now visualize a calendar in the terminal.

Going Further

You could further customize this program. For instance, you could check for the existence of a *$HOME/.calr* configuration file that lists special dates such as holidays, birthdays, and anniversaries. Use your new terminal colorizing skills to highlight these dates using bold, reversed, or colored text.

The manual page mentions the program `ncal`, which will format the months vertically rather than horizontally. When displaying a full year, `ncal` prints three rows of four months as opposed to four rows of three months like `cal`. Create an option to change the output of `calr` to match the output from `ncal`, being sure that you add tests for all the possibilities.

Consider how you could internationalize the output. It's common to have a LANG or LANGUAGE environment variable that you could use to select month names in the user's preferred language. Alternatively, you might allow the user to customize the months using the aforementioned configuration file. How could you handle languages that use different scripts, such as Chinese, Japanese, or Cyrillic? Try making a Hebrew calendar that reads right to left or a Mongolian one that reads top to bottom.

The original `cal` shows only one month or the entire year. Allow the user to select multiple months, perhaps using the ranges from `cutr`. This would allow something like -m 4,1,7-9 to show April, January, and July through September.

Finally, I mentioned the date command at the beginning of the chapter. This is a program that shows just the current date and time, among many other things. Use **man date** to read the manual page, and then write a Rust version that implements whichever options you find tantalizing.

Summary

Here's a recap of some of the things you learned in this chapter:

- The `chrono` crate provides a way to find today's date and perform basic date manipulations, such as finding the previous day of a given date (in `last_day_in_month`).
- The `Vec::chunks` method will return groupings of elements as a slice. The challenge program used this to gather weekdays into groups of seven and the months of the year into groups of three.
- The `Iterator::zip` method will combine the elements from two iterators into a new iterator containing a tuple of values from the sources. The `itertools::izip` macro allows you to expand this to any number of iterators.
- `ansi_term::Style` can create terminal text in various colors and styles, such as reversing the colors used for the text and background to highlight the current date.

In the next chapter, you will learn more about Unix file metadata and how to format text tables of output.

CHAPTER 14

Elless Island

Now you know that the girls are just making it up
Now you know that the boys are just pushing their luck
Now you know that my ride doesn't really exist
And my name's not really on that list

    — They Might Be Giants, "Prevenge" (2004)

In this final chapter, you'll create a Rust clone of the *list* command, ls (pronounced *ell-ess*), which I think is perhaps the hardest-working program in Unix. I use it many times every day to view the contents of a directory or inspect the size or permissions of some files. The original program has more than three dozen options, but the challenge program will implement only a few features, such as printing the contents of directories or lists of files along with their permissions, sizes, and modification times. Note that this challenge program relies on ideas of files and ownership that are specific to Unix and so will not work on Windows. I suggest Windows users install Windows Subsystem for Linux to write and test the program in that environment.

In this chapter, you will learn how to do the following:

- Query and visually represent a file's permissions
- Add a method to a custom type using an implementation
- Create a module in a separate file to organize code
- Use text tables to create aligned columns of output
- Create documentation comments

How ls Works

To see what will be expected of the challenge program, start by looking at the manual page for the BSD `ls`. You'll see that it has 39 options. I'll include only the first part, as the documentation is rather long, but I encourage you to read the whole thing:

```
LS(1)                    BSD General Commands Manual                    LS(1)

NAME
     ls -- list directory contents

SYNOPSIS
     ls [-ABCFGHLOPRSTUW@abcdefghiklmnopqrstuwx1%] [file ...]

DESCRIPTION
     For each operand that names a file of a type other than directory, ls
     displays its name as well as any requested, associated information.  For
     each operand that names a file of type directory, ls displays the names
     of files contained within that directory, as well as any requested, asso-
     ciated information.

     If no operands are given, the contents of the current directory are dis-
     played.  If more than one operand is given, non-directory operands are
     displayed first; directory and non-directory operands are sorted sepa-
     rately and in lexicographical order.
```

If you execute `ls` with no options, it will show you the contents of the current working directory. For instance, change into the *14_lsr* directory and try it:

```
$ cd 14_lsr
$ ls
Cargo.toml      set-test-perms.sh* src/            tests/
```

The challenge program will implement only two option flags, the `-l|--long` and `-a|--all` options. Per the manual page:

```
The Long Format
 If the -l option is given, the following information is displayed for
 each file: file mode, number of links, owner name, group name, number of
 bytes in the file, abbreviated month, day-of-month file was last modi-
 fied, hour file last modified, minute file last modified, and the path-
 name.  In addition, for each directory whose contents are displayed, the
 total number of 512-byte blocks used by the files in the directory is
 displayed on a line by itself, immediately before the information for the
 files in the directory.
```

Execute `ls -l` in the source directory. Of course, you will have different metadata, such as owners and modification times, than what I'm showing:

```
$ ls -l
total 16
-rw-r--r--  1 kyclark  staff  217 Aug 11 08:26 Cargo.toml
-rwxr-xr-x  1 kyclark  staff  447 Aug 12 17:56 set-test-perms.sh*
drwxr-xr-x  5 kyclark  staff  160 Aug 26 09:44 src/
drwxr-xr-x  4 kyclark  staff  128 Aug 17 08:42 tests/
```

The -a *all* option will show entries that are normally hidden. For example, the current directory . and the parent directory .. are not usually shown:

```
$ ls -a
./                Cargo.toml        src/
../               set-test-perms.sh* tests/
```

You can specify these individually, like **ls -a -l,** or combined, like **ls -la.** These flags can occur in any order, so -la or -al will work:

```
$ ls -la
total 16
drwxr-xr-x   6 kyclark  staff  192 Oct 15 07:52 ./
drwxr-xr-x  24 kyclark  staff  768 Aug 24 08:22 ../
-rw-r--r--   1 kyclark  staff  217 Aug 11 08:26 Cargo.toml
-rwxr-xr-x   1 kyclark  staff  447 Aug 12 17:56 set-test-perms.sh*
drwxr-xr-x   5 kyclark  staff  160 Aug 26 09:44 src/
drwxr-xr-x   4 kyclark  staff  128 Aug 17 08:42 tests/
```

 Any entry (directory or file) with a name starting with a dot (.) is hidden, leading to the existence of so-called *dotfiles*, which are often used to store program state and metadata. For example, the root directory of the source code repository contains a directory called *.git* that has all the information Git needs to keep track of the changes to files. It's also common to create *.gitignore* files that contain filenames and globs that you wish to exclude from Git.

You can provide the name of one or more directories as positional arguments to see their contents:

```
$ ls src/ tests/
src/:
main.rs   owner.rs

tests/:
cli.rs  inputs
```

The positional arguments can also be files:

```
$ ls -l src/*.rs
-rw-r--r-- 1 kyclark  staff  8959 Feb 25 12:09 src/main.rs
-rw-r--r-- 1 kyclark  staff   313 Feb 25 12:03 src/owner.rs
```

Different operating systems will return the files in different orders. For example, the *.hidden* file is shown before all the other files on macOS:

```
$ ls -la tests/inputs/
total 16
drwxr-xr-x  7 kyclark  staff  224 Aug 12 10:29 ./
drwxr-xr-x  4 kyclark  staff  128 Aug 17 08:42 ../
-rw-r--r--  1 kyclark  staff    0 Mar 19  2021 .hidden
-rw-r--r--  1 kyclark  staff  193 May 31 16:43 bustle.txt
drwxr-xr-x  4 kyclark  staff  128 Aug 10 18:08 dir/
-rw-r--r--  1 kyclark  staff    0 Mar 19  2021 empty.txt
-rw-------  1 kyclark  staff   45 Aug 12 10:29 fox.txt
```

On Linux, the *.hidden* file is listed last:

```
$ ls -la tests/inputs/
total 20
drwxr-xr-x. 3 kyclark staff 4096 Aug 21 12:13 ./
drwxr-xr-x. 3 kyclark staff 4096 Aug 21 12:13 ../
-rw-r--r--. 1 kyclark staff  193 Aug 21 12:13 bustle.txt
drwxr-xr-x. 2 kyclark staff 4096 Aug 21 12:13 dir/
-rw-r--r--. 1 kyclark staff    0 Aug 21 12:13 empty.txt
-rw-------. 1 kyclark staff   45 Aug 21 12:13 fox.txt
-rw-r--r--. 1 kyclark staff    0 Aug 21 12:13 .hidden
```

 Due to these differences, the tests will not check for any particular ordering.

Notice that errors involving nonexistent files are printed first, and then the results for valid arguments. As usual, *blargh* is meant as a nonexistent file:

```
$ ls Cargo.toml blargh src/main.rs
ls: blargh: No such file or directory
Cargo.toml   src/main.rs
```

This is about as much as the challenge program should implement. A version of `ls` dates back to the original AT&T Unix, and both the BSD and GNU versions have had decades to evolve. The challenge program won't even scratch the surface of replacing `ls`, but it will give you a chance to consider some really interesting aspects of operating systems and information storage.

Getting Started

The challenge program should be named `lsr` (pronounced *lesser* or *lister*, maybe) for a Rust version of `ls`. I suggest you start by running **cargo new lsr**. My solution will use the following dependencies that you should add to your *Cargo.toml*:

```
[dependencies]
anyhow = "1.0.79"
chrono = "0.4.31" ❶
clap = { version = "4.5.0", features = ["derive"] }
tabular = "0.2.0" ❷
users = "0.11.0" ❸

[dev-dependencies]
assert_cmd = "2.0.13"
predicates = "3.0.4"
pretty_assertions = "1.4.0"
rand = "0.8.5"
```

❶ chrono will be used to handle the file modification times.

❷ tabular will be used to present a text table for the long listing.

❸ users will be used to get the user and group names of the owners.

Copy *14_lsr/tests* into your project, and then run **cargo test** to build and test your program. All the tests should fail. Next, you must run the bash script *14_lsr/set-test -perms.sh* to set the file and directory permissions of the test inputs to known values. Run with -h|--help for usage:

```
$ ./set-test-perms.sh --help
Usage: set-test-perms.sh DIR
```

You should give it the path to your new lsr. For instance, if you create the project under *~/rust-solutions/lsr*, run it like so:

```
$ ./set-test-perms.sh ~/rust-solutions/lsr
Done, fixed files in "/Users/kyclark/rust-solutions/lsr".
```

Defining the Arguments

I suggest you update *src/main.rs* to add the following struct for the program's arguments:

```
#[derive(Debug)]
pub struct Args {
    paths: Vec<String>, ❶
    long: bool, ❷
    show_hidden: bool, ❸
}
```

❶ The paths argument will be a vector of strings for files and directories.

❷ The long option is a Boolean for whether or not to print the long listing.

❸ The show_hidden option is a Boolean for whether or not to print hidden entries.

There's nothing new in this program when it comes to parsing and validating the arguments. Annotate the struct for the `clap` derive pattern or use this outline for `get_args` you can use:

```
fn get_args() -> Args {
    let matches = Command::new("lsr")
        .version("0.1.0")
        .author("Ken Youens-Clark <kyclark@gmail.com>")
        .about("Rust version of `ls`")
        // What goes here?
        .get_matches();

    Args {
        paths: ...
        long: ...
        show_hidden: ...
    }
}
```

Start your `main` function by printing the arguments:

```
fn main() {
    let args = get_args();
    println!("{args:?}");
}
```

Make sure your program can print a usage like the following:

```
$ cargo run -- -h
Rust version of `ls`

Usage: lsr [OPTIONS] [PATH]...

Arguments:
  [PATH]...  Files and/or directories [default: .]

Options:
  -l, --long     Long listing
  -a, --all      Show all files
  -h, --help     Print help
  -V, --version  Print version
```

Run your program with no arguments and verify that the default for `paths` is a list containing the dot (.), which represents the current working directory. The two Boolean values should be `false`:

```
$ cargo run
Args { paths: ["."], long: false, show_hidden: false }
```

Try turning on the two flags and giving one or more positional arguments:

```
$ cargo run -- -la tests/*
Args { paths: ["tests/cli.rs", "tests/inputs"], long: true, show_hidden: true }
```

Stop reading and get your program working to this point.

I assume you figured that out, so here is my `get_args`. Be sure to include `use clap::{Arg, ArgAction, Command}` for the following code. It's similar to that used in previous programs, so I'll eschew commentary:

```
fn get_args() -> Args {
    let matches = Command::new("lsr")
        .version("0.1.0")
        .author("Ken Youens-Clark <kyclark@gmail.com>")
        .about("Rust version of `ls`")
        .arg(
            Arg::new("paths")
                .value_name("PATH")
                .help("Files and/or directories")
                .default_value(".")
                .num_args(0..),
        )
        .arg(
            Arg::new("long")
                .action(ArgAction::SetTrue)
                .help("Long listing")
                .short('l')
                .long("long"),
        )
        .arg(
            Arg::new("all")
                .action(ArgAction::SetTrue)
                .help("Show all files")
                .short('a')
                .long("all"),
        )
        .get_matches();

    Args {
        paths: matches.get_many("paths").unwrap().cloned().collect(),
        long: matches.get_flag("long"),
        show_hidden: matches.get_flag("all"),
    }
}
```

For the derive pattern, add `use clap::Parser` and the following:

```
#[derive(Debug, Parser)]
#[command(author, version, about)]
/// Rust version of `ls`
struct Args {
    /// Files and/or directories
```

```
    #[arg(default_value = ".")]
    paths: Vec<String>,

    /// Long listing
    #[arg(short, long)]
    long: bool,

    /// Show all files
    #[arg(short('a'), long("all"))]
    show_hidden: bool,
}
```

Bring in the run function from earlier programs. Add use anyhow::Result to your imports for the following code:

```
fn main() {
    if let Err(e) = run(Args::parse()) {
        eprintln!("{e}");
        std::process::exit(1);
    }
}

fn run(_args: Args) -> Result<()> {
    Ok(())
}
```

Next, you'll figure out how to find the input files.

Finding the Files

On the face of it, this program seems fairly simple. I want to list the given files and directories, so I'll start by writing a find_files function as in several previous chapters. The found files can be represented by strings, as in Chapter 9, but I've chosen to use a PathBuf, like I did Chapter 12. If you want to follow this idea, be sure to add std::path::PathBuf to your imports:

```
fn find_files(
    paths: &[String], ❶
    show_hidden: bool ❷
) -> Result<Vec<PathBuf>> { ❸
    unimplemented!();
}
```

❶ paths is a vector of file or directory names from the user.

❷ show_hidden indicates whether or not to include hidden files in directory listings.

❸ The result might be a vector of PathBuf values (*https://oreil.ly/Mth0r*).

My find_files function will iterate through all the given paths and check if the value exists using std::fs::metadata (*https://oreil.ly/VsRxb*). If there is no metadata, then I print an error message to STDERR and move to the next entry, so only existing files and directories will be returned by the function. The printing of these error messages will be checked by the integration tests, so the function itself should return just the valid entries. I struggled here with printing the errors rather than returning them as I cannot write a unit test that verifies the expected errors are detected, but writing the function in this way replicates the behavior of the original tool. In the parlance of purely functional programming, printing is a side effect because it is not reflected in the function's return values.

The metadata can tell me if the entry is a file or directory. If the entry is a file, I create a PathBuf and add it to the results. If the entry is a directory, I use fs::read_dir (*https://oreil.ly/m95Y5*) to read the contents of the directory. The function should skip hidden entries with filenames that begin with a dot (.) unless show_hidden is true.

> The filename is commonly called *basename* in command-line tools, and its corollary is *dirname*, which is the leading path information without the filename. There are command-line tools called basename and dirname that will return these elements:
>
> ```
> $ basename 14_lsr/src/main.rs
> main.rs
> $ dirname 14_lsr/src/main.rs
> 14_lsr/src
> ```

Following are two unit tests for find_files that check for listings that do and do not include hidden files. As noted in the chapter introduction, the files may be returned in a different order depending on your OS, so the tests will sort the entries to disregard the ordering. Note that the find_files function is not expected to recurse into subdirectories. Add the following to your *src/main.rs* to start a tests module:

```
#[cfg(test)]
mod test {
    use super::find_files;

    #[test]
    fn test_find_files() {
        // Find all nonhidden entries in a directory
        let res = find_files(&["tests/inputs".to_string()], false); ❶
        assert!(res.is_ok()); ❷
        let mut filenames: Vec<_> = res ❸
            .unwrap()
            .iter()
            .map(|entry| entry.display().to_string())
            .collect();
```

```rust
        filenames.sort(); ❹
        assert_eq!( ❺
            filenames,
            [
                "tests/inputs/bustle.txt",
                "tests/inputs/dir",
                "tests/inputs/empty.txt",
                "tests/inputs/fox.txt",
            ]
        );

        // Find all entries in a directory
        let res = find_files(&["tests/inputs".to_string()], true); ❻
        assert!(res.is_ok());
        let mut filenames: Vec<_> = res
            .unwrap()
            .iter()
            .map(|entry| entry.display().to_string())
            .collect();
        filenames.sort();
        assert_eq!(
            filenames,
            [
                "tests/inputs/.hidden",
                "tests/inputs/bustle.txt",
                "tests/inputs/dir",
                "tests/inputs/empty.txt",
                "tests/inputs/fox.txt",
            ]
        );

        // Any existing file should be found even if hidden
        let res = find_files(&["tests/inputs/.hidden".to_string()], false);
        assert!(res.is_ok());
        let filenames: Vec<_> = res
            .unwrap()
            .iter()
            .map(|entry| entry.display().to_string())
            .collect();
        assert_eq!(filenames, ["tests/inputs/.hidden"]);

        // Test multiple path arguments
        let res = find_files(
            &[
                "tests/inputs/bustle.txt".to_string(),
                "tests/inputs/dir".to_string(),
            ],
            false,
        );
        assert!(res.is_ok());
        let mut filenames: Vec<_> = res
            .unwrap()
```

```
            .iter()
            .map(|entry| entry.display().to_string())
            .collect();
        filenames.sort();
        assert_eq!(
            filenames,
            ["tests/inputs/bustle.txt", "tests/inputs/dir/spiders.txt"]
        );
    }
}
```

❶ Look for the entries in the *tests/inputs* directory, ignoring hidden files.

❷ Ensure that the result is an Ok variant.

❸ Collect the display names into a Vec<String>.

❹ Sort the entry names in alphabetical order.

❺ Verify that the four expected files were found.

❻ Look for the entries in the *tests/inputs* directory, including hidden files.

Following is the test for hidden files:

```
#[cfg(test)]
mod test {
    use super::find_files;

    #[test]
    fn test_find_files() {} // Same as before

    #[test]
    fn test_find_files_hidden() {
        let res = find_files(&["tests/inputs".to_string()], true); ❶
        assert!(res.is_ok());
        let mut filenames: Vec<_> = res
            .unwrap()
            .iter()
            .map(|entry| entry.display().to_string())
            .collect();
        filenames.sort();
        assert_eq!(
            filenames,
            [
                "tests/inputs/.hidden", ❷
                "tests/inputs/bustle.txt",
                "tests/inputs/dir",
                "tests/inputs/empty.txt",
                "tests/inputs/fox.txt",
            ]
```

```
        );
    }
}
```

❶ Include hidden files in the results.

❷ The *.hidden* file should be included in the results.

 Stop here and ensure that **cargo test find_files** passes both tests.

Once your `find_files` function is working, integrate it into the `run` function to print the found entries:

```
fn run(args: Args) -> Result<()> {
    let paths = find_files(&args.paths, args.show_hidden)?; ❶
    for path in paths { ❷
        println!("{}", path.display()); ❸
    }
    Ok(())
}
```

❶ Look for the files in the provided paths and specify whether to show hidden entries.

❷ Iterate through each of the returned paths.

❸ Use `Path::display` (*https://oreil.ly/apWTZ*) for safely printing paths that may contain non-Unicode data.

If I run the program in the source directory, I see the following output:

```
$ cargo run
./Cargo.toml
./target
./tests
./Cargo.lock
./src
```

The output from the challenge program is not expected to completely replicate the original `ls`. For example, the default listing for `ls` will create columns:

```
$ ls tests/inputs/
bustle.txt  dir/        empty.txt   fox.txt
```

If your program can produce the following output, then you've already implemented the basic directory listing. Note that the order of the files is not important. This is the output I see on macOS:

```
$ cargo run -- -a tests/inputs/
tests/inputs/.hidden
tests/inputs/empty.txt
tests/inputs/bustle.txt
tests/inputs/fox.txt
tests/inputs/dir
```

And this is what I see on Linux:

```
$ cargo run -- -a tests/inputs/
tests/inputs/empty.txt
tests/inputs/.hidden
tests/inputs/fox.txt
tests/inputs/dir
tests/inputs/bustle.txt
```

Provide a nonexistent file such as the trusty old *blargh* and check that your program prints a message to STDERR:

```
$ cargo run -q -- blargh 2>err
$ cat err
blargh: No such file or directory (os error 2)
```

 Stop reading and ensure that **cargo test** passes about half of the tests. All the failing tests should have the word *long* in the name, which means you need to implement the long listing.

Formatting the Long Listing

The next step is to handle the -l|--long listing option, which lists metadata for each entry. Figure 14-1 shows an example of the output with the columns numbered in bold font; the column numbers are not part of the expected output. Note that the output from your program will have different owners and modification times.

```
$ cargo run -- -l tests/inputs/
-  rw-r--r-- 1 kyclark staff   0 Mar 12 21 10:12 tests/inputs/empty.txt
-  rw-r--r-- 1 kyclark staff 193 May 31 21 16:43 tests/inputs/bustle.txt
-  rw------- 1 kyclark staff  45 Aug 12 21 10:29 tests/inputs/fox.txt
d  rwxr-xr-x 4 kyclark staff 128 Aug 10 21 18:08 tests/inputs/dir
1  2         3 4       5     6   7               8
```

Figure 14-1. The long listing of the program will include eight pieces of metadata.

The metadata displayed in the output, listed here by column number, is as follows:

1. The entry type, which should be d for directory or a dash (-) for anything else
2. The permissions are represented using r for read, w for write, and x for execute for user, group, and other
3. The number of links pointing to the file
4. The name of the user that owns the file
5. The name of the group that owns the file
6. The size of the file or directory in bytes
7. The file's last modification date and time
8. The path to the file

Creating the output table can be tricky, so I decided to use tabular (*https://oreil.ly/ 5HBqP*) to handle this for me. I wrote a function called format_output that accepts a list of PathBuf values and might return a formatted table with columns of metadata. If you want to follow my lead on this, be sure to add use tabular::{Row, Table} to your imports. Note that my function doesn't exactly replicate the output from BSD ls, but it meets the expectations of the test suite:

```
fn format_output(paths: &[PathBuf]) -> Result<String> {
    //          1   2     3     4     5     6     7     8
    let fmt = "{:<}{:<}  {:>}  {:<}  {:<}  {:>}  {:<}  {:<}";
    let mut table = Table::new(fmt);

    for path in paths {
        table.add_row(
            Row::new()
                .with_cell("") // 1 "d" or "-"
                .with_cell("") // 2 permissions
                .with_cell("") // 3 number of links
                .with_cell("") // 4 user name
                .with_cell("") // 5 group name
                .with_cell("") // 6 size
                .with_cell("") // 7 modification
                .with_cell("") // 8 path
        );
    }

    Ok(format!("{table}"))
}
```

You can find much of the data you need to fill in the cells with `PathBuf::metadata` (*https://oreil.ly/2G3en*). Here are some pointers to help you fill in the various columns:

- `metadata::is_dir` (*https://oreil.ly/qhXWX*) returns a Boolean for whether or not the entry is a directory.

- `metadata::mode` (*https://oreil.ly/LuKo4*) will return a u32 representing the permissions for the entry. In the next section, I will explain how to format this information into a display string.

- You can find the number of links using `metadata::nlink` (*https://oreil.ly/f2RyC*).

- For the user and group owners, add `use std::os::unix::fs::MetadataExt` so that you can call `metadata::uid` (*https://oreil.ly/P8YpO*) to get the user ID of the owner and `metadata::gid` (*https://oreil.ly/ggddm*) to get the group ID. Both the user and group IDs are integer values that must be converted into actual user and group names. For this, I recommend you look at the `users` crate (*https://oreil.ly/nuvE8*) that contains the functions `get_user_by_uid` (*https://oreil.ly/gaDwI*) and `get_group_by_gid` (*https://oreil.ly/qFRSD*).

- Use `metadata::len` (*https://oreil.ly/129cs*) to get the size of a file or directory.

- Displaying the file's `metadata::modified` (*https://oreil.ly/buVC9*) time is tricky. This method returns a `std::time::SystemTime` struct (*https://oreil.ly/GIiqd*), and I recommend that you use `chrono::DateTime::format` (*https://oreil.ly/TUBOK*) to format the date using `strftime` syntax (*https://oreil.ly/075dF*), a format that will likely be familiar to C and Perl programmers.

- Use `Path::display` (*https://oreil.ly/8tnwX*) for the file or directory name.

I have unit tests for this function, but first I need to explain more about how to display the permissions.

Displaying Octal Permissions

The file type and permissions will be displayed using a string of 10 characters like `drwxr-xr-x`, where each letter or dash indicates a specific piece of information. The first character is either a d for *directory* or a dash for anything else. The standard `ls` will also use l for a *link*, but the challenge program will not distinguish links.

The other nine characters represent the permissions for the entry. In Unix, each file and directory has three levels of sharing for a *user*, a *group*, and *other* for everyone else. Only one user and one group can own a file at a time. For each ownership level, there are permissions for reading, writing, and executing, as shown in Figure 14-2.

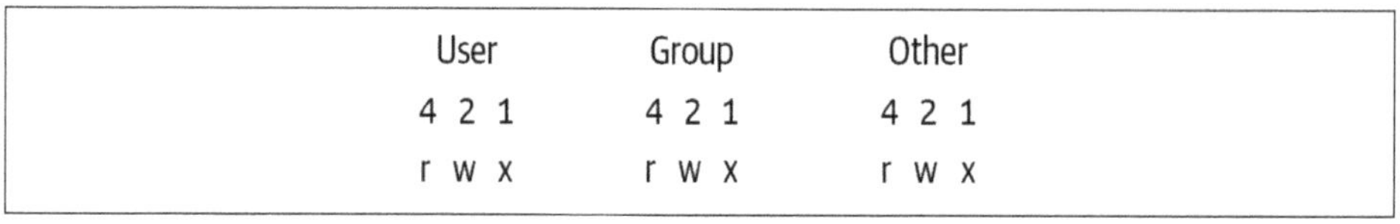

User	Group	Other
4 2 1	4 2 1	4 2 1
r w x	r w x	r w x

Figure 14-2. Each level of ownership (user, group, and other) has permissions for read, write, and execute.

These three permissions are either *on* or *off* and can be represented with three bits using 1 and 0, respectively. This means there are three combinations of two choices, which makes eight possible outcomes because $2^3 = 8$. In binary encoding, each bit position corresponds to a power of 2, so 001 is the number 1 (2^0), and 010 is the number 2 (2^1). To represent the number 3, both bits are added, so the binary version is 011. You can verify this with Rust by using the prefix 0b to represent a binary number:

```
assert_eq!(0b001 + 0b010, 3);
```

The number 4 is 100 (2^2), and so 5 is 101 (4 + 1). Because a three-bit value can represent only eight numbers, this is called *octal* notation. You can see the binary representation of the first eight numbers with the following loop:

```
for n in 0..=7 { ❶
    println!("{n} = {n:03b}"); ❷
}
```

❶ The ..= range operator includes the ending value.

❷ Print the value n as is and in binary format to three places using leading zeros.

The preceding code will print this:

```
0 = 000
1 = 001
2 = 010
3 = 011
4 = 100
5 = 101
6 = 110
7 = 111
```

Figure 14-3 shows that each of the three bit positions corresponds to a permission. The 4 position is for *read*, the 2 position for *write*, and the 1 position for *execute*. Octal notation is commonly used with the chmod command I mentioned in Chapters 2 and 3. For example, the command chmod 775 will enable the read/write/execute bits for the user and group of a file but will enable only read and execute for everyone else. This allows anyone to execute a program, but only the owner or group can modify it. The permission 600, where only the owner can read and write a file, is often used for sensitive data like SSH keys.

User	Group	Other	User	Group	Other
4 2 1	4 2 1	4 2 1	4 2 1	4 2 1	4 2 1
r w x	r w x	r - x	r w -	- - -	- - -
7	7	5	6	0	0

Figure 14-3. The permissions 775 and 600 in octal notation translate to read/write/ execute permissions for user/group/other.

I recommend you read the documentation for `metadata::mode` (*https://oreil.ly/ LuKo4*) to get a file's permissions. That documentation shows you how to mask the mode with a value like `0o200` to determine if the user has write access. (The prefix `0o` is the Rust way to write in octal notation.) That is, if you use the binary *AND* operator `&` to combine two binary values, only those bits that are both set (meaning they have a value of 1) will produce a 1.

As shown in Figure 14-4, if you `&` the values `0o700` and `0o200`, the *write* bits in position 2 are both set and so the result is `0o200`. The other bits can't be set because the zeros in `0o200` will *mask* or hide those values, hence the term *masking* for this operation. If you `&` the values `0o400` and `0o200`, the result is 0 because none of the three positions contains a 1 in both operands.

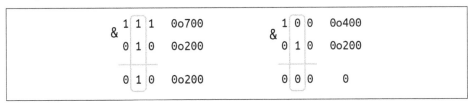

Figure 14-4. The binary AND operator & will set bit values in the result where both bits are set in the operands.

I wrote a function called `format_mode` to create the needed output for the permissions. It accepts the `u32` value returned by `mode` and returns a `String` of nine characters:

```
/// Given a file mode in octal format like 0o751,
/// return a string like "rwxr-x--x"
fn format_mode(mode: u32) -> String {
    unimplemented!();
}
```

The preceding function needs to create three groupings of `rwx` for user, group, and other using the mask values shown in Table 14-1.

Table 14-1. Read/write/execute mask values for user, group, and other

Owner	Read	Write	Execute
User	0o400	0o200	0o100
Group	0o040	0o020	0o010
Other	0o004	0o002	0o001

It might help to see the unit test that you can add to your `tests` module:

```
#[cfg(test)]
mod test {
    use super::{find_files, format_mode}; ❶

    #[test]
    fn test_find_files() {} // Same as before

    #[test]
    fn test_find_files_hidden() {} // Same as before

    #[test]
    fn test_format_mode() {
        assert_eq!(format_mode(0o755), "rwxr-xr-x"); ❷
        assert_eq!(format_mode(0o421), "r---w---x");
    }
}
```

❶ Import the `format_mode` function.

❷ These are two spot checks for the function. Presumably, the function works if these two pass.

Stop reading and write the code that will pass **cargo test format _mode**. Then, incorporate the output from format_mode into the format_output function.

Testing the Long Format

It's not easy to test the output from the `format_output` function, because the output on your system will necessarily be different from mine. For instance, you will likely have a different user name, group name, and file modification times. We should still have the same permissions (if you ran the *set-test-perms.sh* script), number of links, file sizes, and paths, so I have written the tests to inspect only those columns. In addition, I can't rely on the specific widths of the columns or any delimiting characters, as user and group names will vary. The unit tests I've created for the `format_output` function should help you write a working solution while also providing enough flexibility to account for the differences in our systems.

The following helper function, which you can add to your `tests` module, will inspect the long output for any one directory entry. Be sure to add `pretty_assertions::assert_eq` to your imports to make failing tests easier to read:

```
fn long_match( ❶
    line: &str,
    expected_name: &str,
    expected_perms: &str,
    expected_size: Option<&str>,
) {
    let parts: Vec<_> = line.split_whitespace().collect(); ❷
    assert!(parts.len() > 0 && parts.len() <= 10); ❸

    let perms = parts.get(0).unwrap(); ❹
    assert_eq!(perms, &expected_perms);

    if let Some(size) = expected_size { ❺
        let file_size = parts.get(4).unwrap();
        assert_eq!(file_size, &size);
    }

    let display_name = parts.last().unwrap(); ❻
    assert_eq!(display_name, &expected_name);
}
```

❶ The function takes a line of the output along with the expected values for the permissions, size, and path.

❷ Split the line of text on whitespace.

❸ Verify that the line was split into an expected range of fields.

❹ Verify the permissions string, which is in the first column.

❺ Verify the file size, which is in the fifth column. Directory sizes are not tested, so this is an optional argument.

❻ Verify the filepath, which is in the last column.

I use `Iterator::last` (*https://oreil.ly/mvd2C*) rather than try to use a positive offset because the modification date column has whitespace.

Expand the tests with the following unit test for the `format_output` function that checks the long listing for one file. Note that you will need to add `use std::path::PathBuf` and `format_output` to the imports:

```
#[test]
fn test_format_output_one() {
    let bustle_path = "tests/inputs/bustle.txt";
    let bustle = PathBuf::from(bustle_path); ❶

    let res = format_output(&[bustle]); ❷
    assert!(res.is_ok());

    let out = res.unwrap();
    let lines: Vec<&str> =
        out.split("\n").filter(|s| !s.is_empty()).collect(); ❸
    assert_eq!(lines.len(), 1);

    let line1 = lines.first().unwrap();
    long_match(&line1, bustle_path, "-rw-r--r--", Some("193")); ❹
}
```

❶ Create a `PathBuf` value for *tests/inputs/bustle.txt*.

❷ Execute the function with one path.

❸ Break the output on newlines and verify there is just one line.

❹ Use the helper function to inspect the permissions, size, and path.

The following unit test passes two files and checks both lines for the correct output:

```
#[test]
fn test_format_output_two() {
    let res = format_output(&[ ❶
        PathBuf::from("tests/inputs/dir"),
        PathBuf::from("tests/inputs/empty.txt"),
    ]);
    assert!(res.is_ok());

    let out = res.unwrap();
    let mut lines: Vec<&str> =
        out.split("\n").filter(|s| !s.is_empty()).collect();
    lines.sort();
    assert_eq!(lines.len(), 2); ❷

    let empty_line = lines.remove(0); ❸
    long_match(
        &empty_line,
        "tests/inputs/empty.txt",
        "-rw-r--r--",
        Some("0"),
```

```
    );
    let dir_line = lines.remove(0); ❹
    long_match(&dir_line, "tests/inputs/dir", "drwxr-xr-x", None);
}
```

❶ Execute the function with two arguments, one of which is a directory.

❷ Verify that two lines are returned.

❸ Verify the expected values for the *empty.txt* file.

❹ Verify the expected values for the directory listing. Don't bother checking the size, as different systems will report different sizes.

> Stop reading and write the code to pass `cargo test format _output`. Once that works, incorporate the long output into the run function. Have at you!

Solution

This became a surprisingly complicated program that needed to be decomposed into several smaller functions. I'll show you how I wrote each function, starting with find_files:

```
fn find_files(paths: &[String], show_hidden: bool) -> Result<Vec<PathBuf>> {
    let mut results = vec![]; ❶
    for name in paths {
        match fs::metadata(name) { ❷
            Err(e) => eprintln!("{name}: {e}"), ❸
            Ok(meta) => {
                if meta.is_dir() { ❹
                    for entry in fs::read_dir(name)? { ❺
                        let entry = entry?; ❻
                        let path = entry.path(); ❼
                        let is_hidden = ❽
                            path.file_name().map_or(false, |file_name| {
                                file_name.to_string_lossy().starts_with('.')
                            });
                        if !is_hidden || show_hidden { ❾
                            results.push(entry.path());
                        }
                    }
                } else {
                    results.push(PathBuf::from(name)); ❿
                }
            }
```

```
        }
    }
    Ok(results)
}
```

❶ Initialize a mutable vector for the results.

❷ Attempt to get the metadata for the path.

❸ In the event of an error such as a nonexistent file, print an error message to STDERR and move to the next file.

❹ Check if the entry is a directory.

❺ If so, use `fs::read_dir` to read the entries.

❻ Unpack the `Result`.

❼ Use `DirEntry::path` (*https://oreil.ly/koDWO*) to get the `Path` value for the entry.

❽ Check if the basename starts with a dot and is therefore hidden.

❾ If the entry should be displayed, add a `PathBuf` to the results.

❿ Add a `PathBuf` for the file to the results.

Next, I'll show how to format the permissions. Recall Table 14-1 with the nine masks needed to handle the nine bits that make up the permissions. To encapsulate this data, I created an `enum` type called `Owner`, which I define with variants for `User`, `Group`, and `Other`. By default, all the variables and functions in a module are private, which means they are accessible only to other code within the same module, so I must use the `pub` (*https://oreil.ly/Jmj7b*) keyword to make this visible to the rest of the program. Additionally, I want to add a method to my type that will return the masks needed to create the permissions string. I would like to group this code into a separate module called `owner`, so I will place the following code into the file *src/owner.rs*:

```
#[derive(Clone, Copy)]
pub enum Owner { ❶
    User,
    Group,
    Other,
}

impl Owner { ❷
    pub fn masks(&self) -> [u32; 3] { ❸
        match self { ❹
            Self::User => [0o400, 0o200, 0o100], ❺
```

```
                Self::Group => [0o040, 0o020, 0o010], ❻
                Self::Other => [0o004, 0o002, 0o001], ❼
            }
        }
    }
```

❶ An owner can be a user, group, or other.

❷ This is an implementation (`impl`) block for `Owner`.

❸ Define a method called `masks` that will return an array of the mask values for a given owner.

❹ `self` will be one of the `enum` variants.

❺ These are the read, write, and execute masks for `User`.

❻ These are the read, write, and execute masks for `Group`.

❼ These are the read, write, and execute masks for `Other`.

> If you come from an object-oriented background, you'll find this syntax is suspiciously similar to a class definition and an object method declaration, complete with a reference to `self` as the invocant.

To use this module, add `mod owner` to the top of *src/main.rs*, then add `use owner::Owner` to the list of imports. As you've seen in almost every chapter, the `mod` keyword (*https://oreil.ly/GqfkT*) is used to create new modules, such as the `tests` module for unit tests. In this case, adding `mod owner` declares a new module named `owner`. Because you haven't specified the contents of the module here, the Rust compiler knows to look in *src/owner.rs* for the module's code. Then, you can import the `Owner` type into the root module's scope with `use owner::Owner`.

> As your programs grow more complicated, it's useful to organize code into modules. This will make it easier to isolate and test ideas as well as reuse code in other projects.

Following is a list of all the imports I used to finish the program:

```
mod owner;

use anyhow::Result;
use chrono::{DateTime, Local};
use clap::Parser;
use owner::Owner;
use std::{fs, os::unix::fs::MetadataExt, path::PathBuf};
use tabular::{Row, Table};
use users::{get_group_by_gid, get_user_by_uid};
```

I added the following mk_triple helper function, which creates part of the permissions string given the file's mode and an Owner variant:

```
/// Given an octal number like 0o500 and an [`Owner`],
/// return a string like "r-x"
fn mk_triple(mode: u32, owner: Owner) -> String { ❶
    let [read, write, execute] = owner.masks(); ❷
    format!( 
        "{}{}{}", ❸
        if mode & read == 0 { "-" } else { "r" }, ❹
        if mode & write == 0 { "-" } else { "w" }, ❺
        if mode & execute == 0 { "-" } else { "x" }, ❻
    )
}
```

❶ The function takes a permissions mode and an Owner.

❷ Unpack the three mask values for this owner.

❸ Use the format! macro to create a new String to return.

❹ If the mode masked with the read value returns 0, then the *read* bit is not set. Show a dash (-) when unset and r when set.

❺ Likewise, mask the mode with the write value and display w if set and a dash otherwise.

❻ Mask the mode with the execute value and return x if set and a dash otherwise.

Following is the unit test for this function, which you can add to the `tests` module. Be sure to add `super::{mk_triple, Owner}` to the list of imports:

```
#[test]
fn test_mk_triple() {
    assert_eq!(mk_triple(0o751, Owner::User), "rwx");
    assert_eq!(mk_triple(0o751, Owner::Group), "r-x");
    assert_eq!(mk_triple(0o751, Owner::Other), "--x");
    assert_eq!(mk_triple(0o600, Owner::Other), "---");
}
```

Finally, I can bring this all together in my `format_mode` function:

```
/// Given a file mode in octal format like 0o751,
/// return a string like "rwxr-x--x"
fn format_mode(mode: u32) -> String { ❶
    format!(
        "{}{}{}", ❷
        mk_triple(mode, Owner::User), ❸
        mk_triple(mode, Owner::Group),
        mk_triple(mode, Owner::Other),
    )
}
```

❶ The function takes a u32 value and returns a new string.

❷ The returned string will be made of three triple values, like `rwx`.

❸ Create triples for user, group, and other.

 You've seen throughout the book that Rust uses two slashes (`//`) to indicate that all text that follows on the line will be ignored. This is commonly called a *comment* because it can be used to add commentary to your code, but it's also a handy way to temporarily disable lines of code. In the preceding functions, you may have noticed the use of three slashes (`///`) to create a special kind of comment that has the #[doc] attribute (*https://oreil.ly/VP1AV*). Note that the doc comment should precede the function declaration. Execute `cargo doc --open --document-private-items` to have Cargo create documentation for your code. This should cause your web browser to open with HTML documentation as shown in Figure 14-5, and the triple-commented text should be displayed next to the function name.

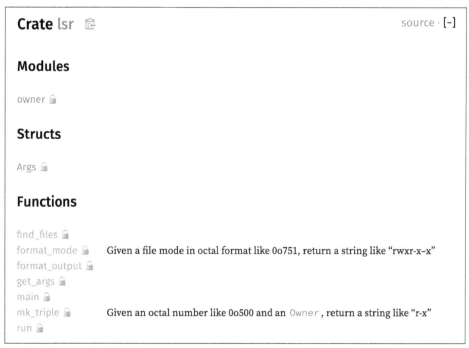

Figure 14-5. *The documentation created by Cargo will include comments that begin with three slashes.*

Following is how I use the `format_mode` function in the `format_output` function:

```
fn format_output(paths: &[PathBuf]) -> Result<String> {
    //       1   2    3     4    5    6    7    8
    let fmt = "{:<}{:<}  {:>}  {:<}  {:<}  {:>}  {:<}  {:<}";
    let mut table = Table::new(fmt); ❶

    for path in paths {
        let metadata = path.metadata()?; ❷

        let uid = metadata.uid(); ❸
        let user = get_user_by_uid(uid)
            .map(|u| u.name().to_string_lossy().into_owned())
            .unwrap_or_else(|| uid.to_string());

        let gid = metadata.gid(); ❹
        let group = get_group_by_gid(gid)
            .map(|g| g.name().to_string_lossy().into_owned())
            .unwrap_or_else(|| gid.to_string());

        let file_type = if path.is_dir() { "d" } else { "-" }; ❺
        let perms = format_mode(metadata.mode()); ❻
        let modified: DateTime<Local> = DateTime::from(metadata.modified()?); ❼
```

```
        table.add_row( ❽
            Row::new()
                .with_cell(file_type) // 1
                .with_cell(perms) // 2
                .with_cell(metadata.nlink()) // 3 ❾
                .with_cell(user) // 4
                .with_cell(group) // 5
                .with_cell(metadata.len()) // 6 ❿
                .with_cell(modified.format("%b %d %y %H:%M")) // 7 ⓫
                .with_cell(path.display()), // 8
        );
    }

    Ok(format!("{table}")) ⓬
}
```

❶ Create a new `tabular::Table` (*https://oreil.ly/z73wW*) using the given format string.

❷ Attempt to get the entry's metadata. This should not fail because of the earlier use of `fs::metadata`. This method is an alias to that function.

❸ Get the user ID of the owner from the metadata. Attempt to convert to a user name and fall back on a string version of the ID.

❹ Do likewise for the group ID and name.

❺ Choose whether to print a d if the entry is a directory or a dash (-) otherwise.

❻ Use the `format_mode` function to format the entry's permissions.

❼ Create a `DateTime` struct using the metadata's `modified` value (*https://oreil.ly/buVC9*).

❽ Add a new `Row` (*https://oreil.ly/Mrmvg*) to the table using the given cells.

❾ Use `metadata::nlink` (*https://oreil.ly/f2RyC*) to find the number of links.

❿ Use `metadata::len` (*https://oreil.ly/129cs*) to get the size.

⓫ Use `strftime` format options (*https://oreil.ly/075dF*) to display the modification time.

⓬ Convert the table to a string to return.

Finally, I bring it all together in the `run` function:

```
fn run(args: Args) -> Result<()> {
    let paths = find_files(&args.paths, args.show_hidden)?; ❶
    if args.long {
        println!("{}", format_output(&paths)?); ❷
    } else {
        for path in paths { ❸
            println!("{}", path.display());
        }
    }
    Ok(())
}
```

❶ Find all the entries in the given list of files and directories.

❷ If the user wants the long listing, print the results of `format_output`.

❸ Otherwise, print each path on a separate line.

At this point, the program passes all the tests, and you have implemented a simple replacement for `ls`.

Notes from the Testing Underground

In this last chapter, I'd like you to consider some of the challenges of writing tests, as I hope this will become an integral part of your coding skills. For example, the output from your `lsr` program will *necessarily* always be different from what I see when I'm creating the tests because you will have different owners and modification times. I've found that different systems will report different sizes for directories, and the column widths of the output will be different because you are likely to have shorter or longer user and group names. The most that testing can do is verify that the filenames, permissions, and sizes are the expected values while assuming the layout is kosher.

If you read *tests/cli.rs*, you'll see I borrowed some of the same ideas from the unit tests for the integration tests. For the long listing, I created a `run_long` function to run for a particular file, checking for the permissions, size, and path:

```
fn run_long(filename: &str, permissions: &str, size: &str) -> Result<()> { ❶
    let cmd = Command::cargo_bin(PRG)? ❷
        .args(&["--long", filename])
        .assert()
        .success();
    let stdout = String::from_utf8(cmd.get_output().stdout.clone())?; ❸
    let parts: Vec<_> = stdout.split_whitespace().collect(); ❹
    assert_eq!(parts.get(0).unwrap(), &permissions); ❺
    assert_eq!(parts.get(4).unwrap(), &size); ❻
    assert_eq!(parts.last().unwrap(), &filename); ❼
    Ok(())
}
```

❶ The function accepts the filename and the expected permissions and size.

❷ Run `lsr` with the `--long` option for the given filename.

❸ Convert STDOUT to UTF-8.

❹ Break the output on whitespace and collect it into a vector.

❺ Check that the first column is the expected permissions.

❻ Check that the fifth column is the expected size.

❼ Check that the last column is the given path.

I use this function like so:

```
#[test]
fn fox_long() -> Result<()> {
    run_long(FOX, "-rw-------", "45")
}
```

Checking the directory listings is tricky, too. I found I needed to ignore the directory sizes because different systems report different sizes. Here is my `dir_long` function that handles this:

```
#[allow(suspicious_double_ref_op)] ❶
fn dir_long(args: &[&str], expected: &[(&str, &str, &str)]) -> Result<()> { ❷
    let cmd = Command::cargo_bin(PRG)?.args(args).assert().success(); ❸
    let stdout = String::from_utf8(cmd.get_output().stdout.clone())?; ❹
    let lines: Vec<&str> =
        stdout.split("\n").filter(|s| !s.is_empty()).collect(); ❺
    assert_eq!(lines.len(), expected.len()); ❻

    let mut check = vec![]; ❼
    for line in lines {
        let parts: Vec<_> = line.split_whitespace().collect(); ❽
        let path = parts.last().unwrap().clone();
        let permissions = parts.get(0).unwrap().clone();
        let size = match permissions.chars().next() {
            Some('d') => "", ❾
            _ => parts.get(4).unwrap().clone(),
        };
        check.push((path, permissions, size));
    }

    for entry in expected {
        assert!(check.contains(entry)); ❿
    }
}
```

```
        Ok(())
    }
```

❶ This annotation asks Clippy to ignore the warning "using .clone() on a double
    reference, which returns &str instead of cloning the inner type."

❷ The function accepts the arguments and a slice of tuples with the expected
    results.

❸ Run lsr with the given arguments and assert it is successful.

❹ Convert STDOUT to a string.

❺ Break STDOUT into lines, ignoring any empty lines.

❻ Check that the number of lines matches the expected number.

❼ Initialize a mutable vector of items to check.

❽ Break the line on whitespace and extract the path, permissions, and size.

❾ Ignore the size of directories.

❿ Ensure that each of the expected paths, permissions, and sizes is present in the
    check vector using Vec::contains (*https://oreil.ly/PnrUd*).

I use the dir_long utility function in a test like this:

```
    #[test]
    fn dir1_long_all() -> Result<()> {
        dir_long(
            &["-la", "tests/inputs"], ❶
            &[
                ("tests/inputs/empty.txt", "-rw-r--r--", "0"), ❷
                ("tests/inputs/bustle.txt", "-rw-r--r--", "193"),
                ("tests/inputs/fox.txt", "-rw-------", "45"), ❸
                ("tests/inputs/dir", "drwxr-xr-x", ""), ❹
                ("tests/inputs/.hidden", "-rw-r--r--", "0"),
            ],
        )
    }
```

❶ These are the arguments to lsr.

❷ The *empty.txt* file should have permissions of 644 and a file size of 0.

❸ The *fox.txt* file's permissions should be set to 600 by *set-test-perms.sh*. If you forget to run this script, then you will fail this test.

❹ The *dir* entry should report d and permissions of 755. Ignore the size.

In many ways, the tests for this program were as challenging as the program itself. I hope I've shown throughout the book the importance of writing and using tests to ensure a working program.

Going Further

The challenge program works fairly differently from the native ls programs. Modify your program to mimic the ls on your system, then start trying to implement all the other options, making sure that you add tests for every feature. If you want inspiration, check out the source code for other Rust implementations of ls, such as exa (*https://oreil.ly/2ZWIe*) and lsd (*https://oreil.ly/u38PE*).

Write Rust versions of the command-line utilities basename and dirname, which will print the filename or directory name of given inputs, respectively. Start by reading the manual pages to decide which features your programs will implement. Use a test-driven approach where you write tests for each feature you add to your programs. Release your code to the world, and reap the fame and fortune that inevitably follow open source development.

In Chapter 7, I suggested writing a Rust version of tree, which will find and display the tree structure of files and directories. The program can also display much of the same information as ls:

```
$ tree -pughD
.
├── [-rw-r--r-- kyclark  staff      193 May 31 16:43]  bustle.txt
├── [drwxr-xr-x kyclark  staff      128 Aug 10 18:08]  dir
│   └── [-rw-r--r-- kyclark  staff       45 May 31 16:43]  spiders.txt
├── [-rw-r--r-- kyclark  staff        0 Mar 19  2021]  empty.txt
└── [-rw------- kyclark  staff       45 Aug 12 10:29]  fox.txt

1 directory, 4 files
```

Use what you learned from this chapter to write or expand that program.

Summary

One of my favorite parts of this challenge program is the formatting of the octal permission bits. I also enjoyed finding all the other pieces of metadata that go into the long listing. Consider what you did in this chapter:

- You learned how to summon the metadata of a file to find everything from the file's owners and size to the last modification time.

- You found that directory entries starting with a dot are normally hidden from view, leading to the existence of *dotfiles* and directories for hiding program data.

- You delved into the mysteries of file permissions, octal notation, and bit masking and came through more knowledgeable about Unix file ownership.

- You discovered how to add `impl` (implementation) to a custom type `Owner` as well as how to segregate this module into *src/owner.rs* and declare it with `mod owner` in *src/main.rs*.

- You learned to use three slashes (`///`) to create doc comments that are included in the documentation created by Cargo and that can be read using **cargo doc**.

- You saw how to use the `tabular` crate to create text tables.

- You explored ways to write flexible tests for programs that can create different output on different systems and when run by different people.

Epilogue

No one in the world / Ever gets what they want / And that is beautiful /
Everybody dies / Frustrated and sad / And that is beautiful

    — They Might Be Giants, "Don't Let's Start" (1986)

You made it to the last page, or at least you flipped here to see how the book ends. I hope that I've shown that combining a strict language like Rust with testing allows you to confidently write and refactor complicated programs. I would encourage you to rewrite these programs in other languages that you know or learn in order to determine what you think makes them a better or worse fit for the task.

I've had more than one person say that telling people to write tests is like telling them to eat their vegetables. Maybe that's so, but if we're all going to "build reliable and efficient software" like the Rust motto claims, it is incumbent on us to shoulder this burden. Sometimes writing the tests is as much work (or more) as writing the program, but it's a moral imperative that you learn and apply these skills. I encourage you to go back and read all the tests I've written to understand them more and find code you can integrate into your own programs.

Your journey has not ended here; it has only begun. There are more programs to be written and rewritten. Now go make the world a better place by writing good software.

Index

Symbols

types
  casting, 84
  inferring, 87
  naming conventions in Rust, 149
  string variables in Rust, 39
  types option in findr, 154
    finding all the entry types, 158
  values in vectors, 31

U

u64 type, 75, 269
  -s option parsed as in fortuner, 288
Unicode, 83, 95, 172
  multibyte character Ö, 252
  multibyte character ś, 253
unimplemented! macro, 182
uniq program, 119-140
  how it works, 119-124
  writing uniqr version
    defining the arguments, 125
    getting started, 124
    going further, 139
    processing input files, 132-133
    solution, 134
    testing the program, 127-131
unit tests, 6
  creating for count function, 106-108
  creating for cutr utility, 182
  test for extract_fields function, 194
  test_count_lines_bytes function, 267
  test_find_files in fortuner, 292
  test_find_files in lsr, 339
  test_format_mode in lsr, 348
  test_format_month in calr, 321
  test_format_output in lsr, 350
  test_get_start_index function, 269
  test_last_day_in_month in calr, 322
  test_mk_triple function in lsr, 355
  test_parse_month in calr, 315
  test_parse_num function, 260
  test_read_fortunes in fortuner, 295, 297
unit type, 20, 37
  return by if expression without else, 32
Unix
  conditionally testing Unix versus Windows
    for findr, 162-165
  files and directories, levels of sharing and
    ownership, 345

ls command and ideas of files and owner-
    ship, 331
  newlines, 82
unknown character, 252
unreachable! macro, 190
unsigned integers, 75, 259
UpperCamelCase, 149
usage statement, 5
  calr program, 312
  commr utility, 232
  cutr utility, 175
  fortuner program, 287
  lsr program, 336
  tailr utility, 255
  uniqr program, 125
User enum, 352
user time, 278
users, 335, 353
users crate, 345
usize type, 75, 187, 292
  casting to i64, 273
UTC (Coordinated Universal Time), 319
UTF-8 character encoding, 83
  byte selection producing invalid UTF-8
    string, 197
  String type and, 86

V

-V and --version flags, 26
ValueEnum trait, 149
value_error closure, 187
variables (Rust), 8
  shadowing, 68
Vec type, 29, 41, 154, 195
vec! macro, 30
Vec::chunks, 326, 327
Vec::contains, 360
Vec::dedup function, 293, 301
Vec::extend function, 300
Vec::first function, 181
Vec::get function, 195
Vec::join function, 30
Vec::len method, 90
Vec::push function, 195
Vec::sort function, 293, 301
Vec::windows, 139
Vec<&str>, 198
Vec<Range<usize>>, 182
Vec<String>, 324

About the Author

Ken Youens-Clark is a software developer, teacher, and writer. He began his undergraduate studies at the University of North Texas, initially with a focus in jazz studies (drums) and then changing his major several times before limping out of school with a BA in English literature. Ken learned coding on the job starting in the mid-1990s and has worked in industry, in research, and at nonprofits. In 2019, he earned his MS in biosystems engineering from the University of Arizona. His previous books include *Tiny Python Projects* (Manning) and *Mastering Python for Bioinformatics* (O'Reilly). He resides in Tucson, Arizona, with his wife, three children, and dog.

Colophon

The animal on the cover of *Command-Line Rust* is a fiddler crab, a small crustacean sharing a common name with more than 100 species in the family Ocypodidae, made up of semiterrestrial crabs.

Fiddler crabs are perhaps best known for the oversized claw that distinguishes males and that is used for communication, courtship, and competitive behaviors. Fiddlers eat microorganisms, algae, decaying plants, and fungi, sifting through sand and mud for edible matter. They live relatively short lives—generally no more than two to three years—and can be found in the salt marshes and beach habitats of several regions around the world.

Many of the animals on O'Reilly covers are endangered. While fiddler crabs are not rare, they, like all animals, are important to the world and the ecosystems of which they are a part.

The cover illustration is by Karen Montgomery, based on an antique line engraving from *Brehms Thierleben*. The cover fonts are Gilroy Semibold and Guardian Sans. The text font is Adobe Minion Pro; the heading font is Adobe Myriad Condensed; and the code font is Dalton Maag's Ubuntu Mono.

Milton Keynes UK
Ingram Content Group UK Ltd.
UKHW052003240924
448803UK00002B/4